BUDDHIST TRANSLATIONS

BUDDHIST TRANSLATIONS
Problems and Perspectives

Edited by

DOBOOM TULKU

MANOHAR
2026

First published 1995
Reprinted 2020, 2021, 2022, 2023, 2026

ISBN 978-93-88540-90-2

Published by
Ajay Kumar Jain *for*
Manohar Publishers & Distributors
4753/23 Ansari Road, Daryaganj
New Delhi 110 002

Printed at
Replika Press Pvt. Ltd.

Acknowledgements

This volume is the outcome of the International Seminar on "Buddhist Translations: Problems and Perspectives" which was organised by Tibet House in February 1990. This Seminar was funded by the Ford Foundation and supported by the Indian Council for Cultural Relations and the India International Centre.

The success of the Seminar and the preparation of the materials for this volume are the result of the interest, effort and kindness of many people and organisations.

At the concluding session of the Seminar the participants credited its enormous success to the efforts made by Tibet House. It was also remarked that this seminar had been a milestone in the history of Buddhist translations. Certainly Tibet House was able to bring all the necessary components together for this seminar which was the first of its kind, but the contributions of the participants, their co-operation and encouragement will go a long way in advancing the translation and dissemination of Buddhist literature and knowledge. We deeply appreciate the kindness of the contributors to this volume who took the time and trouble to prepare these valuable papers and recommendations. I am also very grateful to Dr. Peter Della Santina, Dr. Renuka Singh and Ms. Hilary Shearman for their generous assistance in providing researched materials. Finally, I wish to thank Prof. C. Mani for providing the diacritical marks for Sanskrit words, Mr. Lobsang Gyaltsen Shastri of the Library of Tibet House for checking the Tibetan words of the text, and Mr. Tshering Wangyal for surveying the manuscripts of this volume.

Contents

Introduction

In the course of the last few decades, there has been a considerable increase in the quantity of translation of Tibetan Buddhist literature. This indicates a growing desire in many parts of the world to know more about Buddhism, in the way it developed and is practised in the Tibetan tradition. The task of transmitting any religious or philosophical knowledge and truths embedded in an old language like Tibetan, to a modern one like English, is enormously difficult. This is so because from whatever angle one looks at these two languages—their grammar, syntactical arrangement of words, the social and geographical backgrounds in which they developed—they are totally different. So much so indeed that perhaps all that a devoted translator can hope to achieve in his or her translation is to convey the contents of a Tibetan text without much distortion or confusion. Even that is often too much to hope. A very conscientious translator may have to be satisfied with conveying, in the target language, no more than some particular aspect or aspects of the original whole—such as he or she thinks is the most important.

Translators of course come from diverse backgrounds and they approach their difficult tasks with different aims in mind. This is no doubt as it should be. But those who hope to learn, through reading translations, something about Tibetan Buddhism are often confused by the varied styles and nature of translation of many Tibetan texts. Some of these classical texts are abstruse even to a Tibetan scholar and they become more so in translation if the translator's understanding of them is insufficient, surmounted by the problem that there is no standardisation of translated Tibetan terminology.

Situations such as this prompted Tibet House to organize a seminar, to which scholars working on the translations of Buddhist texts from both India and abroad were invited to attend and speak about their work and experiences. The seminar received monetary and organizational support from the Ford Foundation, the Indian

Council for Cultural Relations, and India International Centre. The seminar, called "An International Seminar on Buddhist Translations: Problems and Perspectives," was held in Delhi in February 1990. All the twenty-two papers included in this volume were read at the seminar in which about fifty scholar-translators participated. Later, the authors were requested to revise their papers if necessary for publication. Some took the opportunity to do so and sent revised versions. Keeping the entire collection in mind, it was thought necessary to edit a number of papers. However, care has of course been taken to avoid any distortion of meaning.

Before the papers are briefly introduced, I would like to say a few words about the history of the translation of Buddhist texts from Sanskrit and Tibetan. This can be divided into three phases. A fourth phase can probably be projected for the immediate future.

The first phase covers the early years of the colonial period on the Indian subcontinent, when Christianity and Christian values were an integral part of the colonial mentality. During this time the translations of Buddhist texts into English from Pali, Sanskrit and Tibetan were often done by missionaries, or, if not by missionaries, by persons who were deeply committed to and influenced by Christianity. These translations, therefore, contain a very high degree of Christian colouring in the language of the translations and in the interpretation of the original material. Kern's early translation of the Lotus Sutra, *Saddharmapuṇḍarīka,* is one of the best or worst examples of this period. In it the phrase "the flesh pots of Egypt," which is taken straight from the Bible, is used to indicate, presumably, the idea of sensual corruption. What is even more damning to the translation is Kern's insistence on using "death" for *Nirvāṇa.* This is not only an incorrect translation; it also betrays an unconscious evaluation, or devaluation, of the highest goal in Buddhism.

Another example of the overwhelming influence of biblical values upon an early translator of Buddhist texts are Rhys David's translations taken from Pali sources. She found, in spite of all the evidence to the contrary, an affirmation of the existence of the Soul in the teaching of the Buddha!

Waddell can also be classified in this group although, to my knowledge, he did not produce much in the way of actual translations. His term *Lamaism* is full of Christian prejudice against Buddhism. While he was in Tibet, Waddell is believed to have been quite favourable towards Buddhism; but at the time of writing his book in England, the prevailing Christian attitude towards non-Christian, especially non-biblical religions, changed his views and he produced a book that conformed to the then prevailing attitude.

In the second phase of translation of Buddhist texts, which may be taken to cover roughly the first half of this century, the Christian influence is not as dominant. During this period, although the colonial, political and economic domination of many Buddhist lands in Asia continued, the influence of Christianity and Christian values on western translators faded into the background. Perhaps this development can be partly explained by the decline in the credibility of Christianity among western intellectuals which accompanied the advances of science and the rise of Marxism. In this phase the categories and concepts of traditional western philosophy became dominant and most translators were powerfully influenced by Kant. However, the introduction of Kantian categories and concepts into the translation and interpretation of Buddhist texts did not help to reveal the real object and purpose of these texts.

An example of a translator who worked extensively on Buddhist materials during this period and whose translations are deeply influenced by Kantian ideas is Stcherbatsky. His repeated use of the phrase "the thing in itself" comes directly from Kantian metaphysics. He uses it to refer to, as it does in Kantian metaphysics, the absolute or ultimate reality. However, whether it is a helpful phrase for understanding the Buddhist conceptions of *paramārtha* or *tathatā* is very doubtful. It may be mentioned that Kant was also influenced in his translations of Yogācāra texts like the *Madhyāntavibhaṅga* by another western philosopher, Berkeley, who was the first among western philosophers to propose the existence of only mind. This association was not helpful, for Berkeley was a bishop who wanted to prove that nothing could exist except in the mind of God, and therefore God had to be accepted as the supreme architect of the world. Most contemporary scholars now recognize that Buddhist mentalist philosophers, particularly Asaṅga and Vasubandhu, have a very different outlook from that of the traditional western idealism.

Another example of a western translator who, despite producing a great deal of very useful work, allowed Kantian ideas to creep into his translation and interpretations of Buddhist texts is Conze.

His insistence upon the use of the term "the absolute" to translate *paramārtha* is again a direct imposition of Kantian terms and concepts upon Buddhist thought. In line with the point made earlier about the decline in the influence of Christianity during this phase of English translations of Buddhist texts, it may be pointed out that Stcherbatsky, although a Russian, was educated in Germany and it could be surmised that he was conditioned to abandon Christian values and replace them with those of Kant and Marx. Conze too belonged to that period.

The third phase of translation of Buddhist texts into English from Sanskrit and Tibetan sources is marked by the introduction of still more models and conceptual schemes taken from the western intellectual and philosophical tradition. This phase can be said to run roughly from the middle of the twentieth century to the present, as is evident from the translations of some western scholars. In these Kant and Marx, as well as Berkeley, are largely abandoned. The new fashion has been to look to western psychology, as taught primarily by Freud and Jung, for conceptual schemes to be used in the translation and interpretation of Buddhist materials. There has also been a new tendency to adopt the concepts of linguistic relativism, particularly as propounded by Wittgenstein, for help in the work of translating Buddhist texts into English. There are many modern translators who, in their translations of Buddhist texts, have made large-scale use of concepts and terms taken from modern Western psychology and linguistic relativism. The most obvious example of these new influences in the translation of Buddhist texts into English are the works of Guenther; but there are many others who also fall into this category.

What these three phases have in common is the imposition of the Western conceptual scheme upon Buddhist material. In other words, whether it was Christian values or those of traditional Western philosophy or those of modern movements in Western intellectual circles, all of them were marked by the prevalent use of a particularly western scheme of thought in the translation of Buddhist texts. It would not be wrong to say that all the translators working in these three periods have looked at the Buddhist texts through some Western spectacles of one colour or another. The result has inevitably caused some distortion, to a greater or lesser extent of the original genuine Buddhist message.

The problem is not only a Western one. A similar problem arose when Buddhist texts were translated into Chinese from Sanskrit. There Taoist, and to a lesser extent Confucian concepts influenced the translation and interpretation of Buddhist materials, and in some cases seriously distorted the meaning. Perhaps the problem of reading and translating Buddhist texts through one's own particular culture or intellectual spectacles is bound to occur when Buddhist texts and techniques are introduced into a civilization which already has quite a well developed and well-defined intellectual, religious or philosophical culture of its own. Perhaps the remarkable accuracy of the Tibetan translations of Buddhist texts from Sanskrit is due in part to the fact that in the eighth or ninth centuries C.E. Tibet hardly had any well-developed or well-defined intellectual tradition of its own. That is to say, the Buddhist concepts and values embodied in the Buddhist texts were introduced into what was virtually an intellectual vacuum. To put it more positively, the Tibetan translators were able to read, translate and interpret Buddhist texts through spectacles which were not already coloured by their own intellectual preconceptions.

There is now an emerging tendency among a new breed of Western translators to work in close collaboration with authoritative Tibetan scholars belonging to the indigenous tradition and to allow Buddhist texts to speak in English but with an authentic Buddhist voice. Sometimes such attempts lead to overtly literal English translations which become difficult, if not impossible, for the average English reader not familiar with the original language to understand. Still this is a positive development, for such relative difficulty in comprehension is preferable to wrong comprehension. Certainly the confusion which arises in attempting to understand translations of Buddhist texts loaded with Christian or Kantian or even Freudian, Jungian or Wittgensteinian concepts and terms is lessened by this new approach. The goal for which we should all strive is of course translation which will speak with a genuine Buddhist voice, presented in a language and style comprehensible to the average educated reader. Perhaps this is a goal which may be achieved in the newest and latest phase of translation of Buddhist texts into English; this is what I have called the fourth phase, and the beginnings of it are already evident in some of the latest translations done in a new spirit of objectivity and respect for the indigenous Tibetan Buddhist tradition, both literary and oral, and its legitimate representatives.

Let me now turn to the papers included in this volume, drawing attention to the salient points made in them.

Lama Chimpa thinks that the most important requirement for achieving satisfactory translation of a Tibetan text into any modern language, such as English, should be team work, for it is difficult to find an authoritative Tibetan scholar who can also write English well, and it is no less difficult to find someone who is a master of English, as well as a qualified scholar of classical Tibetan. Other prerequisites for satisfactory translation, according to Lama Chimpa, are the standardization of Tibetan terminology in the target language, standardization of the scheme of transliteration of Tibetan alphabets, and a reliable dictionary.

Rev. Shree N. Singh discusses the factors, a combination of which makes for good translation—language, culture, scholastics, meditative realization on the part of the translator, his personality, grace, and methodology. He also discusses the importance of transliteration and phonetics, and a number of points concerning the relation of Sanskrit and Tibetan that are important for translation.

Elizabeth Napper, unlike Paul Griffiths (one of whose articles is the starting point of her paper), sees no conflict between being a Buddhologist and a Buddhist. She thinks that "the criterion of what gets translated should not be elegance of style, but rather appropriateness as a vehicle to allow full understanding of the Buddhist tradition," and "the most useful translation," she believes, "is one that is quite literal (although not mindless) and that renders technical terms with a precision that allows the complex philosophical discussions that occur in Tibetan to be mirrored in the English translation. We need not be overtly concerned with elegance of expression and adapting the translation to take into account nuances of contemporary English usage and style." She does not see any particular necessity to shift Tibetan terminology into contemporary idiom. For her the most useful translation is one that is quite literal and clear, in which technical terms are rendered with a precision that allows complete philosophical discussion.

S.K. Pathak touches on a number of problems experienced by modern translators—such as free translation versus verbatim, traditional adherence to the concerned text, appropriate equivalence of Buddhist terms in Tibetan with English, maintenance of the flavour of the original—and suggests some formulae to tackle these problems. These are: innovations of systematic methods or guidelines of translation of Buddhist texts from Tibetan into English; methodical exercise in the course of translation; application of mechanical apparatus wherever necessary; organisation of translator-personnels; and publications of the texts translated after codification. He also suggests a scheme necessary for implementing these formulae, comprising compilation of bibliography of all texts translated and reconstructed, preparation of a Tibetan-English concordance, and associating a traditionally trained Tibetan scholar with all undertakings of translation. He suggests some ways of organizing the scheme.

Jośe Ignacio Cabezon first develops an outline of a theory of comparison as a form of knowledge. Comparison becomes both the means and the end of analysis — "means" in so far as it shall be the subject of inquiry. Then he applies the nature and workings of comparison as a form of knowledge to the realm of translation theory, particularly to the translation of Buddhist texts from the Tibetan. Comparison, he argues, is a source of knowledge and translation a form of comparison. Hence translation also is a source of knowledge and "insight" is possible when concepts are stretched beyond their limits, when the semantic implications of a term in one language suggests new ways of perceiving a term in another.

D. Seyfort Ruegg considers some fundamental issues concerning translating Tibetan philosophical texts: the inevitable loss of many connotations and meanings of the original and the inadvertent introduction of some new and undesired connotations in translation, however carefully done. This is due, he thinks, not only to linguistic differences of Tibetan and English but primarily to conceptual and cultural relativism, to the thorny problem of intercultural transmission and reception, of hermeneutics. He also discusses the question of the usefulness of commentaries and of the oral tradition, and states that in many branches of Tibetan studies real progress can be made only in close collaboration with Tibetan scholars. He thinks that "more sustained attempts at analysis and synthesis, and better synchronic and diacronic studies of doctrines and terms with a view to penetrating and interpreting theory and developing an adequate language of theory" are necessary to overcome the difficulties. He maintains that, although it is neither possible nor desirable today to regulate translators and their work by decree, it would be desirable to bring about some uniformity through standardized glossaries and lexicons.

Dr Akira Saito speaks of one interesting aspect of the experience of translating the Tibetan texts of Nāgārjuna's *Mūlamadhyamakakārikā* as cited in its commentaries such as *Akutobhayā,* Buddhapālita's commentary, and the *Prasannapadā.* Sometimes the contents of the translation of a quoted *kārikā* and the commentator's explanation of it, it was noticed, did not agree. This paper aims at clarifying, through the analysis of a number of such instances, how, and in what order, Kluḥi rgyal mtshan and Ñyi ma grags translated the commentaries on the *Mūlamadhyamakakārikā,* including the *Prajñā-nāmā-mūlamadhyamakakārikā,* the *Prajñāpradīpa,* and the above three commentaries.

Peter Della Santina explains that, although within the Buddhist tradition language itself has no direct relation to the real, we use it indirectly in order to eventually induce a direct experience of reality whose consequence is liberation. Since terms acquire their fields of meaning only from a linguistic and conceptual context, that is to say, within a cultural milieu, it is imperative, that an appropriate cultural milieu be created even if the best possible translation of key Buddhist terms are to perform their intended function within the Buddhist project of liberation. The creation of an appropriate cultural milieu, within which selected terms used in the translation of Buddhist texts can acquire proper fields of meaning, is possible only through comprehensive Buddhist education. So, he argues, even the most meticulous selection of terms in translation can have little hope of successfully conveying the intended meanings without the support of an appropriate cultural milieu. It follows from this that translation essentially and generally is reinterpretation of terms and concepts within a new cultural milieu. This is inevitable in case of translation into a foreign cultural milieu because the terminology adopted will of necessity have a prehistory antecedent to its adoption for the purpose of translation.

Dr M.R. Chinchore discusses the rationale of reconstructing in Sanskrit those philosophical and other Buddhist texts which are now available only in Tibetan translations, though written originally in Sanskrit. In the first section of the paper, she gives an outline of the contours of the diversified culture within the framework of the broadly monolithic civilization that flourished in the subcontinent of India. In the second section she discusses the significance of adopting Sanskrit as the common medium of intelligent exchange of ideas and thoughts between different schools of religious and philosophical strands. In the third section she looks into the necessity of reconstructing lost texts in Sanskrit.

Tsepak Rigzin urges the need for compiling a practical Tibetan-English dictionary of Buddhist terminology in order to avoid the confusing variety of renderings currently employed in translation. He discusses the nature, scope, limitations, and the methodology of research necessary for such an undertaking; he also gives many valuable suggestions for organizing a project such as this.

Joe Bransford Wilson considers how Tibetan Buddhist texts should be approached for translation. His response is occasioned by some comments on Buddhology and translation made by a number of scholars. Among the points he discusses are the task of the translator and four schemes of translation methods. He also discusses the assumption that Buddhist texts in Tibetan or in Sanskrit *are* translatable, that whatever is expressed in the source language *can* be re-expressed in the target language, which for him is the twentieth century English.

Georges Dreyfus speaks of his experience of translating, into English, Buddhist concepts rather than the whole of any text. Through the analysis of the problem of translating two terms from the logico-epistemological tradition of Dharmakīrti—*don gcig* and *spyi bye brag*—he concludes that no definite rules can be formed for tackling such problems; only some guidelines may emerge for translating.

Professor Shunzo Onoda deals with the usage of the pronoun "khyod" which originally and normally means "you" as the second person pronoun in the daily use of ordinary Tibetan. In the monastic debate terminology, however, it has a special usage as a variable logical operator. Further, he tries to distinguish between the homological (self-description) and heterological (non self-description) conceptual phenomena which was also one of the early philosophical distinctions made in Tibet.

Chogkhang Thubten Tandhar points to the different interpretations put on the key term *pratītyasamutpāda* by different Buddhist schools and that it is also differently translated by different translators leading to considerable confusion. If, he thinks, a standard

Tibetan-English dictionary could be developed by a group of distinguished scholars, and if the English equivalents of such important terms could be standardized and used in translation, that would go a long way towards solving the confusion often created by using, in translation, a variety of expressions for a single term in the original, with precise meaning. That would also help, he thinks, in presenting the Dharma and Buddhist studies in a better focus.

Karma Monlam discusses three factors that are behind all problems of translation — linguistic, cultural, and geographical. Keeping this in mind, he enumerates the necessary qualifications and requirements of a competent translator. Although he is not in favour of imposing any impractical system of standardization in matters of translation, he feels that there is perhaps an excess of freedom and utter lack of coordination among translators with their totally different cultural and philosophical backgrounds, and that there should be some kind of central body to coordinate the flood of ever-increasing translations of Buddhist texts.

Professor C. Linctner's paper focuses on editors and readers of translation rather than on the task of the translator. Before a Buddhist text is translated it is essential that an authentic and critical edition of it is prepared. The editor ensures this. As an editor, his highest goal is to present before the public any given text in the form in which he believes it has left either the original author or the previous editors or translator. As far as possible, questions and problems relating to authenticity, authorship, chronology, etc. should be settled. The translator should go about his task with the potential readers in mind, of which there are roughly three groups— the scholarly, the not-so-scholarly, and the general, educated reader.

Ven. M. Tsering maintains that Tibetan translations of the Tripiṭaka, tantra and the works of Indian Buddhist masters would not have been so accurate had it not been the products of joint efforts by the utterly dedicated Tibetan *lotsawas* and Indian *paṇḍitas*. According to him, the outcome of the exertion of several minds can be expected to be superior to that of a single mind.

Sharpa Tulku thinks that the faithful rendering and excellent quality of translations from Sanskrit texts to Tibetan were possible owing partly to the cooperative method of work by Indian *paṇḍitas* and Tibetan *lotsawas,* and partly to the standardization of terminology. Now that so many translations are being produced, more attention should be given to the advantages of cooperative efforts and the importance of standardization of terminology in translation.

Glenn H. Mullin speaks of what he thinks to be a neglected aspect of translation from Tibetan. He takes the focus from the usual textual content to the context of the author's presence in his writings. He talks of his experiment with translating some Tibetan material as good literature (albeit somewhat spiritual and exotic), such as the writings of the early Dalai Lamas. He explains how a translator should prepare himself to be able to capture in the translation the subtle and elusive character of the original writing— a particularly difficult task in view of "the distance between Tibetan and English literary sensitivity, and the different ways in which the two languages work."

Ven. Tenzin Dorjee confines his discussion to three styles of translation—what he calls conceptual, thematic, and literary —and he thinks that the best result can be achieved by adopting a judicious mixture of all three; which is what he himself does. To him accuracy of rendering is more important than elegance, although a translation should be readable and intelligible, and it must convey the original sense as in the source language. The syntax and semantic difference between Tibetan and English languages are a major problem area. He thinks that textual ambiguity is a common characteristic of Tibetan writing and that this aspect should not be totally eliminated in translation. Lack of standardized equivalents in English of Tibetan technical terms may be overcome by defining and explaining them in footnotes where necessary.

Bhiksu Jampa Tenzin gives an account of the development and aims of the Dharma Centre in Hamburg in the field of translation of texts relating to Tibetan Buddhism. He speaks mainly about their seven-year study programme for lay students and also about a dictionary project for Tibetan religious terms. He explains the difference in the approach to translation of practicing Buddhists and that of an academic scholar; and how each can be, and is, valuable to the other, particularly the possibility of mutual exchange and support in the dictionary project.

This might be the most appropriate place, to record the recommendations which emerged from the conference.

1. We recommend the encouragement of teamwork between Tibetan and non-Tibetan scholars, as well as, whenever possible, consultation with Sanskritists and philologists, in the translation of Tibetan texts.
2. We recognize the importance of the lexicons being prepared by different institutions, and we recommend increased communication between these groups; here at this early stage of translation work we accept the importance of a plurality of approaches in the treatment of technical terminology, as well as an expansive documentation of the treatment of terms.
3. We recommend publication in Tibetan of the important lexicographical materials, such as: (*a*) Sgra-sbyor-bam-gngis; (*b*) Li-shi-gur-khang; (*c*) Za-ma-tok; (*d*) Chos-kyi-rnam-grangs; (*e*) the lexicons of Lcang-skya and Klong-dol blama; and so forth. Hopefully these could all be brought out in one volume or edition, as an important work-tool for translators, philologists and lexiconographers.
4. We recommend and recognize the importance to Indian culture of the reconstruction/retranslation into Sanskrit of the Kangyur and Tangyur texts that is in progress.
5. Finally, we acknowledge the importance of the following points made at the conference:

    (i) no one definitive system of translation has emerged, and in fact this plurality is both valid and useful to the development of languages of translation;

    (ii) at least one member of the translation team should have the source language as their mother tongue, and at least one member should have the target language as their mother-tongue;

    (iii) that translation should be made with as much knowledge of the Sanskrit and Pali traditions as possible;

    (iv) that translation informed by a knowledge of the implications of a doctrine, the historical background of the terms encountered, the life and perspective of the author, etc. is advisable; and

(v) that the usage of apparatus such as introduction, footnotes, glossaries, etc. is useful.

It will be of great interest to all those who participated to meet again in the not too distant future, to continue the work initiated. To this effect we decided to form a Steering Committee. The Steering Committee is comprised of Venerable Samdong Rinpoche, Venerable Roland Steffan, Dr Elizabeth Napper, Mr Gyatso Tsering and Professor Jeffrey Hopkins with Dr Seyfort Ruegg and myself as co-conveners.

Because these papers are specifically about approaches to translation, which include how to resolve issues of transliteration and phoneticization, we have not attempted to impose a standard system of transliteration across all the papers in this volume.

Doboom Tulku

New Delhi

The Methodology of Translations from Classical Tibetan

Lama Chimpa

A satisfactory translation of a classical Tibetan text into any other language, particularly into English, must be a team work. For it is almost impossible to find a good Tibetan scholar who can also write good English; it is no less difficult to find someone who is a master of the English language and at the same time can deal with ease with classical Tibetan which even an ordinary Tibetan scholar finds quite complex. A thorough knowledge of classical Tibetan is acquired by long study in the traditional way. For understanding any piece of ancient Tibetan writing one is required to gain special knowledge through a long period of serious study. And this is possible only under the guidance of a highly qualified teacher. Then, of course, not every qualified teacher is capable of teaching every work in Tibetan, for these classical works are on diverse subjects. To add to the difficulty, an identical expression or passage occurring in a medical text may have a different meaning when it appears in a *tantra*-text. And the same may have still another meaning when it occurs in a philosophical work. Therefore, having some knowledge of the Tibetan language without a traditional base does not qualify one to undertake the task of translating any work from classical Tibetan, particularly into English, for the syntax of these two languages is totally different. Not only that. Even a Tibetan-speaking scholar who has a good grasp of the Tibetan philosophy finds it hard to explain a medical text in his own language. Therefore, how can he be expected to translate the same into English which is neither his mother tongue, nor a language that he studied in school.

In view of this situation, Tibetan scholars entrusted the work of translation of all Indian classics to a team of translators. None of the works contained in the Tibetan Kanjur and Tanjur is the work of any one person. Usually three scholars were involved in a translation: an Indian pandit, a Tibetan writer and another Tibetan scholar who revised the draft translation.

The main task of the Indian pandit who took part in such translation was to explain the meaning of the text to his Tibetan colleague *(lotsāwa)*, who then translated it into Tibetan, his own tongue. The draft translation was then closely examined making necessary corrections by the Shu-chen-gyi *lotsāwa*—the *reviser*-translator and approved. By this method it was possible, more than a thousand years ago when most of the population of the world were illiterate, to produce satisfactory translation of a large number of works, and these have been carefully preserved. These valuable translations are available in monumental collections called Kanjur and Tanjur. They comprise three hundred and thirty volumes, containing more than five thousand separate works. It would be interesting to know such details about these translation works as the names of the Indian pandits and Tibetan translators who collaborated in producing these, and when and where they worked. Some other details are sometimes given in the colophons of some of the works.

In this connection, it may be mentioned that, though most of the treatises in Kanjur and Tanjur are Buddhist works, not all of them are so. There are among them many important works of secular interest, such as astrology, astronomy, medical science, poetry and what not. Unfortunately, the original texts of these works like *Amṛitāṣṭāṅga-hṛidya* are lost. However, Kālidāsa's *Meghadūta*, Daṇḍi's *Kāvyādarśa* and some other famous works are also among those translated into Tibetan. It would seem that the Tibetan scholars of those days translated whatever literary works they could collect from India into Tibetan with the help of those panditas who fled to Tibet during the Muhammadan attack on the Buddhists in India around the twelfth century A.D.

Most of the original texts in Sanskrit and Pali thus translated into Tibetan are lost, and so in a sort of reverse situation, scholars, particularly Indian scholars, should try to restore these lost treasures of knowledge from their existing Tibetan versions with the help of Tibetan scholars who have come over to India as a consequence of the Chinese occupation of Tibet.

As already mentioned, a satisfactory translation into a modern language of a work in classical Tibetan on any subject can be achieved only with the help of Tibetan scholars educated in a monastery on the concerned subject. This is so because it was in Tibetan monasteries that serious classical texts, like *Pramāṇa vārttika*, *Prajñāpāramitā*, *Madhyamaka-śāstra*, *Abhidharma-koṣa*, Vinaya and *tantra*-treatises were studied thoroughly. Only those therefore who studied any particular text in the proper way in Tibetan monasteries can explain or translate it. Not only that. Even such a Tibetan scholar is hard put to express the basic ideas of the author of that particular text in a language he does not know well. There was no facility in any Tibetan monastery for teaching and learning any modern language. However, a scholar such as this can make his co-translator understand the full sense of an author's expression by various means. This enables the co-translator to put the sense in fine language that he knows well. In this way, a satisfactory translation can be produced.

Apart from these difficulties with regard to translation from Tibetan texts, there are some other problems that outsiders dealing with the Tibetan language may have to face, such as poorly made xylographs or block-printings and illegible hand-writings. While reading translations of Tibetan works, I have noticed that some translators not only misunderstand the basic meanings of passages and sentences in many places but also confuse some letters that look somewhat similar, leading to their getting some wrong sense. Sometimes, for instance, the translator takes the letter 'ng' for 'da', or 'pa' for 'ba' and so on. I cannot go into much detail in this short paper, but by way of an example, I would like to mention a small error made by a great scholar.

The following line occurs in Obermiller's English translation of the *History of Buddhism* by Bu-ston:

> " ... and to place the burning lamp before the tutelary deity. If thou shalt address an entreaty, the *serpent* of Dharmapāla will throw the lamp away, and at the place (where it falls) the temple must be built." (*Buddhism in India and Tibet* by Bu-ston, II part, translated from Tibetan into English by Dr E. Obermiller, Heidelberg 1932).

The original of this passage in Tibetan reads: " ... mar me sbar ba yi dam gyi mdun du bshag ste gsol ba btab na chos skyong gi sprul pas Kong bu gang du skyur pa der lha khang rtsigs shig." The translator has obviously taken the Tibetan *sprul pas* as "*sbrul pas*" and found its meaning in his dictionary to be "serpent" or "snake", while the meaning of the earlier word, '*sprul pas*', is "incarnation" or "miraculous form", and that is the right expression in the context. So the correct translation would be: "the incarnation of the Dharmapāla will throw the lamp away." If a good Tibetan scholar had been associated with this translation, he would not have allowed Obermiller to make such an error, even if the xylography had been poor, for he would have long experience of deciphering bad writing and hazy xylographic print. He would also know the context.

By drawing attention to this mistake, my intention is not to criticize any one but to emphasize that a good translation from a classical Tibetan treatise should usually be a team work. As mentioned above, a good Tibetan scholar of the concerned subject and a good writer of the language into which the translation is to be made, can jointly produce a satisfactory translation of such a text. This does not, however, mean that no good translation has ever been done by individual effort. There are many excellent translations such as by Dr George Roerich *(Blue Annals)* and a few others among whom one must include Dr S. K. Pathak who has a long experience of dealing with complex Tibetan texts.

When we translate a serious Tibetan work into English, we use many Sanskrit or Pali equivalents of standard Tibetan terms, of which there are no English equivalents. To mention a few such terms: Buddha, Bodhisattva, Pratyeka-Buddha, Dharmapāla, etc., of which Tibetan equivalents are, respectively: *Sangs rgyas, byang chub sems dpa', rang sangs rgyas, chos skyong,* etc. There are hundreds of such expressions for which no English words are used. Do most of our English readers know Sanskrit and Pali well enough to accept and know the meaning of these terms as such? If not, why don't we straightaway retain the Tibetan words in English translations?

Many scholars maintain that translations from Tibetan must as far as possible be literal. But why is this necessary? The main purpose of any writing is to communicate with the reader, to let the reader know the subject on which the writer writes. The purpose of translating some one's work into another language is to further the transmission of the author's message to readers of that language.

The writing style, the way of expression and the usage of words in Tibetan are very different from those in English. Therefore, if one translates a Tibetan text into English, word by word, including even those Tibetan words that have no English equivalents, the translation can hardly be understood by those who are not accustomed to reading that kind of language. Rather than following that style, we should try to produce translation in a style that is understood by most readers of the language of translation.

If we follow the translation method adopted by the Tibetan scholars who translated the huge Kanjur and Tanjur from Indian texts, it should be possible to produce better works. For this we must look back and find out how it was possible for them to produce such a large quantity of quality work.

When the Tibetan scholars decided to translate the Indian literary works they had in their hands, they first decided, after long consultation among themselves, the method to be adopted for translating. They proceeded by preparing a glossary of not-so-familiar Sanskrit terms and their Tibetan forms or equivalents. They also compiled several Sanskrit-Tibetan dictionaries, including the famous *Mahāvyutpatti* which is still in use. Their translation of Sanskrit words was not always very literal. For example, the word *Bhikṣu* has been translated as *dge slong* literally, "virtue-seeker," a beautiful translation. The literal equivalent of the word *Bhikṣu* in Tibetan is *sloṅg-ba* which means just "Beggar", and this does not, of course, sound as nice as "virtue-seeker." And such words as were not possible to translate into Tibetan, or those that were quite common to the Tibetan readers, or those that would not sound fine if translated were left as they are in Tibetan transliteration. Examples of such words are "vaidūrya", "chandan" and "liṅga."

To follow a proper method of transliteration is also an essential part of good translation. The transliteration of Tibetan letters in Roman script is presently creating some problems. Those who work in this area do not follow the same scheme in transcribing Tibetan letters into Roman letters. The scheme of translitering Tibetan words into Roman letters has not yet been standardized. Some different Tibetan letters represent similar pronunciation, and scholars are trying to distinguish these by using different diacritical marks and by using different Roman letters even for the same

Tibetan letter. For example, some scholars use "h" while others use "'" for the Tibetan small "a" letter (there are two "a" letters in Tibetan). This creates much confusion. Diacritical marks do not appear to be much useful for a layman like myself, who is weak in the science of phonetics. A good uniform rule for transcribing Tibetan words and letters in Roman script is badly needed. For this, if it is not possible to invent some new Roman letter to represent some equivalent Tibetan letters, we should try to follow the method of transliterating Lancha and Vartula scripts in Tibetan, which is as follows. There are 30 alphabets in Tibetan script. This is not enough for transliterating the ancient Indian scripts in Tibetan letters. So the Tibetan scholars of those days adopted a clear method of transcribing such letters as had no equivalent Tibetan letter by the device of reverting the similarly pronounced letters, subjoining the "ha" letter to some other similarly pronounced letters, and in the case of long vowels, doubling the Tibetan vowel signs, etc. Those who want to see them in detail may consult the front pages of Sarat Chandra Das's *Tibetan-English Dictionary*.

Buddhist Translations: Problems and Perspectives

N. Singh

Namo Guru Mañjughoṣāya!

Translation is the process of rendering a piece of literature from its language of origin into the idiom of a distinctly different culture. The process involves, on the one hand, a thorough understanding of the primary text by the translator, its assimilation into that person's psyche, and a subsequent regurgitation, an accurate re-creation in a comprehensible and coherent form. I will make an attempt in this paper to analyse some of the key factors involved in this process. What I have to say is based on my empirical observations and analyses conducted over nearly two decades of immersion in Tibetan Buddhism, primarily within the Nyingma-Kagyu traditions, but with an expansive and non-sectarian or Rismed perspective. At the onset, to obviate any confusion in this matter I wish to emphasize that I do not claim to be a translator in the sense used in this paper.

It is in fact difficult to isolate the factors elucidated below because they overlap each other to a considerable degree. However, for the sake of clarity they will be dealt with individually. I will discuss seven factors, viz. language, culture, scholastics, meditative realisation, personality, grace and methodology. The paper will conclude with a critique of a few pertinent terms and suggestions for their re-translation. Three further sub-sections—Sanskrit, Transliteration, and Phonetics—will also be included here, since they are pertinent. Translations of three common prayers—one Sanskrit in origin, another a 'térma', and a third, a direct composition in Tibetan—will be appended as examples.

Language, the first factor, is a fairly obvious consideration. A translator needs to be proficient in two languages, the one from which he translates and the one into which the translation is rendered. Some of the more subtle aspects, unfortunately, are apparently overlooked in the exemplary zeal evinced by westerners, particularly in this regard.

Until half a century ago, study curricula placed great emphasis on language. A graduate of a public school in the U.K., corresponding to an elitist private school elsewhere, would thus emerge with a strong foundation not only in English, having been rigorously taught its grammar and composition, but he would also have studied Greek or Latin together with a modern European language. More recently, educationists consider such emphasis on language misplaced. The result is that a frighteningly large number of aspiring translators lack an extensive foundation in their own parent language. Naturally then, their forays into Tibetan lack proper preparation. This is most obvious in terms of their vocabulary limited to perhaps no more than 6,000 words of English, a serious handicap. Unfortunately, however, publishers avidly pick up their efforts, circulating wittingly or otherwise, a plethora of distorted works on Buddhism.

Tibetan and English, together with virtually any other language, have three distinct variants: literary, official, and the vernacular. It need not be mentioned that a philosophical exegesis needs to be rendered as such, whilst an official document must preserve its character in the secondary language. The vernacular, on the other hand, is fair game for the translator as one may express it in any suitable form desired. The unique fascination of Oxbridge English evinced by the late Vidyādhara Dhrungpa Rinpoche of Zurmang is noteworthy. He would constantly emphasize the need for the English-speaking people to go back to their linguistic origins. His rather amusing attempts to educate his American disciples into speaking English correctly, and the elocution booklets he prepared deserve mention here.

This is the only remedy to this problem. Those who aspire to be translators need to study their own parent language first to a degree of acceptable literary proficiency. Simultaneously, they need to have a deep appreciation of their heritage. Only then can they be expected to delve into the intricacies of Tibetan, a language vastly different from their own. It is to the general disadvantage that this is often overlooked.

A bilingual person, moreover, is able to think directly in either or both the languages. This is one way of self-assessment. Another deeper method constitutes dream analysis: should one find oneself dreaming in any language, this is to be construed as an indication of the extent to which it has been assimilated into one's psyche. A qualified translator must necessarily possess these two qualities.

Tibetans have an interesting saying, "We've drunk 'thungpa' together many times during pūjā-assemblies." This leads into the second parameter of culture and aculturization. The question which arises here is, "As a non-Tibetan how well do you know the Tibetan people?"

For the average alien there are two paths open. The most convenient is to have a Tibetan spouse or a boy or girl friend as the case may be. Those accepting the path of renunciation need to immerse themselves without any reservations whatsoever into the sub-culture of their monastery, eating, drinking, sleeping and so on with their Tibetan counterparts, lice and fleas as well. Only then will the aspirant learn to understand their gestures, smiles, moods, and the forces—religious, cultural, and political—which propel them onwards. This aspirant needs to be simultaneously equally mobile in the culture of secondary expression. Where such mobility of consciousness is lacking, translations attempted will be wanting in the vitality and exuberance of the original!

For the Tibetan his culture forms the acmé of human civilization, and must be acknowledged as such by all. This is in direct contrast to people from the west in general who are overtly obsessed with highlighting the *lacuna* in their heritage rather than appreciating its inherent richness. One will find, therefore, that a Tibetan Lama will instruct his disciples to be firmly grounded in his tradition. Westerners on the other hand are involved in the processes of acceptance and rejection. This is fraught with danger for the very same people who turned their backs on their own religion, will similarly, if disillusioned with the Tibetan container environment, not hesitate to spurn the Dharma together with its Tibetan trappings! This is a point Tibetans would do well to heed!

Scholastics. Both the western and eastern hemispheres are exceptionally rich in their traditions of scholasticism. Ancient Greece and Rome produced outstanding thinkers whose works form the very foundations of western consciousness. So has the east. The advent of Christianity brought about profound transformations in an erstwhile "pagan" culture, creating an all-pervasive idiom which *is* its datum. There is no escaping this fact. Similarly the datum in India *is* distinctly Hindu.

What is fascinating is that, in spite of the ancient cultures, one finds a large number of concepts and traits common to them: Learning, for example, in ancient times had always been contained within the framework of religion. The striking difference has been that, in India, religion and science had never been warring factions as they had been in Europe.The two co-existed to the extent that religion, rather its basis, spirituality, has been none other than a scientific investigation into the world of phenomena. However, India too has passed through its Dark Ages when invasion upon invasion enervated what had once been a creative culture. It is most certainly to the credit of the Tibetan people that they have preserved intact within their heritage the wisdom of ancient India in both its scholastic and applicative meditational forms.

The west unfortunately has been sadly deprived of the latter. Fortunately there have been exceptions in the persons of those such as St. Augustine, St. Francis of Assisi, St. Teresa of Avila, St. John of the Cross, and more recently Thomas Merton and Mother Teresa. They are bold statements of the fact that, in spite of oppressive institutions, the grace of the Holy Trinity is still functional, finding expression in the human realm through the lives of these saints, witnesses to that wisdom which cannot be claimed to be the exclusive possession by any given people.

Returning to language one finds that English, for example, has evolved through Chaucer, Shakespeare, the poets of the eighteenth and nineteenth centuries, through Charles Dickens, until more recently Bertrand Russell, Aldous Huxley, and others. Europe too has similarly seen the advent of great literateurs: Rousseau, Dumas, Voltaire, Goethe, Leo Tolstoy and Jean-Paul Sartre are virtually household names there, as also Samuel Becket. Thus there has been no dearth of thinkers there, their works outstanding testimonies to the genius of the west. Their writings, above all, reveal their acumen in the use of language. It is said of Goethe that his genius lay in his ability to express himself succinctly in German to an extent none had done before. Similarly, the works of Russell and Huxley reveal a remarkable degree of maturity and depth in their understanding and use of English.

It stands to reason, therefore, that renditions into English, for example, of Tibetan treatises, primary texts or scholia, cannot be effectively undertaken by people who have little or no grounding in western academia. In this context the translations of the Pali Text Society, London, and the efforts of scholars such as Professor Edward Conze and Professor Herbert V. Guenther amongst others, become exceptionally pertinent. Admittedly, their style may be wanting from certain points of view; however, in spite of these supposed shortcomings, their genius needs to be appreciated. A high level of scholarship in the western tradition is thus a necessary, though not a sufficient, qualification for any who might covet the term "translator" in the Buddhist world.

Coming now to scholarship in the Indo-Tibetan tradition. A mKhas. Pa. or Paṇḍita is defined as an erudite person capable of discerning between right and wrong, truth and falsity, the relative and the absolute, virtue and sin. Implied is that such a person will have a profound understanding of his own language and a deep appreciation of his heritage. One will have studied the Dharma including other branches of learning in the manner they were taught in the ancient Universities of Nālandā and Vikramaśīla. One is expected to have extensively engaged in the tirades of audition, contemplation, and meditation; exposition, debate, and composition; and is therefore sagacious, diligent and magnanimous. Out of compassion, in order to take mother-beings to the other shore, one imparts instructions to disciples urging them similarly on to train their errant egos. This definition of a scholar is peculiar to the Buddhist tradition. The *lotsāwas* of the past were such!

Currently, however, Buddhism in the west is but in a nascent state, hence it is rare to find Paṇḍitas thus qualified. Most non-Tibetans, therefore, are seriously handicapped. Moreover, a distinct western Buddhism is still in the process of being evolved. The situation is both creative and inspiring. An aspiring translator could be fairly successful in his efforts if he attempts to translate from "within" the tradition, rather than from outside of it. This would entail a study of a particular text in a traditional manner, translation being effected subsequently. It is encouraging to note that a number of Khanpos and Géshés are actively engaged in thus instructing their disciples.

It may be mentioned here, however, that H.E. Goshrī Gyaltshab Rinpoche of Tshurphu, after returning once from teaching the Bodhicaryāvatāra at Samye Ling, Scotland, had expressed his disappointment at the intellectual calibre of the disciples there. Such a lack of sophistication is a serious drawback found in most university graduates these days, not to mention those who never ventured that far!

Scholarship, therefore, though a necessary condition, should however be considered as insufficient in itself. The Tibetans themselves maintain that without a direct realization of the Dharma, one is no better than a parrot. It is stated in the Blo-sbyong-don-bdun-ma scholium by Rngul-chu Thog-med:

> "'All dharmas converge to a single purpose.' All the teachings of the Hīnayāna and the Mahāyāna are directed to the subjugation of self-identification. Therefore, could these teachings not become antidotal to it, then any practice accomplished becomes meaningless. On the other hand, if your dharma-practice has become antidotal to self-identification, this then is an indication that your consciousness is being trained and purified. Herein lies the distinction as to whether your practice is really in accordance with the Dharma or not." (excerpted from *Parivarta*, a forthcoming book by this author.)

In direct contrast with western scholasticism where the individual ego is given a free rein for self-expression, Buddhism seeks to give expression solely to the wisdom of egolessness. Therefore, a translator who wishes to be successful in his efforts, needs to be a traveller along the path that leads to the dissolution of the ego, not its enhancement. The *lotsāwas* of the past were not only sagacious and erudite, they were also accomplished saints. For an average person to reach an acceptable proficiency as a translator, some twenty years of intensive study and meditation would constitute a bare minimum. It is encouraging that such facilities are being progressively made more and more available to westerners by various farsighted Masters!

This leads on to the next parameter, that of the *personality* of a translator. Beyond the factors already dealt with above, there are two other requisites: surrender to one's Guru(s) and proper motivation. For a person to be meaningfully expressive in this context, one has no alternative but to be constantly surrendering to one's

Guru(s), constantly unmasking, hence actively training in the two Bodhichittas. It is no hidden secret that only then will scriptures start revealing their multiplicity of nuances to the seeker. This is the more true with the Mantrayāna. Thus only can the perception of one's spiritual environment be enhanced; the more this happens the more discerning one gets. Those who are motivated by the Eight Worldly Dharmas—gain and loss, fame and notoriety, criticism and praise, happiness and suffering—do more disservice to the world than anything else, and should never be called "translators". Derisiveness and the lack of willingness to constantly re-evaluate are none other than ego-functions, hence harmful both to oneself and to others. The outlandish and the common as well both need to be analysed dispassionately, and a "translator" should be able to do so. The personalities of the Masters of the Buddhist traditions stand out as shining examples for aspirants to emulate.

The parameter of *grace* is common to both the east and the west. It is pivotal to the Hindu traditions (which, incidentally, include Buddhism) and Christianity. The years this unknown Indian has spent in the Dharma are themselves a witness to this crucial element, for without it he would have been as faceless as his 800 million compatriots. In modern parlance grace may be defined as a psychic link transcending the boundaries of self-identification. It trasforms an individual's personality, enhancing the perception of a spiritual environment. Ultimately it is none other than the Dharmakāya itself.

There is yet another perspective to this parameter perhaps uncommon elsewhere. The Buddhist Dispensation has been kept alive through the process of the transmission of the Dharma. In terms of the written word this has been done so by Masters reading out texts upon texts to their disciples to maintain an unbroken sequence of vocal transmission. The Tibetan term for this is *lung*. This is important to such an extent that those teachings for which the continuity of *lung* has been interrupted, have ceased to be "alive", even though they might still be extant otherwise. Whereas in the past this unbroken link was transferred to Tibet through the medium of *lotsāwas,* a consensus has yet to be evolved concerning the translations into modern languages. This is a crucial issue indeed and one which will hopefully be resolved during the course of this seminar.

It stands to reason, therefore, that translations attempted in the absence of precious grace, and subsequently taught or used without the existence of a vocal transmission for them, will turn out to be insipid and confused ego-functions. Lacking in the blessings of one's lineage, they will deviate from the purport of the original in that they will fail to accomplish the two Ideals: those of personal accomplishment, and the welfare of others. Such works cannot but be retrogressive, a cause for the furtherance of entrapment in *saṃsāra*!

One of the aspects of grace is traditionally known as Byin. Gyis. rLabs. Pa'i. bK'a., the Dharma which manifests in the being of an aspirant as a function of the blessings of the lineage coming through the medium of one's Principal Guru. The *Heart Sūtras* is an outstanding example of this.

Assuming the above components are replete in an individual who may thus be referred to as "translator," the following methodology deserves serious consideration. Actually it would be superfluous to advise one such, because the person would intuitively adopt this process.

As a matter of course, a Tibetan term needs to be understood together with its Sanskrit equivalents. This would also indicate its origin which could, without much difficulty, be traced to its Latin and or Greek equivalents. It need not be mentioned that Latin and Sanskrit are sister languages of the Indo-Aryan group which includes ancient Persian as well.

To consider an example, the Tibetan Nyan. Thos. is "śrāvaka" in Sanskrit: the verb for the latter is "śṛiṇoti", and its corresponding Latin is "audibilis". Hence "śrāvaka" may be rendered as "audient," a genuine word in English according to the OED. The word, however, might need to be redefined slightly to suit the Buddhist context just as "scholar" has been defined in this paper. The term "listener" generally used for this term is insipid and evokes no imagery whatsoever in the mind of the reader, besides conveying little or no meaning to the English consciousness. This is absolutely the only way a Dharma vocabulary can be built up. The argument that "audient" is archaic or obscure, holds absolutely no water, since both the Tibetan and the Sanskrit are equally obscure, meaning nothing to an ordinary Tibetan, Indian or for that matter a Chinese Buddhist. It is a technical term, not a word in common usage. Similarly, "audition" would be appropriate for Thos. Pa. It is evident, then, that the onus of a translator is to be an educator in, not a popularizer of, the Dharma.

The *lotsāwas* of the Early Translation School had been in a similar situation in the eighth century, that of evolving a language capable of containing the lion's milk of the Buddha's Dispensation. Tibetan had been given its script and grammar only two centuries previously, though the Bon. Po. maintain differently. It fell to the lot of pioneers such as Vairochana and his compatriots to create a new Buddhist vocabulary. This they did uncompromisingly. The intent was not to popularize the Dharma per se in Tibet; it was to establish the Dispensation there without compromising the purport of the Buddha and the scholar-saints of India.

There is perhaps no better way to conclude this paper than to quote the renowned Lotsawa bLoldan Shesrab of the New Translation School, some five centuries later:

"Vairochana's understanding is as expansive as the sky;
Kawa Paltseg's and Chogro Lu'i Gyaltshän's
As brilliant as the sun and the moon—
Mine, no more than the brightness of a firefly!"

We have indeed a long way to go!

TERMS

A considerable Dharma vocabulary has been built up in western languages during the last three years of its induction there. The reference is obviously to the Tibetan tradition. It'll be noticed that a large number of terms have gained currency primarily because of regular usage. This is merely to suggest that a stage of finality has yet to be reached in the codification of the Dharma in English for example, hence it is still viable to incorporate plausible alternatives which might be more expressive. Under the section on methodology, the term 'śrāvaka' has already been dealt with. A few other pertinent terms will be studied here briefly. This would ideally be done, however, as a group endeavour, preferably together with those who know Greek, Latin, and Sanskrit. The standard works of reference used are the *Oxford English Dictionary, Roget's Thesaurus,* and of course the famous work by Sarat Chandra Das.

The first is the term "Buddha śāsana" roughly rendered "the doctrine of the Buddha." This is an extremely inadequate rendition in the Sangs rGyas. Kyi. bsTan. Pa. which is said to constitute two aspects, exposition and the applicative meditational. "Dispensation" includes both these angles, as well as the notion of "reign," also incorporated into "śāsana." It is, moreover, in current usage in the Indian media.

"Mūla Guru" is commonly rendered "Root Lama." The usage of "root" as an adjective is extremely obscure. Nor is it suggestive in the least to an English-speaking person, invoking no imagery whatsoever. Surely "Principal Guru" is a far better choice as it is more connotative, and immediately comprehensible. Similarly, "primary text" may be considered for "root text"; "fundamental breach" instead of "root downfall" for rTsa. lTung. is far more replete with imagery.

The word "samaya" could also easily be rendered "vajrayāna covenant," which is what it is in actuality, or simply "covenant"—Dam. Tshig. It is really futile to harp on the point that this is a Judaeo-Christian term, two thousand years of European history cannot be erased. Buddhists need to learn to function meaningfully within the context of their own heritage. Yes, they might choose to suitably redefine a given word to suit the Buddhist context, an ancient ploy used extensively by scholars and philosophers in India. The word 'dharma', for instance, may be understood in one or often different ways depending upon the context. Why then should Judaeo-Christian words be rejected outright, handicapping the evolution of Buddhist English. Moreover, in India, various Hindu traditions have used the same words, redefined, to express concepts peculiar to the one but unmaintainable by others. Even Buddhism has done so in India. Hence what the Mīmāṃsā school might understand by the word "prakṛiti" is most certainly not what a Buddhist might understand by it.

Thus there is absolutely no reason to reject "sin" as translation for "pāpa." The reader has merely to refer to a dictionary of any of the fifteen major languages in India to find that "pāpa" is defined as "sin" in English. The term may, however, be elucidated to rid it of its Christian overtones, and express the Buddhist view. The word may also be used interchageably with "negative action: where it is understood that "action" may be corporeal, vocal, or psychical, already a usage peculiar to Buddhism. It may be noted here that the thrust of Buddhism is thorough understanding, a far cry beyond the processes of acceptance.

bLo. is commonly translated as "mind" and perhaps justifiably so. However, in the instance of bLo. sByong. the term "consciousness" or "psyche" would be far more expressive. sByong, rendered as "training" misses out on the other aspect of its meaning "purification." Hence "the training and purification of the consciousness/ psyche" instead of "mind training" as commonly used.

Kun. Khyab. or "sarva vyāpak" may be rendered as "all pervading and all-encompassing" for obvious reasons.

bZang. Po. or "bhadra" is a more difficult term, but "magnanimous" is an extremely appropriate translation for it. Thus for bZang. sPyod. "magnanimity" could be used without any reservations whatsoever.

sKu. "kāya" on the other hand almost defies translation. Here again is an example of how a relatively common Sanskrit word has been used in an extremely profound metaphysical way, peculiar only to Buddhism. Ordinarily it refers merely to the physical body, "Lus.", and is extant in Indian languages as such. Used in the context of the Five Kāyas the word undergoes a tremendous transformation, becoming pivotal in the Mahāyāna. It refers to "identity:" the absolute and transcendent, the Dharmakāya; and the two forms Rūpakāyas in which egoless compassion spontaneously express itself, the imagery of the Saṃbhogakāya, and its extension in the physical plane, the Nirmāṇakāya, a psychosomatic complex; Svābhāvikakāya, the composite existence of these three.

Other viable suggestions are "demesne" for Zhing. Khams. and "wight" for 'ḥGro. Wa. even though the latter may only be found in the *OED*. But this is exactly what is being proposed in this paper. Similarly, there exists a distinction between "essential" and "essentificial," and I am more inclined to use the latter as being more connotative adjective of Ngo. bo. "svabhāva," or "essence."

SANSKRIT

The peculiarities of the Tibetan language and culture have produced its own version of this ancient language. In India itself, the Mahāyāna had been codified into what is termed Buddhist Hybrid Sanskrit, a looser variant of the classical. As in India currently, few Tibetans have any knowledge of this exalted language. The Tibetan tongue, moreover, finds itself pathetically incapable of getting around Sanskrit syllables. Hence "vajra" is distorted to "benza," "satva" to "sato," and "prajvala" to "ṭra-dzo-la." whilst compound letters are split up into their single components and given full letter value: "adhyāya" would be pronounced "adhi-ya-ya" or "adha-ya-ya." Texts are extant in Tibetan on Sanskrit pronunciation, but few are knowledgeable in it. A person who knows Sanskrit would thus find it extremely difficult to follow the chanting of Tibetan *mantras.* This needs to be taken into consideration by Tibetans now, should they ever wish to establish meaningful relations with the Indian academia.

A well-known story often told in this context is that of Jo. Bo. rJe. "Swāmī Śrīmān" Atīśa. When he once fell sick in Tibet, a tāntrika had to be summoned to heal him. The latter, chanting *mantras* in his own unique fashion, caused the Swāmījī to burst out into a guffaw, being cured of his ailment immediately. This elicited comment from him: "You Tibetans, your pronunciation of Sanskrit is horrendous; even so you preserve the blessings of the lineage!"

Europeans should therefore be urged to say "Oṃ maṇi padme hūṃg" instead of "Om mani päme hung!"

Another problem here was created by Tonmi-Sambhota himself. It is not clear why he chose Tsa. Tsha. Dza. as equivalents for the Sanskrit consonants "ca cha ja," since these sounds exist in Tibetan also. Hence Tibetans say "tsitta" instead of "citta" and "dzala" for "jala". It does not really make sense that Europeans who trace their linguistic roots back to the Indo-Aryan languages should not revert to the more Aryan pronunciation rather than accept blindly the Mongolian distortions of Sanskrit. There is no reason whatsoever to suspect for a moment that the blessings of the lineage will be lost should this be done.

The last is a more complex problem and an extremely serious one. During the centuries of the use of *mantras* in Tibet, errors have crept into their transliterations in Tibetan. Reading Sanskrit in Tibetan script is trying, since it is almost impossible to discern where a vowel should be short, or where it should be long, and where a word might begin or end. *Mantras,* moreover, are found in a curious admixture of Sanskrit, Prākṛit, Apabhraṃśa, Piśāca, and Tibetan. As a result it is extremely difficult to follow them, or correct them. One is left with really no option other than to go back to their sources in the bK'a. 'Gyur. and bstan. 'Gyur. for their correct versions, an exceptionally tedious process no doubt. Simultaneously, before reducing *mantra* to print, in Roman script, or even in Tibetan for that matter, it should be referred to a scholar of Sanskrit. I have seen many goofs ups in this context in Tibetan and English works accepted as standard, and I am much concerned. It is a serious matter indeed when "hrīḥ" replaces "tṛi," and "divya," the Sanskrit for "heavenly, resplendent" is rendered "adivya," its exact opposite, and used as such.

TRANSLITERATION

Since an accurate system of transliteration of Tibetan in Roman is already in vogue, a couple of things may be pointed out here. The real victim of the current system is the letter "cha" rendered as "ca" leaving the reader in a dilemma as to what it might be. Some pronounce this consonant as "sa," some as "ka," only the knowledgeable as "cha." These needs to be remedied, and the subsequent letter written as "chha." Other suggestions are Nga. for Ṅa., Nya. for Ña., Sha. for Śa., and Ṛi. for Ṛ. I do not yet know why the Sanskrit "wa" as in "swāmī" should be written "svāmī," when currently Sanskrit has no sound equivalent to "va." It may also be suggested here that the compound letter "jña" is pronounced "gya" in a number of Indian tongues. This rendition could be made current since "gyāna" reads far more smoothly than "jñāna", or as the Tibetans would write "dznāna."

PHONETICS

The study of Tibetan phonetics is a hoary issue at the best of times and should form the topic of an independent study. The issue is extremely confused for two reasons. The first is that there is an old system of pronunciation, brDa. rNying-pa., which is still extant in the far eastern parts of Kham. It is amazing to hear a native of Golog speak Tibetan as he is able to pronounce the various letters of a compound letter distinctly as well as differentiate between the various prefixes, and so on. Modern Lhasa is a distinctive dilution of ancient Tibetan, a fact known to all. The other is that intonation and pronunciation vary to such an extent from region to region, that it makes a Tibetan from one utterly incomprehensible to that from another. This is evidence enough of the variations, both ethnic and cultural, in what constitute the Tibetan peoples, and that their stress on pedigree perhaps holds little water on investigation.

Studies have been conducted and attempts made to reduce in Roman script some of these dialects, the sounds of which are wholly foreign to the western ear. In fact the more subtle inflections are more often missed. Some strange and highly inaccurate renditions have come into vogue and it would be unskilful to name them as almost every Tibetan-speaking non-Tibetan has this problem in varying degrees. I would merely like to foreward a few suggestions for consideration.

The third vertical row of the Tibetan consonants contains Ga. Ja. Da. Ba., Dza., and 'a. Ga. is pronounced as a cross between the "ga" and "gha" of Sanskrit, a feat few non-Tibetans can achieve. However, should it have a prefix or be superscribed, the sound reverts immediately to that of "ga." As such to distinguish between these sounds it might be appropriate to render the plain Ga. phonetically as "gha," and the compound Ga. as 'ga'. The same applies to the three following letters. Dza. does not really pose a problem, except that Europeans might have difficulty in pronouncing it the English way. "a" is the most difficult of all, and for the most part I render it as "a." An improvement is definitely possible. Europeans also have problems with Zha. and za. and they need to deal with them individually.

There is also a difference between Grags. and Gra., being pronounced s "ḍhrag" and "ḍra" respectively. Care is also needed to distinguish between the dental sounds of Ta. Tha. and Da. and those of the palatal 'ṭa, ṭha, and ḍa'. Amongst the vowels E. and U. sometimes cause confusion. This may be avoided by ensuring that the former is rendered "é," and the latter "û."

The latter Tsha. presents a problem in that the "sh" is generally not pronounced as an aspirated "s" but "sh." Perhaps a way to work around it would be to render mTsho. as "ts-ho," but never as "tso" as it would be confused with the consonant immediately preceding it in the order.

Hence Bar. Do. would be more correctly rendered "bhar dho," Chos. Grags. rGya. mTsho. the VIIth Gyalwang Karmapa as Chhö Ḍhrag Jamts-ho, 'Brug. Pa. as Ḍrûg pa, and so on.

Of the ten rJe. 'Jug., Ga. and Ba. seem to be a problem. There is no reason why dKon. mChhog. should be rendered as 'kön chhok' instead of 'kön chhog', especially as Tibetans themselves do not pronounce the last letter as "k" but as "g." Ba. is the other victim often rendered as a "p" rather than the "b" it actually is. Hence sKyabs. is phoneticized as 'kyap" or "chap," which is ridiculous.

A consensus also needs to be arrived at concerning the way vowels modified by the rJe. 'Jug. Da., Na., La., and Sa. are represented. A simple method is to use the German umlaut, e.g. Khänpo for mKhan. Po., Dhön for Don., Phü for Phud. The first of these however should not be confused with the vowel E. as there is a distinct difference between "ä" and "é," which must be preserved in the phonetics as well.

Now that His Holiness has been awarded the Nobel Peace Prize for 1989, the time is opportune for correcting the misrepresentation for decades of his title—Tāla'i Lama is what it should be, and it could be used from now on, and the world would soon accept it.

Styles and Principles of Translation

Elizabeth Napper

This paper is in many respects a belated response to an article by Paul Griffiths entitled "Buddhist Hybrid English: Some Notes on Philology and Hermeneutics for Buddhologists," that appeared in the *Journal of the International Association of Buddhist Studies* in 1981 (4/2, pp. 17-33). It was an article that was inflammatory in tone, deliberately I believe, within a certain school of scholarly interchange, and carried with it not only some offensive comments about Buddhist literature in general, but also a great deal of scarcely disguised hostility to Buddhists working as translators and as Buddhologists as well as a generalized disdain for the Buddhist literature of Tibet. However, when one gets beyond Griffiths' tone to the substance of his remarks, he makes a number of rather good points, as well as others that I disagree with. Thus I will take his article as a starting point from which to set forth my own thoughts about the endeavour of translation. Griffiths' article was primarily concerned with translation of Buddhist texts from Sanskrit; my remarks are going to address issues to do with translation from Tibetan, and will be particularly concerned with the translation of Buddhist philosophical literature.

Although I am about to set forth opinions on translation that I hold quite strongly, this in no way means that I think all translators should follow them or that they should work on the sort of Tibetan literature that I consider important, in the ways that I consider important. Diversity of styles and approaches to translation enhances the work of all of us, and what I would very much like to see, and would hope is one of the results of this gathering here, is more active acknowledgment that we can be very committed to our own particular approach without feeling that this diminishes the validity and helpfulness of other quite different ones. I make these points in the spirit of initiating a dialogue, seeking to open up conversation that will enable all of us, whatever our philosophy of translation, to become more clear about how and why we undertake the often slow and tedious work of translation.

That said, let me turn to a consideration of Paul Griffiths' article. To summarize his main points, Griffiths sets forth a threefold process that he feels is the responsibility of a Buddhologist handling Buddhist Sanskrit texts: the first is to understand what the text is about; the second to contextualize the text, both within the tradition from which it comes and within the corpus of writings of the author; and the third is to appropriate the meaning of the text, which essentially involves restating the meaning of the text in terms other than those employed by the text itself. Griffiths makes the very good point that "the Buddhologist, as an academic, has a real duty to communicate," and deplores a "tendency in contemporary Western Buddhology to retreat behind an impenetrable shield of technical vocabulary comprehensible only to co-specialists, and to make no effort to reach out to colleagues in related fields" (p. 20). Griffiths then moves to a point that I know from personal conversation with him he feels strongly about; he says, "the Buddhologist *qua* Buddhologist cannot be a religious enthusiast, proselytizer, or even, one might go so far as to say, Buddhist" (p. 21). He says this largely because he believes, and says in the article, that most Buddhists are "uncritically religious" and hence incapable of this "rigorous historico-philological enquiry" (p. 22) that he sees as essential to the search for truth that is the mission of the Buddhologist. The final part of his article is devoted to a discussion of the sorts of texts that he feels should be translated. Griffiths takes as his goal a translation that results in "clear, precise, and elegant English" (p. 24) and essentially concludes that any Sanskrit original that cannot be translated into such English is probably better off not translated—since such a translation will be nothing more than the Buddhist Hybrid English Griffiths so much deplores—but rather should be summarized and interpreted, with only the expert who can refer to the text in its original language ever seeing the full text. He sees translation as a religiously motivated act "amassing great merit for the doer," that "makes the saving word of the Buddha available for whole new cultures" (p. 25). The criterion of the Buddhologist, on the other hand, who is considering translating a text should be whether or not the text has any literary merit. Buddhologists should creatively study and interpret texts and leave translation to those who wish to perform it as an "act of religious supererogation" (p. 26).

In responding to Griffiths' article, I will begin with his final point concerning the validity and appropriateness of translation, although even to begin this discussion requires addressing another of his primary points, whether one can be both a Buddhologist and a Buddhist. I believe one *can*, although I would not go so far as to say that one *should* be, and I stand here before you as someone who is trying to be both. There is no question that this dual role affects what I say: however, because I believe the mission of both the Buddhologist and the Buddhist to be the quest for truth, I see no conflict in these two roles. And, in contrast to Griffiths, I believe that for both the Buddhologist and the Buddhist, translation is important. The Tibetan Buddhist tradition has within it much of import and interest to the Western world, whether one's primary focus is religion, philosophy, or intellectual history, and those ideas will only truly become available to the West if Tibetan Buddhist texts are translated into English. Griffiths speaks of the importance of reaching out to an audience wider than just that of the specialized Buddhologist; in fact, this is an important aspect of his belief that texts should not be translated, because he does not feel they can communicate anything important to a non-specialist audience.

I believe the opposite, and feel that just this is the reason why translation is so important. Rather than offering an interpretation, a summary, something that forces the reading public to trust my judgement as to what is relevant or helpful, it is important to translate these texts into English and let an educated public read them and make their own decisions as to meaning, importance and so forth. I further feel that as many texts as possible should be translated, so that decisions as to meaning can be made on the basis of the best possible evidence. My doctoral dissertation was a translation of a portion of Tsong kha pa's *Great Exposition of the Stages of the Path,* specifically the beginning section of the "special insight" *(lhag mthong, vipaśyanā)* portion of the text, in which Tsong kha pa sets forth his interpretation of Mādhyamika philosophy, an interpretation he supports with copious citation of Indian sources, particularly the writings of Nāgārjuna, Āryadeva, and

Candrakīrti. As a part of my dissertation, I contrasted Tsong kha pa's Mādhyamika interpretation with interpretations current in Western scholarship. There were of course considerable differences, and without getting into the question of which interpretations are more supportable, one factor that became obvious to me as I looked into the bases for the varying interpretations was that Tsong kha pa was working from a far larger body of material than has been with any Western author. In addition, he was working from material that had been translated into his own language, a fact that I would argue considerably enhanced his capacity to absorb, contemplate, and creatively interpret the material. Whereas most Western scholarship has ben done on the basis of the few extant works in Sanskrit, or if Tibetan materials are utilized, on simply the writings of Nāgārjuna. Tsong kha pa had access to all the works of Nāgārjuna widely accepted as genuinely written by him as well to the full commentarial tradition descended from Nāgārjuna—the writings of Āryadeva, Buddhapālita, Bhāvaviveka, Candrakīrti, and others. If these writings are going to be understood—and eventually creatively interpreted—in the West, there has to be the same sort of access to the texts. Further, it should be access for any one with a willingness to struggle to understand them, not just those with the linguistic skills to read them in the original language.

In terms of Tibetan Buddhism, this immediately opens up the question of the enormity of the project. The Tibetan *Kan-'gyur (bka' 'gyur)*, the translation of the word of Buddha, fills one hundred and eight volumes; the *Ten-'gyur (bstan 'gyur)*, the Indian commentaries on Buddha's word, another two hundred volumes; and Tibetan commentaries on both of these as well as independent synthetic treatises run to thousands of volumes. The collected writings of Tsong kha pa alone fill eighteen Tibetan volumes, which I estimate would require approximately one hundred volumes to translate into English. The writings of the great authors of the other main orders of Tibetan Buddhism are equally extensive. Thus we are contemplating a project of enormous scope and the magnitude of the task has to shape the way it is undertaken.

My first point is that the criterion for what gets translated should not be elegance of style, but rather appropriateness as a vehicle to allow full understanding of this Buddhist tradition. Much of this material is philosophical and technical in nature, often not elegant, often not poetic. Philosophy is difficult in any language; it will be so also in an English translation from Tibetan. It is asking too much to demand that all translations be in elegant, easy prose. Robert Bly has written an interesting book called *The Eight Stages of Translation*. Speaking primarily about the translation of poetry, he sets forth principles of a translation process that moves in stages from an initial literal translation through a steady series of refinements so that translation becomes less literal as it instead utilizes the nuances, imagery, metaphors and so forth of the language of translation. Bly concludes that because language changes constantly and quickly—and it does; I don't argue with his basic point—translations thus need to be redone every twenty or thirty years. This too is asking too much. Given the vast body of material to be translated, most texts will only be translated once. Therefore they need to be translated in a way that will be as lasting as possible.

What form should this translation take? I believe that the most useful translation is one that is quite (although not mindlessly) literal and that renders technical terms with a precision that allows complex philosophical discussions that occur in the Tibetan to be mirrored in the English translation—this is why I feel the two word translation of the Tibetan term *rten 'byung (pratītya-samutpāda)* as "dependent-arising" works better than a translation term such as "relativity," and why the Tibetan term *dgra bcom pa (arhant)* is better translated by, for instance, "Foe Destroyer," term that makes meaningful the traditional etymology of such a being as "one who has overcome the foe of the afflictions," rather than a translation equivalent to such as "Worthy One" that mirrors a widely used Sanskrit etymology but ignores the choice of the translators from Sanskrit into Tibetan. I do not propose that we have always to be literal, however. Sometimes a meaning translation works better than a literal one. Joe Wilson argues convincingly for "fundamental consciousness" as a translation for *kun gzhi (ālaya-vijñāna)*; I myself use "subsequent cognizer" for the rather problematic term from the epistemological literature, *bcad shes*.

Further, I believe we are better served by translation equivalents that simply translate the Tibetan term rather than seeking to find a comparable term within the Western philosophical tradition. Because the Eastern and Western philosophical traditions are so different, seeking to use cognate terms, I believe, often creates more confusion than clarity. We need to find the best terms that we can and allow their meaning to be developed through consistent use, rather than trying to lay over a conceptual structure from another, and very different, system of thought and terminology.

I do not believe we need be concerned with elegance of expression or with adapting the translation to take account of nuances of contemporary English usage and style. Of course translations should be as clear and communicative as possible. And, for this to occur, the first of Griffiths' criteria of what a Buddhologist handling a text should accomplish is obviously required—the translator must understand the text. And, this is a dialogic process. Translation improves as understanding improves, and understanding improves as translation improves.

A good translation requires making many decisions as to the meaning of the text. For instance, the Tibetan genitive particle *(kyi, gyi, gi, 'i, yi)*, the most widely used grammatical particle in Tibetan, often occurring many times in a single sentence, is frequently rendered in English as "of", in fact this particle has at least nineteen possible meanings and the translation of it will vary accordingly—as "of", "which is", "to", "from", "where", "s", "by", and even, in its non-case usage, as "but" or "and". Clearly an accurate and communicative translation is not possible without understanding the meaning. Furthermore, we should be bound by the grammar and syntax of the language we are translating into. Tibetan sentences are extremely long, essentially paragraphs. They must be turned into sentences that are workable in English grammar, shorter sentences with appropriate transitions between them. Tibetan makes extensive use of the passive, or "involuntary" voice; this is not equivalent to the passive in English and thus it is inappropriate to always render it as such in translation. We need to translate Tibetan texts into accurate, readable English, in which decisions have been made as to the meaning of the text so that the translation is unambiguous. Such English may not be elegant, because the Tibetan it is translating may not be elegant, but if it communicates the meaning of the text, it has performed its necessary function.

Further, I do not believe that we should be seeking to shift Tibetan terminology into the current idiom of our culture. Because languages are in a constant state of change, too much concern with being current leads to translations that are quickly dated. Our culture is one in which fads and styles change quickly—throughout the culture, and including the world of academia and the world of Buddhology. The buzzwords of a particular period—some of our current ones being "hermeneutics" and "deconstructionism"—quickly change and are replaced by new ones. The secondary literature on Mādhyamika is filled with attempted comparisons with the philosopher of the moment, from Whitehead to Wittgenstein to Derrida. Although there is value and some intrinsic interest to these comparisons, this is not the sort of work that continues to be utilized and referred to over a long period of time, nor are translations that have been made using the terminology of such comparative work of long term usefulness. Thus I feel that the most useful translation, and the one that will continue to be useful far into the future, is one that simply translates the text as accurately and as literally as possible.

Griffiths' second point about the responsibilities of a Buddhologist is that one should contextualize the text, both within the tradition it comes out of and within the corpus of writings of the author. I think that he is quite right. We are translating not only into the language of the West but into the culture of the West, and as such we are bound by the conventions and expectations of that culture. Western culture (and I use this term with reservation, since it now dominates far more than simply the West) has become an historical one; we see the world in historical terms and we need context. Further, in translating into English, we are bound by the scholarly standards of Western culture. Tibetans may not have written their texts with footnotes, with explanations of technical terms and unclear referents, with reference to the Sanskrit of a passage where available, but we, in translating into the idiom of our culture, must. Part of the difference comes because, within the Tibetan tradition, there is an expectation that texts are not just read, but are accompanied by the commentary of the very rich oral tradition. Since that oral tradition is an essential part of the full meaning of a text, we need to capture in our translation as much of what it contributes as we can. Hence I believe that we need whenever possible to avail ourselves of the opportunity to check the meaning of these texts through consultation with Tibetan scholars who partake of and can share with us this rich and living tradition. I have never translated anything in which my translation was not enhanced and improved by the oral explanation I received from a Tibetan scholar from within the Buddhist tradition.

Griffiths' third aim of a Buddhologist is to appropriate the meaning of the text, which he takes to mean restating its meaning in terms other than those employed and enters into the realm of what must happen if the meanings contained within a text are to take on vitality and life within a new language and culture. Just as there is a vast difference between the Tibetan that is a translation from Sanskrit and the Tibetan that was written originally in Tibetan, so there must necessarily be a difference between English that is translation from Tibetan and English in which these topics are expressed with full use of the range and syntax of the English language, within the concepts being expressed having been digested, reworked, and set forth freely and naturally in a new language. Yes, translations are frequently wooden, frequently stilted, usually not elegant. But they perform a necessary and essential function. They permit us to know what the texts in the original language said, and this is essential if we are going to understand the meaning of those texts. The Tibetan translations from Sanskrit were so systematic and so literal, that it has to some extent been possible, in the light of the subsequent destruction of many of the Sanskrit originals, to reconstruct the original Sanskrit, although, as Professor Ruegg points out with his comparison of two different Tibetan translations of one Sanskrit original, we should not take this too rigidly. The situation with the translation of Tibetan texts into English is so different from that of the eleventh-century Tibet that such could probably never happen, but it is not a model to be discarded lightly. There is real value in translations so literal and so accurate that one can reconstruct the language of origin from them. Interpretation, analysis, critical thought, rethinking of concepts, comparisons—all these are important and necessary. However, they will only be successful, they will only truly enhance our understanding of Buddhism rather than add more layers of obscurity and unclarity, if they take place upon a basis of and in reference to, clear and careful translation.

Some Formulae for Translating: Buddhist Texts from Tibetan

S.K. Pathak

Multidimension of the Tibetan Buddhist Literature

About six thousand Buddhist texts of India and China were translated into Tibetan between the seventh to fourteenth century A.D. These translated texts are available, though most of the original texts are now lost. The Tibetans regard these as their sacred scriptures, as the sayings of the Buddha (Bka'-'gyur) and the teachings of Buddhist teachers (Bstan-'gyur). Besides these translated texts a large number of indigenous writings by Tibetan authors on Buddhism have given rise to a multidimensional Buddhist literature in Tibetan. It may not be out of place to mention here that the wide range of the Buddhist literature in Tibetan has been rightly displayed by E. Gene Smith in his *Tibetan Catalogue*, pt. I of the Washington University Tibetan Collection, Seattle, 1969. A specimen of the classification of subjects has been drafted in my article entitled "Classification of Buddhist Literature in Tibetan," Samyagvak Series V, Central Institute of Higher Tibetan Studies, Sarnath, 1990.

The task of translating the Buddhist literature into English is stupendous. This is so not only because of the colossal number of these texts, but also because of the varieties of subjects, the manifold styles of composition and the diversity in the modes of expressions. Moreover, the Tibetan Buddhist literature has currently taken a new shape for obvious reasons. When I say this I have in mind the writings of the eminent Tibetan scholars who have been living outside of Tibet for the last thirty years or so. On top of that many academicians in the West and the East have themselves engaged in translating the Buddhist literature from Tibetan into English for exploring the hidden treasure of learning that have so long remained inaccessible. Many Tibetan-knowing scholars either individually or in collaboration with a traditionally trained Tibetan teacher, have ventured into this field enthusiastically. In this regard Tarthang Tulku and his associates deserve a mention. The Andin International also have taken a project for translation of the Tibetan Tripiṭaka. In elucidating the objective of such endeavours it may be remarked that th translation of the Buddhist literature from Tibetan into English will unfold the material and spiritual traits of varied cultures of Asia of the past and the present.

It may be added that most of the Indian texts which are preserved in the Bka'-'gyur and the Bstan-'gyur are not found in the Indian languages in which they were originally written. That refers to another difficult task: how to reconstruct them in the Indian languages. Some modern scholars in India have devoted themselves to the task of constituting these lost texts even though the constituted or reconstructed texts cannot be claimed to be the original ones. It is true, however, that such attempts at reconstruction always help towards a better understanding of the text concerned, prior to its English rendering. It has been seen that the sensitivity and fervour of Buddhist scriptures are adequately preserved in the restored text from Tibetan into Indian language, preferably in Sanskrit.

Broadly speaking, the Tibetan Buddhist literature has developed through the following phases:

1. Early phase (snga-dar) prior to the standardization of terminology for translation (seventh to eighth century A.D.).
2. The First Buddhist Council in Tibet and the standardization of the language for canonical writings. Indigenous writings belonging to the rNying-mapa Buddhist scholars appeared in classification of *chos (dharma),* mdo (*sūtra*) and *rgyud* (*Tantra*) in addition to the translation-work of the rNying-'bum and other texts of the Tripiṭaka during the Btsan-rulers like Khri Srong lde btsan, Ralpacan (eighth to ninth century A.D.).
3. The later spread of Buddhism (phyi-dar), Mi-la's songs and Marpa's compositions.
4. The last phase of the translation literature and growth of the indigenous Sar-ma-pa writings during the Sa-skya period.

5. Ecclesiastical writings of the different Buddhist schools in Tibet including the yab-sras gsung 'bum and the Kargyud-pa teachers' works, etc.
6. The period of assimilation led by rGyalwa-*lnga-pa* and others.
7. The Mongolian Buddhist teachers' contributions in Tibetan.
8. The contemporary Buddhist writings (divided into two streams, namely (1) translation works in modern languages and (2) essays with didactic integrated compositions by the eminent personalities)
9. The interim phase of the Buddhist literature observed in the works of Mi-fam, Gedun chosphel, rGyalwa-*lnga-pa,* rGyalwa bcu-sumpa and others deserves a mention.

The history of Buddhist literature that has come down to us is not complete. Mostly fragmentary specimens of writings of many Tibetan authors show a variety of subjects within the periphery of Buddhism, having manifold styles in composition in the process of development through the ages.

Problems experienced by a modern translator

While translating a Buddhist text from Tibetan a translator experience manifold problems, some of which are as follows:

1. *Whether it will be a free translation or verbatim*

The Tibetan translations of Buddhist texts from both the Chinese and Indian sources were verbatim in the true sense. For instance, the Commentary of the *Lankāvatārasūtra* from the Chinese source and that from Sanskrit may be cited to locate the difference here. Many other texts may also be referred to. In the case of the Indian texts several experiments were made with a view to maintaining as far as possible serenity of letters and the sensitivity of a text in the Tibetan translation.

But that does not mean that the endeavours made by the Chinese translators for free translation were futile.

2. *Traditional adherence to the text concerned*

A Buddhist text whether 'Buddhavacana' (Bka'-'gyur) or 'śāstra' (Bstan-'gyur), pertains to a specific ' ecclesiastical heritable' tradition. For instance, the Vinaya tradition in Tibetan belonged to the Mūla-sarvāstivāda in general. But there were three lineages in Tibet up to the post-Atīśa period (*c.* twelfth century A.D.). Moreover, lineage of the Indian *paṇḍitas* collaborating with the Tibetan *lotsāwas* should also be taken into consideration.

In the case of the indigenous works of a Tibetan author, similar lineage or hierarchy(brgyud) of the spiritual teachers tends to specify his legacy in composition-style and thematic perspective. In this regard, Gos Lotsāwa, Sumpa mkhan po and Mkhas-grub rje focus a light on determining the order of their contemporary lineages of Tibetan scholars belonging to different traditions.

3. *Appropriate equivalence of the Buddhist terms in Tibetan and in English*

This is an important factor for translating correctly any Buddhist text from Tibetan into English. The Buddhist terms have special connotations with reference to their derivations and usage with reference to the thematic context. For instance, 'nyams' has no less than five meanings as the noun (ming), e.g. 1. thought, apprehension of ideas; 2. mind or spirit as an entity; 3. manner, state, degree, condition, extent; 4. appearance 'nyams thabs' or 'nyams dgu'; 5. the soul (occasionally). Whereas, nyams-pa (as the participle/ verbal attributive) suggests; 1. injured, hurt, damaged, impaired, imperfect; 2. defiled, polluted (nyams gyur pa); 3. degeneration referring to 'nyams pa gsum' three kinds of ethical and ritual deteriorations or impairments. Also, 'nyams pa drug'.

Similarly, terms like 'rtog-pa' and 'rtogs' (imperative), 'rtogs' and 'rtogs-pa' refer to various connotations in various context.

In this regard Indian scholars since the pre-Christian days have thrashed out the problem of the relation of words with their meanings. Different viewpoints were held by grammarians and the logicians belonging to the Buddhist and the non-Buddhist schools. Yāska (*c.* second century B.C.) justified the inherent capacity of a word, if properly used, to convey appropriately those ideas that one intends to express by depending upon expediency and parsimony in the linguistic usage (Nirukta 1.2).

The eternal and indivisible word-essence (*sphoṭa*) generates meaning-awareness of a particular word in the mind of the listener due to momentary sound-unit *(śabda pada)* in an expression. The word-essence *(sphoṭa)* thus constitutes a word used for sensible communication. It tends to establish the identity (*śabdādhyāsa)* of a particular word with its meaning(s) as real entities. The Buddhist logicians, however, repudiated the cognizing of real entity between a word and its meaning. Such conceptual cognitions are but thought construction *(vikalpa).*

The Tibetan *lotsāwas* were conversant with the Buddhist logic as well as with the grammars of Sanskrit and Tibetan. Therefore, while translating an Indian text into Tibetan, the *lotsāwas,* in collaboration with the Indian *paṇḍitas,* could not ignore the grammarians' viewpoints in spite of their allegiance to the Buddhist logicians. The *lotsāwas* therefore endeavoured to translate word by word, corresponding etymological equivalents as far as practicable. As a result of that no dual entities in a sound unit is cognized in verbatim translation from the Indian languages or Chinese into Tibetan. But it is to be noted that the translations done in the post-Atīśa period (*phyidar*) show more awareness of contextual relevance and propriety where necessary.

Moreover, the grammatical structure and rules of syntax of the two languages, Tibetan and English, are quite different. This should always be taken into consideration.

4. *Maintenance of the serenity in translation and fervour of texts under translation*

Not only should the translation be lucid, the serenity and fervour of the original must be captured. It is here relevant to recall what Anagarika Govinda said about the difficulty faced by a translator brought up in a cultural milieu different from that from which the original text sprang. Anagarika Govinda observed:

> Therefore it requires an extraordinary degree of sensitivity to translate an ancient religious literature without identifying ourselves with the contents and tradition of a still religious experience. Unfortunately, this sensitivity is lacking with most translators and interpreters.

5. *Prospective formulae for translation*

Some formulae have been suggested below to help overcome the above problems. These may be classified under five heads:

- (i) Innovation of systematic methods or guidelines for translation of Buddhist texts from Tibetan into English.
- (ii) Methodical exercise in course of translation.
- (iii) Application of mechanical apparatus, where suitable.
- (iv) Organization of translator-personnels—either individual or institutional guild— at two levels.
- (v) Publications of the texts translated after codification.

In order to implement these formulae a primary need is to formulate the methods of standardization of the translation work. The following methods are suggested:

- (a) Compilation of an uptodate bibliography of the texts translated in the Western and Eastern languages together with those reconstructed in Indian or other languages. It should include the Tripiṭaka texts translated into Tibetan as well as the indigenous works composed by Tibetan and the Mongolian erudites.
- (b) Preparation of a Tibetan-English concordance with Sanskrit equivalents where available. The *Mahāvyutpatti, Prajñā,* and other Sanskirt-Tibetan lexicons may be translated into English. In this respect, *Tibetan-Sanskrit Śatapiṭaka-Dictionary,* compiled by Lokesh Chandra on the basis of many bilingual glossaries that were available to him, may be given a priority.
- (c) Associating a Tibetan scholar trained in the same tradition to which the text belongs. This should ensure sensitivity in translation and help avoiding such subjective mistakes as an un-aided non-Tibetan translator may make owing to his different cultural backgroumd. The association of a non-Tibetan-speaking translator is no less important as he is expected to have a wider knowledge in the field of Buddhism and the related subjects.

In the case of an English-knowing Tibetan scholar with modern education, it will be advisable to associate with the task of translation a non-Tibetan scholar-translator having knowledge of Buddhism.

(d) As regards the standard method of translation, certain general guidelines may be framed after allowing some freedom to the translators in respect of particular cases. The terms used in translation may be restricted mostly to the proposed Tibetan-English Concordance, though the translator will have the privilege to select the appropriate equivalent terms after inserting suitable notes for readers as necessary. Similar notes may also be added wherever needed for clarification of the translation. Annotations on grammatical, thematic, cryptic symbolic expressions are also required.

(e) The traditional method of interpreting a Buddhist text should always be kept in view. In Sanskrit its sixfold enumerations are:

 (i) Cryptic expressions (*sandhyā / sandhāya bhāṣā*).
 (ii) Candid expressions (*no-sandhyā*).
 (iii) Inferential significance (*neyārtha*) of expressions.
 (iv) Condensed significance (*nītartha*) to avoid verbiage.
 (v) Appropriately signified (*yathā-rutam*) by requisite terms.
 (vi) Unuttered implied significance (*nārutam*)

 In addition the local or popular method of interpreting a theme or a particular tradition cannot be overlooked if relevant.

(f) Overall lucidity of the language in translation is very important and should always be kept in mind.

(g) Appendices added to a translation work should explain such difficulties as have been experienced by the translators.

Attention is drawn to three more important aspects as follows:

 (i) As regards the application of the mechanical apparatus in translation, some agency dealing in computers may be consulted, when required. Moreover, a key-book may be prepared on the basis of the Tibetan-English Concordance mentioned above.
 (ii) An organization at the international level may be set up as the 'Summit' body for co-ordinating the tasks undertaken by an individual or an institution. Trans-

lators at the 'base' level may be treated as 'Translators' Cell', designed and coordinated various projects of translating Buddhist texts from Tibetan into English.

(iii) Lastly, the translation work done at different levels in various countries may be published through private publishing agencies or through research institutes or learned bodies sponsored by governments of many countries.

A hill-type model of research

In fine, the research model of translating Buddhist literature from Tibetan into English may be conceived as a mountain with five-peaks representing the five-fold formulae drafted above. Definitely a hard task for the translators who will take part in the programme at different levels. The band of scholars who dedicate themselves to the programme may be respected as *kalyaṇammitra* (dge ba'i bshes) for the advancement of learning and the extension of teachings of the Buddha.

NOTES

No hard and fast rules can be laid down about retranslating from Tibetan or Chinese or Mongolian texts into Sanskrit, Prakrit or Apabhraṁśa. It mostly depends on the preference of an editor and the text which has been transmitted in earlier days. For example, priority may be given to re-translate the Apabhraṁśa, the Dohā and Vajragīti texts, if possible. It may be mentioned that the Lokānanda Nâṭakam has been reconstructed by the late Biswanatha Bhattacharya into Prākṛit where necessary. Some specimens of retranslation of the Tantra texts are shown in Appendix 'C'.

(i) A passage from 'Dpal ye shes snying po zhes bya ba'i rnal 'byor chen mo'i rgyud kyi rGyal po'i rgyal po (Śrījñānagarbha nāma yoginīmahātantra rājātirāja) from Bkaḥ'-'ḥgyur, Rgyud collection.

(ii) An excerpt from 'Rig sṅags kyi rgyal mo rma bya-chen mo (Mahāmāyūrī-Vidyārājñī) from the Bka'-'gyur, rGyud collection in order to point out the variation of style in composition.

(iii) A passage from 'Dpal rdo rje rnal 'byor ma'i tshigs kyi 'khor lo'i cho ga zhes bya ba (Śrī Vajrayoginī-gaṇacakra-vidhi nāma) ascribed to Śabaripā(da) and translated by Gautamabhadra and Nyma rgyalmtshan from the Bstan 'gyur, rGyud 'grel (JPC 52/2272).

Attention may be invited to the following words here.

(i) Blo daṅ ldan pa : 1.lo varṣa (year); 2. mati (arch) form of blo; 3. varṣiṇī or varaṣaṇa (specially meant here).

Also, snaṅ ba mchod pa'i raṅ bshin and snaṅ ba thob pa'i rang bzhin may be noted.

(ii) the context of the Vidyārājñī with Ānanda and his blessing as sought herewith deserve mention.

(iii) tshogs gñis : dvi-varga which makes confusion here. bdud rtsi : amṛitabhaṣma and pho mos sbrel pa (spel ba) needs annotations in the tantra context and so on.

In this connection the following methods may be considered.

(a) To maintain Index-cards of the rare use and technical terms which have been found in course of reconstruction.

(b) It is presumed that some glossaries or lexicons having vocabularies from the Tantra are available for reconstruction. Despite that, some terms may signify new connotations in separate context which is to be noted here.

ENGLISH TRANSLATION

1. Śrījñānagarbha nāma-yoginī mahātantra-rājātirāja (The Essence of Proficiency and Eminence: Superior to other Great Tantra-rājas of the Yoginī).

The Divine lady requested thus: Please speak to me about the significance of Mahāmudrā from Śrī-mahāmudrā-tilaka taught by the Divine Lord; what would be a method to obtain its (proper) significance? The Lord said: O Divine Lady, please listen to that which you ask for elucidation. Mahāmudrā is fourfold; such as, Karmamudrā, Samayamudrā, Jñānamudrā and Dharmamudrā.

What is Karmamudrā? It showers the bliss having its self-nature of effulgence.

What is Samayamudrā? It showers the base of effulgence by its self-nature.

What is Jñānamudrā? It showers the basic elements of effulgence by its self-nature.

What is Dharmamudrā? It is the radiant effulgence by self-nature.

2. Vajrayoginī-gaṇacakra-vidhināma: (Esoteric) Practice in the Vajrayoginī-Assembly. Salutation to Vajrayoginī.

On the festive occasion of the heroes, the Practice in the Assembly (gaṇacakra) is narrated to pay homage to Sugata, who moves in the air when the practitioners meet together (a male and a female) for nourishment of the Samayayoga.

Human-skull-bowls or colourful painted auspicious pots would be there; the requisite articles will also be placed in those bowls or pots, such as, assorted meat in five kinds, mixture of fivefold ambrosia (amṛta), and other articles for the Samaya. Moreover, various kinds of food, edible commodities, drinks, and other enjoyable objects would be procured and covered by a piece of red cloth.

After taking their bath the male and the female practitioners would anoint them with the ambrosia-mixture and perfume, dress in new cotton garments, decorate in ornaments and flower-garlands on their heads with unguent.

Then male and female practitioner each would be engaged in the practice of their self-control power to start with and enter into the Bhagavatī-yoga (esoteric practice in favour of the Divine-lady); and, according to the Five-orders of worship (Pancakrama) of the Kriyātantra offerings should be submitted thereafter.

3. Mahāmāyūrī-vidyārājñī: The chiefmost Vidyā (Secret Science)[1] named Mahāmāyūrī (the Great Pea-hen).

Thus was said: The Lord addressed to Ānanda; O Ānanda, please narrate the Chiefmost Vidyā, uttered by the Tathāgata, which you had heard about the seizure of the malignant selfish beings, like the wrathful god, the demon, the evil deity (presiding) over wind, the celestial bird (garuḍa), the smell-eater (gandharva), the vile-person (kinnara), the big reptile (creeping on its breast), the evil spirit (jambha) inclined on evil deeds of living beings, the goblin, the departed spirit, the meat-eater spirit (piśāca), the ghost, the deformed (headless trunklike) goblin (kabanda), the fiendess (pūtanā), the corpse-like fiendess (Kaṭapūtanā), the drought-causing demon, the spirit causing a fainting fit, the seizing by shadow of harpy (chāyāgraha), the epilepsy and the diseases caused by evil spirit,[2] the wrathful deity like Yamāntaka and others dexterous in hypnotic mirage e.g. Kakhoda, Kiṭi, Vetāḍa, Cicchu, Vesavara, bad appetite, odourous excrement, pale look, weak disposition (in body), consuming physique, melancholia, fatigue (continued), daily fever, alternate-day fever and relapsing fevers by the third alternate day, the fourth, the week-end, the fortnightly, the monthly fever, the daytime fever, intermittent fever, remittent fever, malignant fever under the influence of a ghost, that of a man and that of a non-human being, rheumatic fever, that (on account of disorderliness) of bile and of phlegm, ailment due to derangement of three humours of the body (sannipāta) so that the monk Sāriputra be protected from all kinds of illness (by listing to it). Let Buddhas bring forth welfare (to all).

1. rgyal mo-queen (rajñi), Vidyā is feminine while tantra is masculine; Tatrarāja and Vidyārājñī. It suggests the chiefmost of all Vidyās. M. Winternitz translates Vidyā as the Secret-Science (*A History of Indian Literature,* Calcutta University, 1934, p. 385f).
2. gdon (graha) refers to malignant spirit causing mischief and disease of living beings when they are in wrath. About twenty among them are mentioned here out of twentyeight occasionally enumerated in the Buddhist texts.

Appendix 'C'

Specimens of reconstructed texts from Tibetan

Dpal ye śes sñiṅ po zhes bya ba rnal 'byor ma chen mo'i rgyud kyi rgyal po'i (Śrījñānagarbha nāma yogī mahātatrāti-rāja)

//Bcom ldan 'das mas gsol ba/ gaṅ zhig dpal phyag rgya [3] chen po thig le'i rgyud kyi rgyal po las phyag rgya chen po'i don bstan pa de thob par bya ba'i don du de'i thabs bcom ldan' 'das kyi bdag la bka' rtsal du gsol/bcom ldan 'das kyi bka' stsal ba/khyod kyis bdag la gzig-pa gaṅ'/gcig lha mo [4] rab tu bśad/phyag rgya chen po'i 'dir bzhir dbye ba ste/las kyi phyag daṅ/ye śes kyi phyag rgya daṅ/dam tshig gi phyag rgya daṅ/chos kyi phyg rgya'o//

1. proktam/Bhagavatyā/śrīmahāmudrā-tilaka-tantreṇa/-mahām udrātho deśitaḥ bhagavatā so'rthaprāptyarthamupāyo yo bhavati mam *kathyatam*/bhagavadvacanam : (bhagavānuvāca) - devī tvayā yad pṛṣṭam tadevamprakāṣitam ṣṛṇu/mahāmudrātra caturvidhā yathā hi—karmamudrā, samayamudrā, jñānamudrā dharmamudrā ca/

// Gan zhig las kyi phyag rgya ni snan ba'i raṅ *daṅ ldan pa'o*/ gaṅ zhig dam tshig gi phyag rgya/de ni snaṅ ba mched pa'i raṅ bzhin skye mched kyi *lo daṅ ldan pa'o*/ gaṅ zhig ye śes kyi phyag rgya de ni/snaṅ ba thob pa'i raṅ bzhin khams kyi lo daṅ ldan pa'o/ gan zhig chos kyi phyag gya de ni 'od gsal gyi raṅ bzhin no//

Kā nāma/karmamudrā/ālokasvābhāvānandavarṣiṇīti/katamā samayamudrā? Sā lokavardhanasvabhāv(a) svatanavarṣiṇī/katamā jñānamudrā sāloka alabhasvabhāvadvastu varṣiṇī/katamā karmamudrā ? sā prabhāsavarasvabhāveti//(Bkah-'gyur rgyad kha, $3b_2$4a grul bum g.d./srul po'i g.d/ lus srul gyi g.d./ skes byed ky kyi g.d/ smyo byad khyi 93) g.d./grib gnon gyi g.d./ brjed byed kyi g.d/ gnon gi g.d./ skar ma'i g.d./ gsed byed dan/ sgyu ma'i las byad daṅ/ gweṅs daṅ/ ro laṅdaṅ/ sems sgyur ba daṅ/spod gton daṅ/bza'nes daṅ/ sgyu gnis daṅn gnod grib daṅ/ gnod ltas dan / bri nes daṅ/ bskom nes daṅ/ smad pa rims nin dan gcig dan/nin gnis dan/ nin gsum daṅ/ nin bzhi daṅ/ ñin bdun daṅ/ zla phyed daṅ/ zla ba gcig daṅ/ zla ba gcig daṅ/nin pa daṅ/ yud tsamdaṅ/ rtag pa'i rims pa daṅ/ rims drag po daṅ/ 'byun bo'i rims pa daṅ mi'i rims pa daṅ/mi ma yin pa'i rims pa daṅ/rlun las gyur pa sa khris pa las gyur pa daṅ/bad gan dan las gyur pa daṅ/ 'dus pa las gyur pa daṅ/ rims thams cad las gyur pa daṅ/ slog sa-ri la bsruṅ pa gyis śig ...... kun gyis dge ba dag//

bhasmamparamapi nānāvidhabhojanīya-khādanīya-pāniyādi-bhokta vyāni samāhṛtamapi raktavastreṇā cchāditāni (santi) / ta-tradasu sarva-yoginaḥ yoginyaśca snānam kṛtvā pañcāmṛtam gandhānulelepanāni gatnebyasamlipya navavastrāṇī karpasādi paridhaya ābhuṣaṇāni puṣpamalyanisirasi baddhvā sūtrapatasar-gakāle srtripumsau svādhiṣṭhanādhāya bhagavatiyogamcarantu/ tataḥ kriyācaryena pancakramānusāreṇa pūjām dadyat//

Appendix

Specimens of reconstructed texts from Tibetan

1. Dpal ye śes sñiṅ po zhes pa rnal 'byor ma chen mo'i rgyud kyi rgyal po'i rgyal po (Śrījñānagarbha nāma yoginīmahātantrāti-rāja) [3b:2]

// Bcom ldan 'das mas gsol ba/zhig dpal phyag rgya [3] chen po thig le'i rgyud kyi rgyal po las phyag rgya chen po'i don bstan pa de thob par bya ba'i thabs bcom ldan 'das kyi bdag la bka' rtsal du gsol/bcom 'das kyi bka' stsal ba/kayod kyis bdag la zhl pa gaṅ/ ñon cig lha mo [A] rab tu bśad/ phyag rgya chen po'i 'dir gzir dbyed pa ste/ las kyi phyag rgya daṅ/ ye śes kyi phyag rgya daṅ/ dam tshig gi phyag rgya daṅ/ chos kyi phyag rgya'o//

1. proktaṃ Bhagavatyā /śrīmahāmudrā-tilaka-tantrān/ - mahāmudrārtho deśitaḥ bhagavatā so'rthaprāptyarthamupāyo yo bhavati māṃ *kathyatām* bhagavadvacanam : (bhagavānuvāca) - devī tvayā yad pṛṣṭaṃ tadevamprakāśitaṃśṛṇu/ mahāmudrātra caturvvidha yathā hi— karmamudrā, samayamudrā, jñānamudrā dharmamudrā ca/

//Gaṅ zhig las kyi phyag rgya ni snaṅ ba'i raṅ zhiṅ dga' ba'i lo *can ldan pa'*o/gaṅ zhig dam tshig gi phyag rgya / de ni snaṅ ba mched pa'i raṅ bzhin skye mched kyi *lo daṅ ldan pa'o* / gaṅ shig ye śes kyi ph yag rgya de ni/snaṅ ba thob pa'i raṅ bzhiṅ khams kyi lo daṅ ldan pa'o/ gaṅ zhig chos kyi phyag rgya de ni od gsal gyi raṅ bshin no//

kā nāma/karmamudrā/ālokasvabhāvānandavarṣiṇīti/katamā samayamudrā? Sālokabardhanasvabhāv(a)āyatanavarṣinī/ katamā jñānamudrā sālik(a) ālabhasvabhāvadhātu varṣiṇī/katamā dharmamudrā? sa prabhāsvarasvabhāveti//(Bhaḥ-'gyur rgyud kba, 3b24a) grul bum g.d./srul po'i g.d./lus srul gyi g.d./skem byed kyi g.d./ smyo byed kyi (3) g.d/grib gñon gyi g.d./ brjed byed kyi g.d./gnon gi g.c./ skar maḥi g.d./ gśed byed daṅ/ sgyun ba'ḥi las byed daṅ/ gweṅs daṅ/ ro laṅs caṅ/sens sgyur ba daṅ/ spod gton daṅ./ bza' ñes daṅ/sgyag ñes daṅ/gnod grib daṅ/ gnod ltas daṅ/ bri ñes daṅ/bskom ñes daṅ/ snad pa/daṅ/rims ñin daṅ gcig daṅ/ ñin gñis daṅ/ñin gsum daṅ/ ñin bshi daṅ/ ñin bdun daṅ/ zla phyed daṅ/ zla ba gcig daṅ. ñin pa daṅ/ yud tsampa daṅ/ rtag pa'i rims pa daṅ/ rims drag po daṅ/ 'byuṅ vi'i rims pa daṅ nu;i rims pa daṅ/ mi ma yin pa'i rims pa daṅ/rkuṅ las gyur pas khris pa las gyur pa daṅ/bad han—las gyur pa daṅ/'cus pa las gyur pa daṅ/sloṅ sa-ri la bsruṅ—bgyis śis .... kun gyis dge ba dag// bhasmamparampi nānāvidhabhojanīya-khādanīya-pānīyādi-bhoktvyāni samāhṛtāmapi nānāvidhabhojanīya-khādanīya-pānīyādi-bhoktvyāni samāhṛtāni raktavastreṇācchāditāni (santi)/ tatrādau sarva-yoginaḥyoginyaśca snānam kṛtvā pañcāmṛtaṃ gandhābhyalepanāni gātenabhasaṃlipya navavastrāṇi kārpasād in paridhāyaāv-bhūṣaṇāni puṣpamālyāniśi baddhvā sūtrapāṭasargakāke strīpuṃsau svādhiṣṭhābādhāya bhagavatīyogamcarantu/ tataḥ kriyācaraṇa pañcakramābhsāreṇa pūjāṃ dadyat//

1. Rig snags kyi rgyal mo rma bya chen mo (Mahamayurividyarajn I

//de skad gsol ba daṅ/bcom ldan 'das kyis tshe daṅ lden pa kun dga' bo 'di skad ces bka' stsal to/kun dga' bo (89b.1) de bzhin gsegs pa'i bkas khod son la rigs snags kyi rgyal mo 'di lha'i gdon dan/lha ma yi gdon dan/ rluṅ lha'i dgon dan/dri sa'i g,d,/mi (am c'i g.d./ lto phyo chen po'i g.d./ gnod g.d./sriṅ po yi dags kyi g.d./sa za'i g.d./Ibyun po'i g.d./

Rdo rje rnal ḥbyor maḥi tshogs kyi 'khor lo'i tshogs zhes bya ba (vajrayoginī-gaṇacakra-vidhi-nāma) Dpal rdo rje rnal // byor ma la phyag 'tshal lo/

tshogs gñis tshogs ni bsag pa daṅ/
rnal 'byor dam tshig gso ba daṅ/
bde gsegs mkha' 'gro mchod pa'i phyir/
dpa' bo ston mo tshogs 'khor bcas//

de la ka pa la'am snod(3) sin tu mdzes pas mtshan ñid daṅ ldan pa'i nan du tshogs kyi yo byad sam pa ni sa lna dan/bdud rtsi daṅ/ dam tshig gi gi rdzas bdud tsi ril bu daṅ/ gshan yaṅ zhal zas kyi khyad par rnam la sna tshods/ rnams bza' dan/ (4) btun ba la sogs pa lons spyod bya bsams la ras dmar pos gyogs bzhag go/der dan pr rnal 'byor pho mo thams cad khrus byas te/ bdud rtsi lna dan dri bzaṅ pos lus phyugs te/ gos gsar pa daṅ rus pa la sogs pa'i (5) rgyan daṅ / mgo; me tog bzhag pa'am phren bu bciṅs te thig btab pai le'u tshe'am/pho mos spel ba daṅ/ raṅ gi gnas su 'dug ste/ rje btsun ma'i rnal'byor du bya ste/ de la las kyi slob dpon gyis mchod pa (6) rnam las rim pa ltar 'bul lo //

Vajrayoginyai namaḥ//
gaṇe dvandvam samāsādya samayayoga jīvitam/
khecarasugatam vande gaṇacakram virotsvam //
tatra kapalam vatisobhnalakṣaṇa patra madhye cakrasama sa-

khecarasugatam vande gaṇacakram virotsvam //
tatra kapalam vatisobhnalakṣaṇa patra madhye cakrasama samāhrtya pancamāmsam pancāmṛtam samayasya vastūni amrta
Mahāmāyūrī-vidyārajñī : idam vac yacitam bhagavatā sm Ananada tathāgat bhvantam vidhyārajñryam deśita/ (yathāhi) devegraha-danavagraha-pavanagraha-garudagraha-gandharvagraha-kinnar agraho-ragagraha-yajsagraha-raksasagraha-pretagraha-piśacagraha-bhūtagraha-kabandhagrah putanagrahakatputanigraha-skandagraha-piśunagraha-chaya-graha spasmaragraha-patagraha-tarkagraha- krtyahsca-nivr-tyakrtya-daka (kahkoda) kiti-vetada-ciccha-vesavara-duscarita-durbhavitaavasada-ekajvara dvayajvara-tryahajvara-caturthakajvara-saptahajvara-ardhmāsajvara-māsajvara-divājvara-ksaṇajvara.-nityajvara-viṣamajvarabhutajvara-manusyajvara-amūnusyajvaravatapittakaphajaniata sannipata-sakalajvara bhiksum raksayantu/ ......sarvabuddhakalyāṇaṃ dadātu//

2. Rig snags kyi rgyal mo rma bya chen mo (Mahāmāyūrīvidyārajñī) [890:8]// de skad gsol ba daṅ /bcom - ldan 'das kyis tshe daṅ ldan kun dga' bo di skad ces bka stsal to/ kun dga' bo [89b:1] de bshin gśegs pa'i bkas khyod soṅ la rig sṅags kyi rgyal mo 'di lha'i gdon daṅ/lha yi gdon daṅ, rluṅ lha'i gdon daṅ/(=g.d.) dri sa'i g,d,/mi'am d'i g.d./lto 'phye chen po'i g.d./gnod g.d/srin po yi dwags kyi g.d./śa za' i g.d./'byuṅ bo'i g.d./

3.Rdo rje 'byor ma'i tshogs kyi 'khor lo'i tshogs she bya ba (Vajrayoginī-gaṇacakra-vidhi-nāma)// lpal rdo rje rnal byor ma la phyag ḥtshal lo/

tshogs gñis tshogs ni bsag pa daṅ/
rnal 'byor dam tshig gso ba daṅ/
bde gśegs mkha' 'gro mchod pa'i phyir/
dpa' bo ston mo tshogs 'khor bśad//

de la ka pā la'am snod(3) śin tu mdzes p mtshan ñid daṅ ldan pa'i naṅ du tshogs kyi yo byad bsam pa ni śa lṅa daṅ/ bdud rtsi daṅ/ dam tshing gi rdzas bdud rtsi ril bu daṅ/ gzhan yaṅ zhal zas kyi khyad par rnam pa/sna tshogs/ rnams bza'daṅ (4) btun ba la sogs pa loṅs spyod bya bhams la as dmar pos gyogs bshag go/ der daṅ por rnal 'byor pho mo thams cad khrus byas te/ bdud rtsi lṅa daṅ dri bzaṅ pos lus phyugs te/ gos gsar pa daṅ rys pa la sogs pa'i (5) rgyan daṅ/mgo//la/me tog bzgag pa' am phren bu bciṅs te thig btab pai le'u tshe' am/pho mos spel ba daṅ/raṅ gi gnas su 'dug ste/

rje btsun ma'i rnal 'byor du bya ste/ de la las kyi slob dpon gyis mchod pa (6) rnam lha rim pa ltar 'bul lo//

3. Vajrayoginyai namaḥ//

gaṇe dvandvaṃ samāsādya samayayoga jīvitaṃ/ khecarasugatam vande gaṇacaśraṃ vīritsvaṃ// tatras kapālaṃ vātiśobhanalakṣana-yota...........pātranadgte cajrasāna grīṃ samāhṛya pañcamāmsaṃ samayasya vastiūni amṛta

2. Mahāmāyūrī-vidyārājñī : idam vacūnaṇvācutaṃ bhagavatāyusmananandaṃ / kmnanad tathāgatena bhvantaṃ vidyārājñiyaṃ deśitā/ (yathāhi) devagrāha-dānavagrāha-pavanagrāha-garyḍagrāha-gandharvagrāha-kinnaragrāho-rāgagrāha-yakṣagrāha rakṣasagrāha-pretagrāha-piśacagrāha-bhutagrāha-kabanchagrāha pūtanāgraha-kaṭpūtaṇigrāha-piśunagrāha-chāhāgrāhā-spasmāragrāha-pātagrāha-tārakāgrāha-kṛtyāgśca-nivṛtyajṛtya-ḍāja (kaoda) kiṭi-vetāḍa-cuccha-vesavāraduścarita-durbhāvita-avasāda-ekajvara dvayajvara-tryahajvara-caturthakajvara-saptāhajvara-ardhmāsajvara māsajvara-divājvara-kṣaṇajvara-nityajvara-viṣamajvarabhūtajvara-mānusyajvara-amānusyajvara-vātapittajaohajanita sannipā-sakalajvara bhikṣūn rakṣayantu/ ......sarvabuddhakalyāṇaṃ dadātu//

Comparison as a Principle of Knowledge and its Application to the Translation of Buddhist Texts

José Ignacio Cabezón

Introduction

This paper has two goals. It seeks, first of all, to develop the outline of a theory of comparison as a form of knowledge. In accomplishing this, comparison shall be both the means and the end of the analysis, for we shall come to a theory of comparison through the comparison of different notions of this concept, which is to say, through the analysis of the concept of comparison as it exists in two very different intellectual traditions. Comparison shall be the means in so far as it shall be the method of inquiry, and it shall be the end in so far as it shall be the subject of the inquiry. We shall focus first on the notion of comparison in the writings of a contemporary historian of religion, Jonathan Z. Smith, and then turn to a discussion of the Indian philosophical concept of *upamāna*, usually translated in Western scholarly literature as "analogy" or "comparison". In this way we hope to come to some conclusions about the nature and workings of comparison as a form of knowledge, conclusions which we will apply to the realm of translation theory, and more specifically to the translation of Buddhist texts from the Tibetan.

I. Comparison in Western Intellectual History

Even a survey of the literature on comparison, or analogy, in Western intellectual history, is beyond the scope of this paper. It has, in any case, been outlined elsewhere.[1] For the sake of completeness I shall, however, give a short list of major bibliographical *topoi*.[2]

1. Plato's notion of *anamnesis,*
2. Aristotle's *De memoria et reminiscentia,*
3. Augustine's *Confessions* (10.19),
4. The Late Antique through Renaissance handbooks on visualization,[3]
5. The Law of Association as discussed in the works of Locke, Berkeley, Hume,[4] Hartley, Mill, Charles Sanders Pierce,[5] and William Hamilton,[6]
6. In the history of religions, Rudolph Otto's "law of parallels," Goethe's morphological comparison of religions, E. B. Tylor's application of the law of association to the field of religions,[7] and J. G. Frazer's adaptation of the notion in his *Golden Bough,* where he uses it to explain the psychology of magic in "primitive cultures,"
7. In the philosophy of science, the extensive literature on the commensurability of scientific paradigms and of translatability across paradigms (Feyerabend and Kuhn), a literature which was one of the objects of critique in,
8. Donald Davidsons's influential essay, "On the Very Idea of the Conceptual Scheme,"[8] which has opened up the more general question of translatability across cultures, now in the area of philosophy, and
9. The theoretical discussions of comparison and the comparative method that abound in the fields of anthropology and comparative literature.[9]

Several things are striking about these sources. First of all, the earliest treatments of the topic were psychological, in so far as they treated the subject of comparison or analogy in the process of treating the more general question of memory. The topic was approached from the Empiricist's perspective by Hume but continued to be associated with "ideas" until William Hamilton's more general treatment of the question. Since the time of the early historians of religion the issue of comparison has taken a new turn with the recognition of pluralism. In more recent years this has led to yet another approach to the question, focused on the issue of cultural relativism.

My survey of much of the above literature, which is still ongoing, has proven only marginally relevant to the questions that I shall address concerning translation theory. More interesting is an emergent literature in the area of Comparative Philosophy that is more directly relevant to the questions of translating across cultures.[10]

I intend to forego discussion of both of these areas, however, and instead turn my attention briefly to the work of Jonathan Z. Smith, a historian of religion who is committed to the comparative method and who, perhaps more than anyone else in the field in recent years, has written most extensively and provocatively on the subject of comparison. Though much of his work is prefaced by fascinating discussions of method, where the question of comparison or analogy frequently rears its head, of most interest to us here are two essays in which the question is explicitly raised. In his "Adde Parvum Parvo Magnus Acervus Erit," he suggests a morphology of comparison in which he recognizes four principal ways of engaging in the comparative enterprise. These he calls cultural comparison, historical comparison, comparison aimed at noting and accounting for similarity in terms of a process of assimilation, diffusion or borrowing and comparison as a hermeneutic device.[11]

Smith considers cultural comparison to take place in the meeting of cultures, "upon the living contact between two peoples" (p. 242). Borrowing the we/they duality from the philosopher Robert Redfield, he describes four distinct attitudes that a member of one culture can hold in regard to others, (1) They are LIKE-US, (2) They are NOT-LIKE-US, (3) They are TOO-MUCH-LIKE-US, (4) We are NOT-LIKE-THEM. In our present inquiry, of course, it is not the contact of cultures that will be of most relevance but the contact of concepts and it will become clear in what follows that each of these four categories have the potential to shed light (1) on how concepts are understood cross-culturally and (2) on how they can be translated.

On his "fourth great class of comparison," that is comparison as a hermeneutic device, Smith says: "Here the meaning and function of a particular motif, symbol or custom in one culture may be used as a key to interpret a similar motif, symbol or custom in another culture by moving from what is known to what is unknown." When Smith begins to fill in the details of his theory, its relevance to our present discussion is lost. Nonetheless, the idea that a concept in one culture can serve as a key to new insights when compared with a concept in another is of course what we are after. What is perhaps most interesting is Smith's notion that comparison proceeds from what is known to what is unknown, something that becomes an issue in the Indian sources as well.

In a later essay, "In Comparison a Magic Dwells,"[12] he approaches the same question from another vantage point. He asks why there has never been a literature that presents "rules for the production of comparison," to which he answers:

> Perhaps this is the case because, for the most part, the scholar has not set out to make comparisons. Indeed, he has been most frequently attracted to a particular datum by a sense of uniqueness. But often, at some point along the way, as if unbidden, as a sort of *deja vu*, the scholar remembers that he has seen "it" or "something like it" before; he experiences what Coleridge described in an early essay.... as the result of the "hooks and eyes of memory." This experience, this unintended consequence of research, must then be accorded significance and provided with an explanation. (p. 22)

Rejecting the validity of earlier analyses based on the principles of resemblance, contiguity and causality, analyses which sought to give the psychological fact of comparison objective validity through a "scientific" explanation of its workings, Smith states: "Thus far, comparison appears to be more a matter of memory than a project for inquiry, it is more impressionistic than methodical." (p. 22) It is interesting that Smith never emerges from the skepticism to provide a positive theory for the workings of comparison as a form of knowledge. He concludes his essay with the confession that he has gotten no closer to the " 'how', 'why' and, above all, the 'so what'" (p. 35) of comparison.

II. Indian Theories of Comparison

It seems to me that Indian theories of *upamāna* do provide us with something of a methodical, rule-governed approach to the study of analogy. Embedded as it is in the discussion of the nature and function of *pramāṇa*, or valid knowledge, the Indian approach is more epistemological than it is psychological in tone. Hence, in India, the questions that were asked in the context of the analysis of analogy or comparison were different from what they were in the West. The Indian sources seem more concerned with the epistemic status of comparison, i.e. with whether or not it is a source of knowledge and if so with whether or not it is a *distinct* source of knowledge, a source of knowledge different from both perception and inference. They are concerned with the object(s) of comparison, i.e. with what it is that comparison cognizes, and they are concerned with the relationship of the two *comparanda*.

It is, of course, beyond the scope of this paper to provide a history of the evolution of the idea of *upamāna* in India, as interesting as I think such a project might be. Still, I think it worthwhile to look, albeit impressionistically, at serval sources in order to glean first hand exactly what some of the issues were. The *Nyāya Sūtras* define *upamāna* as "that which establishes for one knowledge of a fact through its similarity to something that is already known to one."[13] The example given is the classical one in which a man, having heard that there is such a thing as a *gavaya*, a wild cow without dewlap, goes to the forest and sees one. Remembering that he had heard of such a thing in the past, he arrives at the conclusion that the animal before him is a *gavaya*. This is the *upamiti*, the knowledge derived from comparison. Hence, a later *sūtra* (v. 108, sūtra 2.1.147) implies that comparison allows us, in effect, to name the entity before us as a *gavayaḥ*, by noticing its similarity to the cow.

Several points are worth mentioning here. First of all, both Smith and the Indian Naiyāyikās share the notion that comparison proceeds from the known to the unknown. Secondly, as in the general discussion in the Western sources, comparison involves memory. The Western sources that discuss the issue in the context of the Association of Ideas, however, are concerned more with the psychological question of explaining how memory arises, whereas the Indian sources are concerned more with explaining how comparison, as a cognition subsequent to the memory, can be an epistemic source. Finally, the claim is being made that comparison is born from a cognition of *similarity*. The later Vedāntins would claim that comparison is not the result of a cognition of similarity but the *cause* of a cognition of similarity.[14] Both Naiyāyikās and Vedāntins would agree, however, that comparison can involve a cognition of difference as well as a cognition of similarity. The Vedāntins, for example, actually held that one could come to a knowledge of Brahman through the process of comparing Brahman to what it is not, i.e. by noticing the differences between Brahman and the material world, for example.

Vātsyāyana comments that comparison is not a case of perception (something held by the Sāṃkhyas), because it involves an understanding, i.e. the naming, of an entire class of animals, the *gavayas,* something that perception cannot do. It is not a case of inference (something held by the Vaiśeṣikās and Buddhists)[15] because, as mentioned above, it leads to knowledge of a perceived thing (the *gavaya*) through its similarity to something else that is perceived (the cow). Inference, on the other hand, proceeds from knowledge of something *unperceived* through the knowledge of something perceived. The Advaitins and Mīmāṃsakās, the other two major schools that accept comparison as a separate source of knowledge,[16] give a different reason for why comparison is not a form of perception. They claim that it is not a case of perception because the most that perception does is to cognize the *gavayaḥ* and its similarity to the cow, whereas comparison, they say, is knowledge, not of *gavaya's* similarity to the cow, but of the subsequent cognition of the cow's similarity to the *gavaya.*[17] Hence, even among the orthodox Hindu schools (Naiyāyikas, Advaitins and Mīmāṃsakās) there was disagreement as to the nature and function of comparison.

Another controversy, brought up in the *Nyāya Sūtras* themselves (v.105, sūtra 2.1.44), portrays an opponent as suggesting that comparison is impossible because of its lack of precise standards. If two things are *completely* similar, then the comparison is tantamount to tautology and is pointless, if they are *similar only in some degree* then likewise the comparison fails, for if two things are only partially similar, can they truly be said to be like each other? Is a buffalo truly like a cow? I find this argument fascinating in part because it underscores Smith's notion that comparison is more like magic than like science. Both for the Naiyāyikās opponent and for Smith there are no rigid standards involved in assessing comparison. For them, a good comparison, like beauty, may be more in the eye of the beholder.

III. Comparison as an epistemic Source

With this brief overview and comparison of the notion of analogy in two quite disparate traditions let us come to some tentative conclusions of our own about comparison as a source of knowledge. Comparison *is,* first of all, a source of knowledge, a point expressed very eloquently by F. Max Müeller when he states:

> What is gained by comparison?—Why, all higher knowledge is acquired by comparison, and rests on comparison. If it is said that the character of scientific research in our age is pre-eminently comparative, this really means that our researches are now based on the widest evidence that can be obtained, on the broadest inductions that can be grasped by the human mind.[18]

Whether the cause or the effect of the knowledge of similarity, comparison nonetheless involves the recognition of similarity in one way or another. Nonetheless, it seems that most of the literature is in agreement in considering the knowledge of dissimilarity to be the other side of the coin. Hence, comparison and contrast are analogues of each other.[19] Comparison involves memory, usually as a trigger. Seeing something new reminds us of something we have seen or heard before. Memory, therefore, yields the objects to be compared but is different from the process of comparison itself. Smith has stated that comparison involves proceeding from what is known to what is unknown. In the sense that comparison is a source of knowledge this must certainly be true at some level. The Naiyāyikas, as we have seen, hold a similar position when they define comparison as that which "establishes for one knowledge of a fact through its similarity to something that is already known to one." It seems from other passages in the *Nyāya Sūtras*, however, that the Nyāya position is more complex than this, for at times the text seems to imply that the process of comparison does not involve knowledge of new thing *per se* but rather new knowledge of something that is already perceived (that the beast one is already witnessing is a *gavaya*). This, it seems to me, is quite profound. It implies, first of all, that the person doing the comparison must have some type of previous knowledge of the two *comparanda*; it also implies that the comparative process is concerned more with deepening one's knowledge with at least one, and I would maintain both, *comparanda*, rather than with gaining complete knowledge of something that was completely unknown.

What happens after the "hooks and the eyes of memory" yield the two elements to be compared? In a sense, this is the point at which true comparison begins. Notice, first of all, the comparison is symmetrical across cultures. It can proceed in either direction. It is possible that in reading a Buddhist text one might come across a concept, the *neyārtha/nītārtha* distinction, for example, that triggers a memory of something similar in a Western context, hermeneutics as a field of inquiry, for example. At the same time, it may be that in contemplating an issue as it has ben treated in the Western academy, the question of canonicity, for example, I may ask myself whether there exists a parallel discussion or a similar concept, "canon," in the Buddhist literature. Hence, comparison does not always operate in a direction away from one's indigenous intellectual tradition. In this sense it is symmetrical.

Notice also that the most interesting form of comparison involves a process in which one proceeds, not from what is known to what is unknown, but from a partial knowledge of the two *comparanda* to a greater knowledge of both. In this sense, I find both Smith's and the Indian discussions limiting. The picture of the process of comparison which they paint is too simplistic. Comparison is not simply a question of broadening our knowledge of a foreign culture's conceptual constructs, it is instead a dialectical process in which the questions raised by the dialogue between two cultures sheds light on our understanding of both. In a recent paper, for example, I have examined criteria that emerge in the Western scholarly treatment of the notion of canon and have concluded that the Indo-Tibetan *siddhānta* schema is very much the functional equivalent of a canon, albeit a philosophical or doctrinal one.[20] This, in turn, raises the question of the extent to which normative doctrine, or dogma, might be considered a canon of sorts, even in Western religious literature, thereby enhancing or broadening the concept of canon in the indigenous intellectual sitting, in the very context from which it arose. The dialectical nature of the comparative enterprise is clear.

Put in another way, we might say that the process of comparison involves the reconciliation of the two *comparanda*, where by reconciliation I mean simply the fullest possible recognition of the similarities *and* differences. Let me also emphasize, however, that comparison *is a process*, so that each of the elements being compared can (and in the most interesting comparisons *do*) change as the comparison proceeds. Although Richard Rorty is more of a skeptic than I am in regard to our ability to understand the issues and concepts that are expounded by a foreign culture, he *does*, it seems to me, express the possibility of mutual influence very well when he states:

> Sooner or later we realize that we shall never read, or know, enough to put ourselves in their shoes (either because there is too little material preserved or too much to get through). So we content ourselves with imposing the grid of our own needs upon the books these men wrote, and blanking out most of their needs. As a result, we fuse our horizons with just a little (usually just a few minutes of arc) of each of theirs. Nevertheless, such tiny fusions may sometimes be turning points in our own intellectual or spiritual lives.[21]

If, as both Smith and at least one Indian opponent of the Naiyāyikas suggests, comparison is more of an art than a science, then it becomes essential to consider criteria for what makes something a good comparison, to develop an aesthetics of comparison, as it were. I think that this is possible, though obviously beyond the scope of this paper. Still, I would like to suggest certain factors that might be considered in such an enterprise. One striking feature of *good* comparison, comparison that is interesting and meaningful, concerns the levels of *abstraction* or *generality* of the concepts being compared. As a general rule we might state that, whether or not the process of comparison begins this way, it must end in such a way that minimizes the relative difference in the levels of abstraction of the two concepts. For example, in considering the question of syllogistic reasoning it would be bad comparison, and poor scholarship, to conclude that Buddhist writers had nothing but the most rudimentary and naive notions of logic by focusing only on the *Nikāyas,* some of the earliest Buddhist scriptures. The point, of course, is that even if we begin with the *Nikāyas as* a starting point it is incumbent upon us to find the most sophisticated/abstract notion of syllogistic reasoning available in the Buddhist literature as a *comparandum.* Not to do so is not only poor scholarship, it is tantamount to sophism. The comparison is naive, and fails, if, among other things, the level of abstraction of the two *comparanda* can be reconciled but never are. To take another example, if there exists a notion of canon in Buddhism more complex and more abstract than that of a mere exemplum of a canon (the *tripiṭaka*), and I have argued in the above mentioned paper that *siddhānta* is such a notion, then in the process of reconciliation it is incumbent upon the comparativist to find a partner for the initial concept that is of a level of abstraction that *comes closest to that of the initial concept.* If the reconciliation of the two *comparanda* can never be accomplished, whether because the concept is simply missing in one tradition or because of irreconcilable philosophical differences (the case with God), then the comparison succeeds so long as the reconciliation is pushed to its limits.

IV. The Role of Comparison in the Translation of Texts

Notwithstanding its portrayal in naive historical accounts, Tibet was neither a linguistic nor a conceptual *tabula rasa* when it first came into contact with Buddhism. The fact that there existed a rich vocabulary from which to construct, albeit at times by force, a Tibetan Buddhist technical lexicon is proof sufficient of this. By comparison to the case of China,[22] however, we must admit that when Buddhism entered Tibet it entered a culture that was, by contrast, philosophically impoverished. This, of course, had both "advantages" and "disadvantages," a discussion of which would take us too far abreast of our present topic to merit further treatment here. Suffice it to point out that the West's encounter with Buddhism is more similar to the case of its entrance into China than of its entrance into Tibet. Both Han China and the modern West were/are cultures with complex philosophical heritages. As was the case with China, when Buddhism becomes understood in the West it becomes understood in the light of a pre-existing nexus of intellectual and philosophical concepts that have long histories and often complex semantic interconnections.

What this means, practically speaking, is that Smith's notion of cultural comparison, or our modified version, "conceptual comparison," is more relevant to the Chinese case, and to the case of Buddhism's emergence in the modern West, than it is to Tibet. In both China and in the West, Buddhist concepts come to be understood by *comparison* to pre-existing concepts, so that the four categories, LIKE-OUR-CONCEPT, and so forth, are the means through which Buddhist ideas become assimilated.[23] What this means, as well, is that the translation of Buddhist technical terms from Tibetan or Sanskrit must take into account the philosophical presuppositions of Western culture by giving due consideration to the philosophical and conceptual ramifications of translation choices. Does this imply that only Westerners can translate Buddhist texts into Western languages? Not at all. It does mean, however, that good translations are going to require expertise, not only in Western languages, but in Western intellectual history as well. We might also add that the West's philosophical complexity vitiates against any attempts at standardizing Buddhist terminology the way it was presumably done in Tibet. The polysemic nature of Buddhist terms and of their Western equivalents, and the disparate nature of possible audiences, makes this impossible *at the theoretical level*. What is more, translators in the West do not, of course, have a single common source of financial support, the case in Tibet at least at certain times. This means that compliance with a fixed translation lexicon is not rewarded financially, and more importantly, that non-compliance is not punished financially. In addition, we tend to be, in part because of our socialization within the academy, an egocentric bunch. Both of these factors makes the enterprise of standardizing Buddhist translation terminology *practically* impossible.

The way we translate is not unlike the way we compare. In fact, a great deal of theoretical work in the area of translation theory is intimately tied to the question of the comparison of concepts across cultures. We might even say that translation is the culmination of comparison in that making a final translation choice is often the end product of considerable comparative reflection. Translation too brings into play the "hooks and the eyes of memory," as our minds sift through different options of words and phrases to convey the desired meaning. Moreover, if we reflect on the process of translation it becomes clear that neither comparison nor translation is as simple as proceeding from "what is known to what is unknown." If anything, the process of translating texts is the exact opposite of this scenario. It is a process that takes us from the unknown to the known, from a source language that is foreign to us, to a target language that is our own. This too is overly simplistic, however, for a source term is never completely unknown, nor is a target term ever totally understood. Therefore, like the theory of comparison that I have tried to outline above, translation is a process that is dialectical in nature. We become confronted initially by what we take to be the uniqueness of a concept or by the uniqueness of a nexus of concepts. Then, to use Smith's phrase, we remember that "we have seen 'it' or something like 'it' "before in our own intellectual milieu and in our own language. From this memory is born our initial choices of words and phrases, the first attempt at translation. The words in the source and target languages, and the concepts for which they stand, are our initial *comparanda*. As we encounter further examples of contexts in which the terms are used, both in the source and in the target languages, there evolves a dialectic in which the two terms or conceptual structures become more refined. Reconciliation is sought, as we begin to understand more fully the semantic interconnections of the two terms in their respective linguistic and intellectual settings.[24] Our initial translation choice may even come to be discarded. Perhaps the target term does not adequately express the complexity of the source term, or perhaps the implications of our translation choice, of the term in the target language, are too manifold, giving to it more complexity than is implied by the source language. Eventually, however, we make a final choice. Having worked through the comparative dialectic, however, our choice is informed, it is a choice that is aware of the similarities and differences of the terms. It has achieved reconciliation.

No translation is perfect. There is no such thing as a one-to-one match, unless of course we are willing to create a target language which is a calculus-like mirror image of the source language. It might be claimed that Buddhist Tibetan *(chos skad)* is just that. I have already argued, however, that Western languages will never be cast in the mould of Tibetan. Both the complexity of the Western intellectual/linguistic milieu and the socio-economic context of the translation enterprise militates against this. The position that all translation is imperfect, however, implies neither skepticism nor relativism. Standards do exist. There are, after all, degrees of imperfection. The least imperfect translation, I would maintain, is an informed one, one in which both the similarities and the differences between the source and target terms are understood—one which has been subjected to the comparative dialectic. In short, it is one in which reconciliation has taken place.

We begin this paper with the claim that comparison is a source of knowledge. I have now made the additional claim that translation is a form of comparison. It follows of course that translation is also a source of knowledge. In the process of translating a passage our knowledge of both source and target concepts are enhanced. The obligation to make a translation choice forces us to test the limits of different possibilities, to become aware of the implications of each possible choice. The source term challenges us to fully understand the implications of the possible target term, while the finite possibilities of target terms forces us to come to an informed conclusion about the source concept. This, in and of itself, is surely knowledge. I believe, however, that in the process of translation something even greater, call it insight if you will, is possible. This occurs when concepts are stretched beyond their limits, when the semantic implications of a term in one language suggest to us new ways of perceiving a term or concept in another. This leads to the asking of new questions, and hopefully to their being answered.

I once entertained the notion that my years among my Tibetan teachers and friends had in many ways made my intellectual outlook more Tibetan than Western. There is some truth to this. The years that I have spent on the debate courtyard of the Byes College of Se ra have, without a doubt, had a permanent influence on the way I think. At times, when I argue philosophy with my colleagues at Iliff, I reflect upon the scenario and I realize what a strange animal I must seem to them ... and justifiably so, for in large measure they are arguing with a voice from fifteenth century Tibet. I also realize, however, that when I argue with my monk friends in Sarnath I am to them, in large part, the voice of the Western academy, and of a scientific outlook to the universe. Both of these traditions have of course influenced me as an intellectual, but because of my commitment to the comparative method, because of my work as a translator, but especially because of my love for pushing concepts to their limits and beyond, I am in a real sense neither Western nor Tibetan. If the reader will permit one final apologetic remark, I will end by saying that I can imagine few more interesting predicaments in which to find oneself.

NOTES

1. In Jonathan Z. Smith, "In Comparison a Magic Dwells," chapter 2 of his collection of essays *Imagining Religion: From Babylon to Jonestown* (Chicago: University of Chicago Press, 1982), pp. 20-22.

2. The list relies heavily on Smith's article (see previous note) and on Heinrich Frick's "The aim of the comparative study of religions," a selection from his *Vergleichende Religionswissenschaft* anthologized in Jacques Waardenburg, ed., *Classical Approaches to the Study of Religion: Aims, Methods and Theories of Research* (The Huge: Moulton, 1973), pp. 480-486.
3. See J.Z. Smith, "In Comparison," p. 139, n. 1.
4. David L. Hume, *Enquiries Concerning Human Understanding and Concerning the Principles of Morals,* L.A. Selby-Biggs, ed., (Third edition, with the revisions and notes of N.H. Nidditch) (Oxford: The Clarendom Press, 1975), pp. 23-24, which is the third section entitled, "On the Association of Ideas."
5. *Collected Papers,* C. Hartshorne and P. Weiss, eds. (Cambridge, Mass.: Harvard University Press, 1931-35), especially vol. V, p. 307ff, "Consequences of Four Incapacities," when he discusses Hume's principles of resemblance, contiguity and causality.
6. See his famous *Note D**,* in his edition of *The Works of Thomas Reid* (Edinburgh: Maclahan and Stewart, 1852), pp. 889-914.
7. In his *Researches into the Early History of Mankind,* third edition (London: 1878), p. 130; and *Primitive Culture* (New York: 1889), vol. I, pp. 115-116.
8. Anthologized in J.W. Meiland and M. Krausz, eds., *Relativism: Cognitive and Moral* (Notre Dame and London: The University of Notre Dam Press, 1982), pp. 66-80.
9. J.Z. Smith, "Adde Parvum Parvo Magnus Acervit Erit," in his *Map is not Territiry: Studies in the History of Religions* (Leiden: E.J. Brill, 1978), p. 264 (Afterword) gives bibliographical references to works in these fields.
10. See Gerald James Larson and Eliot Deutsch, eds., *Interpreting Across Boundaries: New Essays in Comparative Philosophy* (Princeton: Princeton University Press, 1988); see also the reviews by Richard Rorty and John M. Koller in *Philosophy East and West,* vol. 39, no. 3 (1989), pp. 332-337, and 338-352, respectively.
11. He then devotes the remainder of his essay to a discussion of historical example of these four modes, which he now categorizes under the titles: the ethnographic, the encyclopedic, the morphological and the evolutionary. The earlier set of four, especially because of the impressionistic way in which Smith treats them, leaves room for the possibility of their being adapted to our present discussion. When the gaps begin to be filled in by Smith in his historiographic treatment of the general principles, a discussion that leads to his association of the general principles with the more specific and latter set of four, it becomes clear that none

of these forms of comparison are truly relevant to our present concerns. Be that as it may, I see it as a perfectly legitimate exercise to use Smith for what he is worth to us, and in this regard it is clear that his notion of cultural comparison and of comparison as a hermeneutic device are promising.

12. See note 9 above.
13. *prassidhasādharmyāt sādhyasādhanam upamānam* / v. 6, sūtra 1.1.6; M.M. Satisa Chandra Vidyābhūṣaṇa, ed., N. Sinha, rev., *The Nyāya Sūtras of Gotama* [Delhi: Motilal Banarsidass, 1981], p. 4.
14. See, for example, *Vedāntaparibhāśā* (III, 1), where *upamāna* is defined as "the cause of the knowledge of similarity" *(sadṛśyapramākaraṇam)*; see the edition of S.S. Suryanarayana Sastri [Madras: The Adyar Library, 1984], p. 62.
15. For a Jaina viewpoint on this issue see Hemacandra's Pramāṇa-mīmāṃsā (1, 2, 3-4), S. Mookerjee and N. Tatia, trans. (Calcutta: 1946), pp. 86-91.
16. This is a claim made by, for example, Swami Satprakashananda in his classic study, *Methods of Knowledge* (Calcutta: Advaita Ashrama, 1965), p. 154.
17. This definition seems to me to be more an answer to Buddhist and Sāṃkhya polemicist than one motivated by the nature of the process of comparison itself. In this sense I think that the Naiyāyikas are clearer in their analysis of the concept than are the later orthodox Hindu schools.
18. From *Inroduction to the Science of Religion,* anthologized in J. Waardenburg, *Classical Approaches to the Study of Religion* (The Hague and Paris: Moulton, 1973), p. 91.
19. Smith, "In Comparison a Magic Dwells, " p. 21, seems to see an overemphasis on *similarity* in his treatment of the Western sources. He concludes at one point that "the issue of difference has been all but forgotten."
20. See my "The Canonization of Philosophy and the Rhetoric of Siddhānta in Indo-Tibetan Buddhism," in John Keenan and Paul Griffiths, eds., *Buddha Nature* (Reno, Nevada: Buddhist Books International, 1991).
21. Richard Rorty, review of G.L. Larson and E. Deutsch, eds., *Interpreting Across Boundaries: New Essays in Comparative Philosophy,* p. 332.
22. For historical treatments of Buddhism's entrance into China see K Chen, *Buddhism in China: A Historical Survey* (Princeton: Princeton University Press, 1972).
23. Consider, for example, the extensive literature on the *ko-i* method of translation in China.

24. The purpose of reconciliation is not, of course, to find the identical equivalent of a source term in the target language. If this were possible, comparison would never be possible. As the previously mentioned Naiyāyika opponent claims, if the two entities are completely similar, the comparison becomes nothing but a tautology.

On Translating Tibetan Philosophical Texts

D. Seyfort Ruegg

It has often been said that translation is an art rather than a science, and that to translate is to betray *(traduttore traditore).* If the first proposition is intended only to mean that translation is not a mechanical activity, this is surely so: the translator has so often to take into careful consideration a number of contextual and cultural factors that are unexpressed or barely hinted at in the text he is translating. Moreover, syntactical and semantic structures frequently cannot be automatically rendered from a source-language into the target-language. As for the proposition, *traduttore traditore,* even when the translator has proceeded knowledgeably and carefully and succeeds in making what may be called a good and accurate translation, he and his reader might well find that many connotations and meanings of the original have nevertheless been lost in the rendering and perhaps also that new and undesired connotations have been inadvertently introduced. At least to this extent, then, the translator, even a competent and careful one, may find that he has betrayed his text or author. Let us not mention here the so-called 'unfaithful beauties' *(belles infideles),* those egregiously unfaithful translations, or rather creations, in which translators have reworked and recreated their originals to the detriment of the latter.

In order to mitigate and, whenever possible, to eliminate such undesired losses or gains of meaning in the process of translation, professional translators and linguists and also some philosophers have devoted numerous studies to the problem of translation. It will of course not be possible to survey this literature here. Suffice it to say that in this manner much valuable work, both theoretical and applied, has ben carried out on making translation less of an art that may be more or less haphazard and more of a science that is regular and well-founded in both practice and theory.

Now we are often told that an ideal translation should read as if it had been composed originally in the target-language, that is, as if it had not been translated at all. On the face of it this ideal sounds unexceptionable, and it no doubt proves to be an attainable goal when the original and the translation both belong to a common linguistic and cultural milieu.

But if we consider the matter more closely, is this always to be our ideal? That is, can and indeed should (e.g.) an English translation of a Tibetan or Sanskrit philosophical work read exactly as if it had been composed originally in English? If the thesis that there exists a certain essential link between the levels of expression and content is to be taken seriously—even without going so far as to espouse the doctrines of linguistic and cultural relativism and the Sapir-Whorf view of the relation between language and the cultural categories—it is less than obvious that our answer to the question should always be an unqualified affirmative. Of course a translator must avoid not only barbarism and solecisms but also unnecessary calques of his source-text; thus there is generally no reason why a syntactic construction of the source-language should be literally reproduced in the target-language. Nevertheless, it is not clear that the semantic structure of a translation, including its vocabulary, should (or indeed could) be that of some "Standard Average English" writing. In other words, there may be place for certain kinds of calques which take into account the semantic fields of the language and theoretical representations of the source-text.

It may be that it is not such cases that the advocates of total Englishing etc. had in mind when setting up the ideal of having a rendering read just as though it had not been translated at all. But it is not altogether clear what the proponents of such Englishing do mean, and whether they have given due consideration to the fact that translation—and most certainly non-literary translation—cannot necessarily be expected to read like an original English composition. This is probably a matter that requires further thought.

At all events it is well known that bilingualism often brings with it interaction and interference between two languages. And biculturalism (or multiculturalism) in philosophy might be expected to have a similar effect.

Let us just note here a point that is perhaps relevant to this matter. Our Tibetan colleagues who have both an excellent Tibetan education and an outstanding mastery of (e.g.) English sometimes find it possible to say in good English what is written in a Tibetan text that presents difficulties as to its contents—that is, they are able to paraphrase this text—but at the same time they find it hard to translate it in the strict sense. In other words, the Tibetan text is not considered by them to contain something unsayable in (e.g.) English—something that is properly ineffable—but they find they can convey this content to us only in English paraphrase. This curious problem in communication and translation may, of course, be purely contingent in the sense that it is due to nothing more than the fact that Tibetan scholars have been translating their literature into Western languages for only a decade or two. In short, it may simply be a matter of acquiring more practice in translation. That it is a real problem, and not one that is experienced solely by our Tibetan colleagues, is nevertheless suggested by the fact that it has been encountered equally by Western scholars translating from Tibetan into their native languages. Thus, over a number of decades some very competent Western scholars have published renderings of Tibetan philosophical works that can be described as good, but which nevertheless fail at critical points fully to "communicate," that is, to convey the meaning of the original. This is probably the experience of most translators, as it has been mine.

The question then arises: Where do the problems lie? One answer no doubt is that the problem is not exclusively one of linguistic expression but also one of content: philosophical, religious, cultural, etc. This may seem obvious enough, for the level of content is of course generally recognized to be of no less importance for translation than that of linguistic expression; and the problem of the relation of the source-language to the target-language is accordingly not an exclusively linguistic one in the sense of being confined to, e.g., morphology and syntax or, indeed, even to vocabulary.

To refine our question then: How does the translator implement the conveying of the full meaning of his text to the reader or listener? Or to put it in another way, how does he make the text "communicate" to a new audience in another language?

We quickly find that the question of translation raises the twin factors of transmission and reception, and also the matter of intercultural hermeneutics, which are inescapable in any consideration of how to render Tibetan or Sanskrit works into a Western language. Similar problems presumably arise in translating from these languages into a non-Western language such as Japanese. And I suspect that the problems may not be so radically different even when rendering ancient Sanskrit texts into modern Indo-Aryan languages, and that they are only masked by the fact that many translators from Sanskrit into, e.g., Hindi in fact transpose, using *tatsama* forms and substituting Hindi practices for Sanskrit inflexional endings more than they actually translate, on the assumption that the culture of modern Indians is hardly different from that of classical Sanskritic culture, or at least that such transposition renders an ancient Sanskrit work transparent to the modern Indian.

A point that is often raised in connection with translating from Tibetan is the usefulness or necessity of using commentaries and the oral tradition. It seems that a certain amount of confusion may prevail in this matter.

There is, first, the fundamental question of whether commentaries of any kind are to be regarded as reliable guides to understanding and interpreting Tibetan or Sanskrit works, and accordingly whether they can be of any real use to the translator. In the history of Sanskrit studies, the early (and of course some more recent) Indologists had few qualms about making extensive use of later Sanskrit commentaries and of the oral tradition of the pandits. (Reference can be made, for example, to Sir William Jones, Henry Thomas Colebrooke and Horace Hayman Wilson, and also to Theodor Goldstücker whom Ernst Windisch described in this respect as a "frondeur" in his history of Sanskrit philology (p. 246), but who did not actually work personally with paṇḍitas. Later Richard Pischel, whom Windisch also described as "frondeur", differed from Rudolph Röth in his regard for commentaries.) But by the middle of the nineteenth century a very strong, and sometimes quite violent, reaction had set in, and it became practically axiomatic with many Sanskrit philologists that little or no reliance was to be placed on commentaries (unless of course they were autocommentaries or nearly contemporary with the work commented on). (See, for example, the views of Otto Böhtlingk, Rudolph Röth and Albrecht Weber. An extreme case was William Dwight Whitney. This was an attitude that was justified with respect to Vedic

Saṃhitā texts, but very much less in the case of classical Sanskrit texts.) In recent times a more balanced attitude has made its appearance with respect to the use of commentaries when interpreting and translating classical Sanskrit works. It can be summed up by saying that a translator must carefully familiarize himself with the exegetical traditions relevant to his text and textual corpus, even though his task is in the first place to understand and translate his text in its historical context of time and place, not allowing himself to be unduly influenced by the later developments that may be reflected in the commentarial traditions. (It is, however, coming to be widely recognized that such developments in interpretation may be of very considerable interest in their own right.) In sum, the value and interest of the commentarial tradition is being accepted by many Indologists; and for many Western Indologists working with a learned paṇḍita this has come to be regarded as not unusual.

This applies also (and perhaps to an even greater degree) to many Tibetologists. Most regrettably, however, what has been accepted by Tibetologists has yet to be reflected in the academic structure of most universities where Tibetan is taught but where, with only a few exceptions, no provision is made for having the living scholarly and cultural traditions of Tibet represented by a Tibetan. It seems clear that in many branches of Tibetan studies real progress can be made only in close collaboration with Tibetan scholars, following the model, as it were, of the Pandita-Lotsawa teams that produced most of the translations from Indian languages into Tibetan.

As for oral commentary and oral tradition, it has to be said that in very many cases this "orality"is accidental in so far as what it transmits is in fact rooted in the written tradition and can itself easily be recorded in writing. (Cf. for example, the recent commentary by the *dge bšes* rTa mgrin Rab brten on Tsoṅ kha pa's *Legs bśad sñiṅ po.*) For reasons not yet sufficiently explored, however, it has very often not been customary to write down these school-traditions. One reason for this was perhaps the fact that they represented the special interpretations of individual seminaries or teachers, and that they had not (yet) achieved the "official" status or "canonicity" that would have warranted their being written down and eventually printed. But the fact remains that such "oral" commentarial traditions could easily be written down, and that many in fact were sooner or later. (See, for example, the accounts by

Ṅag dbaṅ dpal ldan of the varying interpretations current in the Blo gsal gliṅ and sGo maṅ seminaries of the 'Bras spuṅs monastery near Lhasa.)

Such instances of oral commentarial tradition have therefore to be carefully distinguished from that other form of oral transmission which is properly private and acroamatic, that is, which is to be transmitted individually and privately, in the form of a *sñan brgyud,* from a master or *guru (bla ma)* to each disciple (or group of disciples) and which belongs to Mantrayāna. Such oral tradition is nevertheless not so much "secret" as it is reserved and specific, being destined for individual disciples according to their natures and capacities at a particular time and in specific circumstances. To what extent (if at all) such oral instructions are to be used in preparing a translation is something that has to be decided in each case by their transmitters.

The references made above to the philosophical, religious and cultural specificity of Tibetan or Sanskrit works in connection with intercultural transmission and reception and hermeneutics inevitably raise the thorny questions not only of linguistic relativism but also of conceptual and cultural relativism. These are topics that have been discussed at great length by linguists, philosophers and anthropologists, and they cannot be gone into in detail here.

To simplify a complex matter, it is in my view possible to accept the fact of cultural and philosophical specificity—and perhaps even the theory of a certain incommensurability between cultures—together with the reflection of this specificity in the language and conceptual systems of Tibetan or Sanskrit philosophical or religious texts, without however having to go so far as to maintain the strongest versions of the theses of the indeterminacy of translation and correlation (Quine), cultural relativism, and the influence of language on cultural categories (the Sapir-Whorf hypothesis).

Within Buddhism, the Mahāyānists have in fact generally assumed that translation of their canonical Sūtras—the *buddhavacana*—and the Śāstras—from Sanskrit into Chinese or Tibetan, from Chinese into Korean and Japanese, and from Tibetan into Mongolian—was both desirable and feasible. It is interesting to observe that in this matter the Mahāyānists have proceeded differently from the Theravādins, who retained the Pali canon wherever they migrated in South and Southest Asia and who, though they once had, e.g., an old Sinhalese Aṭṭhakathā, finally transmitted their main commentaries only in Pali. The Buddha himself is indeed deemed to have decreed that each disciple should have the Dharma available in his or her own language. And this use of different canonical languages is completely consistent with Mahāyānist docetism according to which the teaching of the Dharma is carried out by a Buddha's *nirmāṇakāya* in accord with the capacities and requirements of his disciples.

For the Mahāyāna, it is true, absolute reality *(paramārtha)* as such is inexpressible (*anabhilāpya).* Nevertheless, the expositions in both Sūtra and Śāstra presuppose effability (in the frame of, say, *saparyāya-paramārtha* or [*udbhāvanā*-] *saṃvṛti).* And this effability of course implies translatability.

Nevertheless, as already noted, in translating there is frequently to be noticed an unwanted loss or deficit of meaning, and sometimes also an unwanted gain or surplus of meaning. And even if Sūtra and Śāstra are not to be thought of as untranslatable, it seems that there does often exist a kind of incommensurability between the original and the translation, as well as between the translations of the same text into different languages with their culturally determined matrices and (sometimes) even into the same language. (This will have to do with the philosopher's problem of synonymy of propositions in natural languages.)

In considering the translating of philosophical texts from Tibetan or Sanskrit, in addition to the source-language (or object language) or text and the target-language (or subject language) or text, it is necessary to give thought to what Davidson has called the metalanguage ("Radical interpretation," in *Truth and interpretation,* Oxford, 1984, p. 129). This "metalanguage" is "the language of the theory, which says what expressions of the subject language translate which expressions of the object language." Davidson explains (p.129): "When interpretation is our aim, a method of translation deals with a wrong topic, a relation between two languages, where what is wanted is an interpretation of one (in another, of course, but that goes without saying since any theory is in some language)". And he adds (p.130): "The translation manual churns out, for each sentence of the language to be translated, a sentence of the translator's language; the theory of interpretation then gives the interpretation of these familiar sentences. Clearly the reference to the home language is superfluous; it is an unneeded intermediary between interpretation and alien idiom. The only expressions a theory of interpretation has to mention are those belonging to the language to be interpreted." The implications of this and other philosophical treatments of translation and interpretation for our present purposes will require reflection and discussion.

In any case, in our concern with translating and consequently with the source-language/text and its rendering in the target-language, which nowadays characterizes Buddhist studies—and which has indeed characterized them for a century and a half—consideration of theory (which in Buddhism should of course not be understood as exclusive of and antithetical to practice) tends to be neglected. It is for this reason, I think, that we require more sustained attempts at analysis and synthesis, and better synchronic and diachronic studies of doctrines and terms, with a view to penetrating and interpreting theory and developing an adequate language of theory. Amongst other things this involves building up a detailed knowledge of what the Tibetans call *grub mtha'* (Skt. *siddhānta*), that is, not merely "tenets" or sets of dogmas and beliefs, but philosophical systems established by analysis (Tib. *dpyad pa*) and reasoning (Tib. *rigs pa*). Exercise in translation into, e.g., English from Tibetan or Sanskrit doubtless helps towards this end, and this is of course why we engage in translation in university seminars. But such exercises are not sufficient. And sometimes, it seems, the cart has been put before the horse by attempting to translate vast bodies of texts without constructing the firm foundation of a knowledge of the "metalanguage".

Translation of Tibetan or Sanskrit philosophical texts must then involve for us a very radical effort of understanding and interpretation, and also in intercultural transmission and hermeneutics. This need cannot be met simply by turning out translations, however worthy these may be. And a balance will have to be struck between translating on the one side and interpretation, analysis and synthesis on the other side.

I mentioned above that the process of translation is an art in the sense that it cannot be made purely mechanical and automatic. But has it not often been claimed that the Tibetan lotsāwas developed a special form of the Tibetan language in which they imitated and calqued the terminology, and often even the syntax, of their Indian source-texts. And have we not sometimes hard it said that their translations differ radically, for example, from the majority of Chinese translations of Buddhist texts, and especially from the earlier Chinese translations using the method of "meaning-matching" *(ko-i)*, by being not only highly technical but also mechanical?

In the eighth and ninth centuries, the Tibetans did indeed develop a very special language—the so-called *chos skad*—which they used for rendering Sanskrit (and also Pali and Chinese) texts into Tibetan. And a form of this *chos skad* has survived in use up to the present day for writing treatises and commentaries on the Dharma. In its turn this *chos skad* has influenced the language of non-religious official texts and even the colloquial language. But it would be a mistake to overemphasize the artificiality and mechanicalness of Tibetan translations form the Sanskrit, or to regard the *chos skad* as hardly a natural language. This can be demonstrated by comparing two Tibetan translations of (virtually) the same Sanskrit text in the cases (relatively rare it is true) where we have available such parallel translations. (We shall not consider here the case of Tibetan translations from parallel but nevertheless quite distinct versions of a text, such as from the Indian and Chinese versions of the *Mahāparinirvāṇasūtra* and the *Suvarṇabhāṣāsūtra*.)

For this purpose let us briefly compare two Tibetan versions of the *Prajñāpāramitāstotra,* otherwise known as the *Nirvikalpastava,* attributed to Nāgārjuna but no doubt by (his disciple?) Rāhulabhadra. Translation I is by Śāntibhadra and Tshul khrims rgyal ba (1011-) and is found in the Tibetan version of the *Aṣṭasāhaśrikā prajñāpāramitā* (as found in the sPu brag bKa' 'gyur; cf. *Otani Catalogue,* no. 734). Translation II is by Tilakakalaśa (Thig lee bum pa) and rNog Blo ldan ses rab (1059-1109) and is found in the bsTan 'gyur (see *Otani Catalogue,* no. 2018).

We find that there indeed exist significant differences between these two versions. Some of these differences are stylistic; and in II the use of honorific forms is more widespread and consistent than in I. Other differences concern vocabulary. And still others involve interpretation. (No mention will be made here of the instances where the two Tibetan translations are presumably based on distinct versions of the original Sanskrit text.) Here are several examples to illustrate these points:

(i) the word *nirañjanā* as an epithet of Prajñāpāramitā in verse 19 is rendered by *khyad med pa* "undifferentiated" in I, but more literally by *gos med pa* "immaculate" in II;
(ii) the epithet *nirakṣarā* in verse 2 is rendered by *mi 'gyur ba* "immutable" in I, but by *yi ge med* "unsyllabified" (i.e. ineffable, cf. *anakṣara*) in II;
(iii) *bhāvena* in verse 2 is rendered by *ṅo bor* in I, but no doubt more correctly by *bsam yas* (read *bsam pas*) in II; cf. verse 14 where *bhāvatas* is rendered by *yaṅ dag tu* in I (or does *yaṅ dag tu* belong only to *mthoṅ ba*, in which case *bhāvatas* is not translated in I?), but by *bsam pa yis* in I (both sets of translations are possible, though the version by rṄog probably renders the intended meaning better);
(iv) *vidhivat* in verse 5 is translated by *cho ga bzhin* in I but, more accurately, by *tshul bzhin* in II;
(v) *bahurūpā* in verse 9 is rendered by *dṅos maṅ por* in I, but by *tshul maṅ du* in II;
(vi) *prapadya* in verse 4 is rendered by *brten nas* in both I and II; but in verse 14 *prapadya* is translated by *bsgrubs pas* (I) / *bsgrubs pa las* (II), whereas *prapadyante* is there rendered by *grub par byed* (I) / *bsgrubs pa* (II);
(vii) *paśyanti* in verse 14 is rendered by *(yaṅ dag tu) mthoṅ ba* "see" in I. but by *'khums nas* "understand" in II; but in the same context in verse 15, *paśyan* is rendered by *mthoṅ ba* in both I and II (the decision in II to render the connotation 'understand' of *paś-* in verse 14 but not in verse 15 is hard to account for);
(viii) *sunirvṛta* in verse 20 is rendered by *šin tu tshim* in I but by *šin tu mya ṅan 'das* in II (which, unlike I, does not render the desiderative sense in *tuṣṭūṣantas*), both translations being possible but conveying quite different connotations of the word.

These examples of a stylistic, terminological and religio-philosophical character will serve to show that Tibetan translations are not literal to the point of being simply automatic. Incidentally, some of these examples show us, in addition, that it is not always possible to reconstruct the Sanskrit original with perfect confidence from a Tibetan translation. For the Tibetans also, translation has been an art and not an absolutely regular or mechanical science.

But from early times the Tibetan *lotsāwas* sought to develop principles of translation that would preclude imprecision and ambiguity as much as differences of interpretation and the very nature of natural language make this possible. These efforts to develop a technical and truly scientific system of translating find expression in the introduction to the *Madhyavyutpatti* (*Bye brag tu rtogs byed 'briṅ po*), or *sGra sbyor (bam po gñis pa)*, a treatise on translation composed in a horse year *(rta'ilo)* early in the ninth century under the Tibetan monarch Khri lDe sroṅ btsan when the translation of Indian texts into Tibetan was reaching its peak during the early propagation *(sṅa dar)* of the Dharma. This manual for translators contains the principles accepted for rendering Indian texts in the "new language" according to the instructions concerning this decreed standard which were promulgated under the authority of the Tibetan ruler.

Much later, in the eighteenth century, these principles were reproduced and expanded in the introduction to the *Dag yig mkhas pa'i 'byuṅ gnas*, the terminological lexicon prepared when the Tibetan bsTan 'ḥgyur was being translated into Mongolian under the patronage of the Emperor Ch'ien-lung and under the supervision of lCaṅ skya Rol pa 'i rdo rje (1718-1786) and other leading scholars.

No less important for a translator are glossaries and lexicons which allow him to render his texts in as exact, regular and unarbitrary a fashion as possible. The need for such aids to translation was realized by the Tibetans also in the early ninth century when an invaluable glossary of Sanskrit terms with their Tibetan equivalents, the *Mahāvyutpatti*, was composed. The *Mahāvyutpatti* or *Bye brag tu rtogs byed chen po* contains the "official" equivalents accepted for translation according to the principles of the "new language" as decreed by the Tibetan monarch. Later, this glossary had added to it Mongolian and Chinese equivalents.

It is of course not possible today to regulate translators and their work by decree, nor would it be desirable to attempt to impose uniformity by such means. Yet it will be in the interest of translators and their readers to develop systems of terminological equivalences that are as regular, unarbitrary and well thought-out as is humanly possible. Some little progress has been made in this direction, but it would hardly be realistic to expect that a single terminological system can be developed in the foreseeable future for any given target-language.

Given the inspiring precedents mentioned above—and in view of the favourable attitude to translation adopted by both the Śrāvakayānist and Mahāyānist schools of Buddhism which have not hesitated to render their Sūtras and Śāstras into often unrelated languages in Central and East Asia for the sake of peoples of a wide variety of cultures and in view of the fact that these schools are now in the process of doing the same in Europe and America—contemporary translators of Tibetan and also Sanskrit texts have behind them a long tradition of Buddhist scholarship on which they can draw and from the experience of which they must try to learn.

Problems in Translating the *Mūlamadhyamakakārikā* as Cited in its Commentaries

Akira Saito

In our translation work of the Tibetan texts of Nāgārjuna's *Mūlamadhyamakakārikā* as cited in its commentaries such as the *Akutobhayā* (Ga las 'jigs med), Buddhapālita's commentary, and the *Prasannapadā* (Tshig gsal), we sometimes come across those instances where the contents of the translation of a quoted *kārikā* and the commentator's explanation for it do not agree. Through the analysis of such problems, the present paper aims at clarifying how and in what order Klu'i rgyal mtshan and Nyi ma grags translated the commentaries on the *Mūlamadhyamakakārikā*, including the *Prajñā-nāma-mūlamadhyamakakārikā*, the *Prajñāpradīpa* (Shes rab sgron ma), and the above three commentaries.

1

First, let us examine one typical instance as found in the *Mūlamadhyamakakārikā*, chapter II, *kārikā* 2. In the previous *kārikā* (MK II 1) Nāgārjuna says, "There is no [action of] going on that which has been traversed, nor is there [action of] going on that which has not yet been traversed. Apart from what has and has not been traversed, what is being traversed is not known. *(gataṃ na gamyate tāvad agataṃ naiva gamyate / gatāgatavinirmuktaṃ gamyamānaṃ na gamyate //).*" As an objection to this argument, Nāgārjuna sets out the next *kārikā* as follows:

ceṣṭā yatra gatis tatra gamyamāne ca sā yataḥ /
na gate nāgate ceṣṭā gamyamāne gatis tataḥ // (MK II 2)

> "Where there is a motion [*of a going person*, acc. to Buddhapālita and Candrakīrti's understanding (see below)], there is [the action of his] going. And, the motion is [found] on that which is being traversed, but not on that which has already been traversed, nor on that which has not yet been traversed; therefore, [the action of] going exists on that which is being traversed."

To the *Akutobhayā*, Buddhapālita's commentary, and the *Prajñāpradīpa*, the following translation was equally given by Klu'i rgyal mtshan in the early ninth century.

> gang na g-yo ba de na 'gro // de yang *gang gi* bgom pa la / g-yo ba song min ma song min // de phyir bgom la 'gro ba yod //
> (ABh D. Tsa 35bl; BP D. Tsa 168b7; PP D. Tsha 64b1)

On the other hand, Nyi ma grags (1055-) the translator of both the *Prasannapadā* and the *Prajñā-nāma-mūlamadhyamakakārikā*, rendered the same *kārikā* as follows:

> gang na g-yo ba de na 'gro// de yang gang phyir bgom pa la//g-yo ba song min ma song min // de phyir bgom la 'gro ba yod //
> (PSP D. 'A 31b3-4; Prajñā-MK D. Tsa 2b2)

Klu'i rgyal mtshan and Nyi ma grags's translation are mostly quite accurate and very reliable; however, as far as this verse is concerned, their rendering *gang gi* for the underlined *yataḥ* does not correctly reflect the commentators' understandings of this word.

Both the *Akutobhayā* and the *Prajñāpradīpa* take this *yataḥ* as the correlative of *tataḥ* in *pāda d*. On this *kārikā* the *Akutobhayā* comments:

> 'di na gang na g-yo ba snang ba de na 'gro ba yod de / de yang *gang gi phyir* bgom pa la snang gi g-yo ba song ba la yang mi snang / ma song ba la yang mi snang ba *de'i phyir* bgom pa la yang 'gro ba yod do // (ABh D. Tsa 35b1-2)

"In this world, where the motion is found, there exists [the action of] going. *Because* such motion is found on that which is being traversed, but not found on that which has already been traversed, nor on that which has not yet been traversed, *therefore* [the action of] going, too, exists on that which is being traversed.

Likewise, the *Prajñāpradīpa* gives the following explanation to the same *kārikā.*

de la phyogs gang na rkang pa 'degs pa dang / 'jog pa'i mtshan nyid kyi g-yo ba snang ba de na 'gro ba yod de / g-yo ba de yang gang gi phyir bgom pa la snang gi / g-yo ba de song ba la yang mi snang / ma song ba la yang mi snang ba de'i phyir bgom pa la 'gro ba yod do // (PP D. Tsha 64b1-2)

"In this world, [the action of] going exists on a place where the motion characterized by the raising and putting of the foot is found. *Because* such motion is found on that which is being traversed, but not found on that which has already been traversed, nor on that which has not yet been traversed, *therefore* [the action of] going exists on that which is being traversed." It is quite clear that both the author of the *Akutobhaya* and Bhaviveka[1] took the word yataḥ as the correlative of *tataḥ;* therefore, as a suitable translation of *pāda b* they would rather request gang phyir de yang bgom pa la // instead of the above de yang gang gi bgom pa la //.

On the other hand, Buddhapālita took the word yataḥ as a present participle, genitive singular form of √i (to go), "of a going person"; hence on *pāda b* he comments, gang gi zhes bya ba ni 'gro ba po'i zhes bya ba'i tha tshig go // "yataḥ (of a going person) means *gantuḥ* (of a goer) "[D. Tsa 169a1]. This interpretation was later criticized by Bhāviveka for three reasons.[2]

Although modern scholars have never pointed out, Candrakīrti, the author of the *Prasannapadā,* seems to have understood the word yataḥ in the same way as Buddhapālita. After citing *kārikā* 2 he explains it as follows:

tatra ceṣṭā caraṇotkṣepanikṣepalakṣaṇā /[3] *yato vrajato gantur yatra deśe ceṣṭā gatis tatraiava deśe / sā ca ceṣṭā na gate*

> *'dhvani saṃbhavati nāpy agate kiṃ tu gamyamāna eva / tataś ca gamyamāne gatiḥ /* (PSP, p. 94, l. 1-3).
>
> "In this world the motion is characterized by the raising and putting of the foot. [The action of] going exists just on a place where there is the motion *of a going person, of a walker, or a goer.* And the motion cannot be on the path which has already been traversed nor on that which has not yet been traversed, but can only be on that which is being traversed. Therefore [the action of] going exists on that which is being traversed."

That he also takes the *yataḥ* of *pāda b* as a pres. ppl., gen. sg. m. of √i may possibly be confirmed by the fact that just after the word *yataḥ* he puts two words as its synonyms, that is, *vrajataḥ* (pres. ppl., gen.sg.m. of √*vraj* "to walk") and *gantuḥ* (gen. sg. m. of *gantṛ* "goer").

In consequence it may safely be said that as a correct translation of the above *yataḥ* both Buddhapālita and Candrakīrti would rather request *'gro bzhin pa'i* than *gang gi or gang phyir.*

Despite Klu'i rgyal mtshan and Nyi ma grags's misleading translations, Tsong kha pa (1357-1419) comments rightly on this matter: gang gi shes pa Sangs rgyas bskyangs kyis 'gro ba po la bshad de Zla ba'i dgongs par yang snang ngo // "Buddhapālita interprets 'yataḥ' in the sense of a *gantṛ* (goer). This appears to be Candrakīrti's understanding as well." (*Rigs pa'i rgya mtsho,* P. Ta 196a2).[4]

2

However, there still remains another question. Why was such a problematic translation gang gi employed for the above *yataḥ* by Klu'i rgyal mtshan? For solving this problem we can fortunately find a clue in Avalokitavrata's *Prajñāpradīpaṭīkā.* Avalokitavrata explains those two interpretations of the above *yataḥ* in the following way. According to Bhāviveka's understanding, Avalokitavrata explains,

> gang gi shes bya ba'i sgra *gang gi* phyir shes bya bar sbyar te (= yata iti śabdaḥ *yasmāt kāraṇād* [yasya hetor, or yato hetor(?)] iti *saṃbandhaḥ*)/. "The word *'yataḥ'* means 'for which reason (*yasmāt kāraṇāt,* etc.)' in the context." (PPṬ D. Wa 228 a2)

He explains, on the other hand, Buddhapālita's reading as follows:

> gang gi zhes bya ba'i sgra / 'gro ba po gang gi zhes bya bar sbyar te *(=yata iti śabdaḥ* yato *gantur iti saṃbandhaḥ)* / . "The word *'yataḥ'* means 'of a goer who is going *(yato gantuḥ)'* in the context." (PPṬ D. Wa 228a5)[5]

These two explanations of Avalokitavrata's will possibly draw the conclusion that Klu'i rgyal mtshan applied quite mechanically the translation *gang gi* to *yataḥ* in all cases of question since he had already rendered *yasmāt kāraṇāt* [*yasya hetoḥ,* or *yato hetoḥ*] as *gang gi* phyir. This is indeed to be called wrong, or at least misleading. That he puts *yasmāt kāraṇāt,* or the like, into gang gi phyir has no problem at all. However, the problem we find in his translaion is that overlooking such different interpretations as discussed above, he applied the word *gang gi* to every usage of *yataḥ* within the commentaries on the *kārikā* 2.

Although his translation itself is, thus, open to question, this problem has fortunately revealed his way of translation concerning the three commentaries and one subcommentary *(ṭīkā)* on the *Mūlamadhyamakakārikā,* that is, the *Akutobhayā,* Buddhapālita's commentary, the *Prajñāpradīpa,* and the *Prajñāpradīpaṭīkā.* Of those three commentaries Klu'i rgyal mtshan is considered to have first translated the *Prajñāpradīpa* with the constant consultation of Avalokitavrata's subcommentary on it. Or, more strictly, he first rendered the latter text into Tibtan since every passage of the *Prajñāpradīpa* had been cited there. Once having put the *Prajñāpradīpaṭīkā* into Tibetan, Klu'i rgyal mtshan cannot have experienced the slightest difficulty in extracting the quoted sentences of the *Prajñāpradīpa* from there. The way in which he established the translation of the *Mūlamadhyamakakārikā* was probably that he further extracted it from the translation of the *Prajñāpradīpa.*

Afterwards, he must have tried to translate Buddhapālita's commentary and the *Akutobhayā.* Although he should have carefully employed pertinent renderings for the text of each quoted *kārikā* so that they might agree with each of the two commentators' explanations, Klu'i rgyal mtshan gave in actuality almost the same translation to the *Mūlamadhyamakakārikā* as cited in the above three commentaries.

This may probably be the reason why especially in the translations of both Buddhapālita's commentary and the *Akutobhayā* we sometimes encounter those instances where the contents of each *kārikā* text does not exactly accord with the commentator's explanation. In the following diagram are shown those instances.

MK Chap. *kā.* (Tib)	Accordant with	Discordant with
I 4d	PPṬ	ABh, BP, [PP]
8ab	ABh, PP, PPṬ	BP
12	PP, PPṬ	ABh, BP
II 2b	PPṬ	ABh, BP, PP
5c	PP, PPṬ	ABh, [BP]
VII 16ab	ABh, PP, PPṬ	BP
28	PPṬ	[ABh], BP, [PP]
XI 1ab	ABh, PP, PPṬ	BP
XVII 31	PPṬ	[ABh], [BP], [PP]
XXIII 2a	PPṬ	[ABh], [BP], [PP]
XXVII 5	PP, PPṬ	ABh, BP
17c	PP, PPṬ	ABh, BP

It should be noted here that in every instance, where more or less some discordance is found between the contents of each *kārikā* and its *vṛtti*, Klu'i rgyal mtshan's translation of MK is quite agreeable to Avalokitavrata's explanation in his PPṬ. This fact well testifies to the above discussion with regard to Klu'i rgyal mtshan's way of translation.

3

Let us now turn to another example. In MK VII 16ab, Nāgārjuna states as follows:

pratītya yad yad bhavati tat tac chāntaṃ svabhāvataḥ /.

This sentence may be understood differently in accordance with divergent interpretations about the above correlatives: <u>yad</u> *yad* ..., *tat tac* .... The question is whether the underlined yad should be taken as nominative (sg. n.) or accusative (sg. n.). If the former is the case, the above sentence will be rendered: "Whatever originates dependently, it is quiescent of own-nature." Both the *Akutobhayā* and the *Prajñāpradīpa* have taken this interpretation.

Just after the quotation of *kārikā* 16, the *Akutobhayā* explains it:

'di ltar brten nas 'byung ba gang yin pa de ni ngo bo nyid kyis zhi ba de'i phyir ... // (D. Tsa 47b1-2)

"Because what originates dependently is quiescent of own-nature, therefor ...."

Also, to the same *kārikā* the *Prajñāpradīpa* gives a similar explanation as follows:

dngos po rten cing 'brel par 'byung ba gang yin pa de ni don dam par ngo bo nyid kyis zhi ba ste / (D. Tsha 106b7)

"In the highest truth, a thing which originates dependently is quiescent of own-nature."

Klu'i rgyal mtshan's translation of: *rten cing 'byung ba gang yin pa // de ni ngo bo nyid kyis zhi //* is, thereforee, quite suitable for this *kārikā* as cited in both the *Akutobhayā* and the *Prajñāpradīpa*.

The problem lies, however, in the translation of Buddapālita's commentary and also in Nyi ma grags's rendering of *Prasannapadā*. Buddhapālita takes the underlined yad as accusative (sg. n.); hence, after citing *kārikā* 16*ab*, he makes the following explanation.

rten cing zhes bya ba gang yin pa dang / 'byung ba zhes bya ba gang yin pa de dan de gnyis ga ngo bo nyid kyis zhi ba ngo bo nyid dang bral ba ngo bo nyid (P. nyid kyis) stong pa yin no// *(= yat pratītyeti yad bhavatīti tat tac cobhayaṃ śāntaṃ svabhāvataḥ svabhāvarahitaṃ svabhāvaśūnyam /)* (D. Tsa 216a6-7)

"That upon which '[this] is depending' and this which 'originates' are both quiescent of own-nature, bereft of own-nature, and empty of own-nature."

A similar and more detailed explanation was given by Candrakīrti in the following way.

mayā tu yat pratītya bījākhyaṃ kāraṇam yad bhavaty aṅkurākhyaṃ kāryaṃ tac cobhayam api śāntaṃ svabhāvavirahitaṃ pratītyasamutpannaṃ pratipādayatā (PSP p. 160, 1. 6-7) = kho bos ni sa bon zhes bya ba'i rgyu gang shig la brten nas myu gu zhes bya ba'i 'bras bu gang zhig 'byung la / de gnis ga yang rten cing 'brel par 'byang ba zhi ba rang bzhin dang bral bar ston pa na / (D. 'A 54b1-2)

"I have, on the contrary, explained that when, depending upon a cause called 'seed', a result called 'sprout' originates, these two are equally quiescent, dependently-originated, and bereft of own-nature. Then ...."

In the light of these two explanations, Klu'i rgyal mtshan and Nyi ma grags's mistakes are quite obvious. Klu'i rgyal mtshan should have changed the translation of the *kārikā* when he tried to render Buddhapālita's commentary into Tibetan. Also, as far as this *kārikā* is concerned, Nyi ma grags should not have followed Klu'i rgyal mtshan's translation of the *kārikā* in question since both Buddhapālita and Candrakīrti would request a correct rendering such as *gang la rten cing gang 'hbyung ba // de dang de ni rang bzhing zhi //*[6] or the like.

4

Generally, both Klu'i rgyal mtshan and Nyi ma grags's translations are quite accurate and reliable; however, as was discussed above, we cannot be too careful in reading the Tibetan translation of the *Mūlamadhyamakakārikā* as cited in the commentaries especially when the problem is closely related to the translators' way of rendering.

It is deeply interesting to us that in consequences the above investigation has slightly revealed how and in what order the commentaries on the *Mūlamadhyamakakārikā* were translated. The historical order in which Klu'i rgyal mtshan and Nyi ma grags tried to render the *Mūlamadhyamakakārikā* and the commentaraies on it into Tibetan will be summarized in the following diagram.

By Klu'i rgyal mtshan (Early 9th Century) (1) PPṬ, PP, Prajñā-MK [1] (2) BP, ABh
By Nyi ma grags (Late 11th Century) (3) PSP, Prajñā-MK [2]

Concerning the order of (1) and (2), it seems noteworthy that this order agrees with that of Catalogue "lDan dkar ma" where in the section of dBu ma'i bstan bcos, Prajñā-MK, PP, PPṬ, BP, and ABh are listed in the same order.[7] As for the translation of the Prajñā-MK, its colophon tells us that this text was first rendered into Tibetan by the Indian scholar Jñānagarbha and the Tibetan translator Klu'i rgyal mtshan. Klu'i rgyal mtshan appears to have made the translation by extracting it from his rendering of the *Prajñāpradīpa*. Afterwards, it was retranslated by the Indian scholar Hasumati and the Tibetan translator Nyi ma grags (1055-) so that it may accord with the contents of the *Prasannapadā*. This is the reason for the similarity of the present Prajñā-MK and MK as cited in the *Prasannapadā*.[8]

Since the present paper has just outlined the problem in regard to the translations of the *Mūlamadhyamakakārikā* with only a few examples, further minute and comprehensivee investigation will be an urgent need for our future research on this text and also on Nāgārjuna's philosophy in general.

Abbreviations

MK	*Mūlamadhyamakakārikā* (Klu'i rgyal mtshan's translation as found in ABh, BP, PP, and PPṬ)
ABh	*Mūlamadhyamakavṛtty-akutobhayā* D. No. 3829.
BP	*Buddhapālita-mūlamadhyamakavṛtti* D. No. 3842.
PP	*Prajñāpradīpa-mūlamadhyamakavṛtti* D. No. 3853.
PPṬ	*Prajñāpradīpa-ṭīkā* D. No. 3859.
PSP	*Prasannapadā* (D.No. 3860) L. de La Vallée Poussin, *Mūlamadhyamakakārikās (Mādhyamikasūtras) de Nāgārjuna avec la Prasannapadā Commentaire de Candrakīrti,* (Bibliotheca Buddhica IV), St.-Pétersbourg, 1903-1913.

Prajñā-MK *Prajñā-nāma-mūlamadhyamakakārikā* D.No.3824.

Notes

1. See Y. Ejima, "Bhāvaviveka / Bhavya / Bhāviveka", *Journal of Indian and Buddhist Studies,* 38-2, 1990, pp. 838-846.
2. The three reasons are:
 1. de'i phyir zhes bya ba'i sgra'i zla med pa'i phyir "Because [in that case] there will be no correlative of the word *tataḥ*."
 2. bya ba'i gzhi 'khrul pa med pa'i phyir "Because the locus of the action is definite *(avyabhicārin)* [i.e. it does not require such a qualification as yataḥ 'of a going person.'"
 3. song ba dang ma song ba'i 'gro ba po'i 'gro ba dgag pa bstan pa pa'i phyir ro // "Because [in *kārikā* 1, Nāgārjuna] has already explained the negation of the going of a goer on that which has and has not been traversed." (PP D. Tsha 64b3-4). See M. Tachikawa, "A Study of Buddhapālita's *Mūlamadhyamakavṛtti* (1)." *Nagoyadaigaku Bungakubu Kenkyūronshū* 63, 1974, p. 10-11, n. 6.
3. PSP, p. 94, 1.1 : *caraṇotkṣepa[pa]rikṣepalakṣaṇā.* Our reading follows J.W. de Jong, "Textcritical Notes on the Prasannapadā," *Indo-Iranian Journal* 20, 1978, p. 36.
4. See also Jeffrey Hopkins, "Chapter Two of Ocean of Reasoning by Tsong-ka-pa," Library of Tibetan Works & Archives, 1974, p. 10; Tachikawa, *op. cit.,* p. 11.
5. As is obvious in this explanation BP has definitely the reading *yataḥ*. Buddhapālita interprets the word *yataḥ* as meaning "of a going person", and not "whose *(=yasya)*". Cf. Ch. Lindtner, *Nagarjuniana, Studies in the Writings and Philosophy of Nāgārjuna* (Indiske Studier IV), Akademisk Forlag, Copenhagen, 1982, p. 26, n. 79: "[MK] II 2d, Buddhapālita read yasya for yataḥ for which Bhavya rightly criticizes him."
6. Cf. MK XVIII 10ab: *pratītya yad yad bhavati na hi tāvat tad eva tat* / (PSP, p. 375, 1.11) = gang la brten te gang 'byung ba // de ni re zhig de nyid min // (PSP D. 'A 121a2).
7. M. Lalou, "Les textes bouddhiques au temps du roi Khari-sron-lde-bcan," *Journal Asiatique,* 1953, p. 333 (Nos. 573-577).
8. See A. Saito "A Note on the *Prajñā-nāma-mūlamadhyamakakārikā* of Nāgārjuna," *Journal of Indian and Buddhist Studies* 35-1, 1986, pp. 484-487.

Liberation and Language: The Buddha-dharma in Translation

Peter Della Santina

Introduction

The primary, if not the only aim of the vast edifice of Buddhist culture is liberation. Although the primary aim is liberation, even as it was embodied in the figure of the Buddha himself, the foremost vehicle for its expression is language, that is in the teaching of the Buddha, the Dharma. Liberation and language therefore constitute the primary aim as well as the foremost vehicle for communicating the truths associated with the goal of liberation.

In Buddhism, the relationship between language on the one hand and reality and liberation on the other is not direct, but rather indirect, language being directly related only to language and to concepts. Reality, the direct experience of which brings about liberation, is devoid of any conceptual object and therefore beyond the reach of language. Terminology is consequently constituted by usage within a given cultural milieu and has no necessary relation with reality or the liberation that follows upon the direct experience of the latter.

Whenever a cultural phenomenon like the expression in language of the Buddha-dharma changes time and place, which in the case of the former, it must always and of necessity do translation occurs. Translation has of necessity to occur even in situations where the transmission of the Buddha-dharma is intracultural and merely temporal, because the cultural milieu never remains static. Translation is therefore essentially and generally reinterpretation of terms and concepts within a new cultural milieu.

When the process of translation is not only intracultural and temporal, but is intercultural and spatial as well, the fact of reinterpretation is only accentuated but not altered or created afresh. The reinterpretation of language is inevitable in cases of translation into a foreign cultural milieu, because the terminology adopted will of necessity have a prehistory within the foreign cultural milieu antecedent to its adoption for the purpose of translation.

Language, Reality and the Derivatives

From the very period of the Buddha's life onward, Buddhism has been marked by the differentiation and proliferation of doctrines and disciplinary codes. These were soon institutionalized in the form of manifold schools as has been well documented by historians. Nonetheless, notwithstanding the differentiation and proliferation of doctrines and disciplinary codes, the manifold schools of Buddhism retained a common heritage and were able to claim authoritative antecedents in the teaching of the founder of the tradition, the Buddha.

Just as in the case of the differentiation and proliferation of doctrines and disciplinary codes in the centuries following the career of the Buddha, there was a differentiation and proliferation of concepts and terms associated with the principal truths taught by the Buddha. In the course of this process of gradual evaluation, the teaching of the truth of a reality, whose experience ensured liberation, underwent a number of conceptual and linguistic modifications. The truth of *Nirvāṇa,* unborn and beyond decay, illness and death came to be joined by the truths of *suchless* (tathatā), *emptiness* (śūnyatā), the *ultimate* (paramārtha), the *real* (tattvam), the *fulfilled* (pariniṣpanna) and many others. Similarly, the description of the mental derivatives responsible for the creation of bondage in terms of *ignorance* (avidyā), *mental formations* (saṃskāra) and *craving* (tṛṣṇā) were joined by other descriptions like *imagination* (vikalpa), *impressions (vāsanā), construction* (parikalpa) and still others. I have chosen to examine briefly the concepts and terms associated with the truth of reality and the description of the mental derivatives responsible for bondage not because the evolutionary process took place only in their case, but because I believe them to be representative of a phenomenon which affected the entire Buddhist tradition.

The evolution of concepts and terms associated with reality and with the mental derivatives responsible for bondage is reflected in the works of Nāgārjuna, Asaṅga and Vasubandhu, the great exponents of the Madhyamaka and Yogācāra schools. These authors exercise a great degree of freedom in their choice of concepts and terms, and their preferences are evident. The same latitude of expression can also be observed in other authors belonging to other times, but it has obviously not been possible to survey the whole of Buddhist literature for the purposes of this paper. In conclusion, then, we see that the language of the Buddhist tradition was never static, but dynamic. Throughout the centuries of its development, it displayed an uninhibited capacity to adapt to and reflect a changing cultural milieu, and yet without abandoning its fundamental pedagogical function as a conduit toward liberation.

Nāgārjuna indeed encourages us to attain *Nirvāṇa* in the classical fashion.[1] He refers to the Buddha's use of *Nirvāṇa* as synonymous with reality when he says, "The Conquerors proclaimed that *Nirvāṇa* is the only truth..."[2] For this part, Nāgārjuna is careful to define *Nirvāṇa* in a manner consonant with *emptiness* and the doctrine of non-origination (ajātivāda).[3]

The term *thatness* is frequently adopted by Nāgārjuna. He tells us that those who do not see *thatness* assume the world and *Nirvāṇa*, while those who do see *thatness* do not assume them.[4] In the foregoing passage, *Nirvāṇa* is clearly used in a manner not synonymous with its use in the passage quoted above where it is said to be the only truth. In the latter context, there is present an objectified dualistic conception of *Nirvāṇa* in which *Nirvāṇa* does not exhaust reality. The *Nirvāṇa* referred to by Nāgārjuna in the last stanza is therefore the *Nirvāṇa* of the *Hīnayāna*. The stanza just quoted provides me with an opportunity to make an important point about terms and context. In the Buddhist tradition, the field of meaning of terms is determined by the context in which they are used. However, it is not only true to say that alternative terms may have the same field of meaning, without remarking that the same term may have alternative fields of meaning determined by the context.

Not surprisingly the term *emptiness* is very often adopted by Nāgārjuna as we might expect. He declares that all entities are *empty*, because their own-being (svabhāva) is not found anywhere.[5] Again he asserts that whatever is interdependently originated is *empty*. Therefore, there is no factor (dharma) that is not *empty* by nature.[6] However, the term *vacuous* (vivikta) is also occasionally used by Nāgārjuna. He says that everything is *vacuous*. Those who do not understand the real meaning of *vacuity* are lost, because they fail to perform wholesome actions.[7] Obviously for Nāgārjuna *vacuity* is synonymous with *emptiness.*

In the context of the two truths doctrine, the term the *ultimate* (paramārtha) or the *ultimate truth (paramārtha satya)* is found at several places in the works of Nāgārjuna. The most representative are the following famous passages: "The teaching of the Dharma by the Buddhas is based upon the two truths, the conventional truth and the *ultimate truth.* Those who do not understand the distinction between the two truths do not understand the profound reality of the teaching of the Buddha. The *ultimate* is not taught without relying upon the conventional, but without attaining the *ultimate,* one cannot attain *Nirvāṇa.*"[8]

Notwithstanding this clear exposition of the doctrine of the two truths, conventional and *ultimate,* the term the *real* (yaṅ dag) is also used by Nāgārjuna in a manner analogous to his use of the term the *ultimate.* He uses the *real* at several places in order to draw the distinction between the conventional and the *ultimate.* He tells us that origination and destruction as well as existence and non-existence were taught by the Buddha conventionally and not in accord with the *real.*[9] Again, Nāgārjuna affirms that if one understands *emptiness* then one will achieve liberation through that perception of the *real.*[10] Here the *real* is clearly equated with *emptiness,* another epithet of reality, and its perception is plainly regarded as a prerequisite for the attainment of liberation.

Turning to Asaṅga and Vasubandhu, we find that *emptiness* or insubstantiality (niḥsvabhāvatā) appears occasionally.[11] However, the most characteristic of new synonyms of reality is the *fulfilled* or the *fulfilled nature* (pariniṣpanna svabhāva). It occurs at innumerable places in the texts attributed to the two brothers.

In common with Nāgārjuna, Vasubandhu has occasion to refer to *thatness.* He says that the wood which supplies the support of the illusory elephant created by the power of a magician's mantra represents *thatness* or reality.[12] Talking about the *fulfilled,* Vasubandhu remarks that it is the *ultimate truth* of all factors and so it is *thatness.*[13] Here Vasubandhu deliberately defines the *fulfilled* in terms of two well known epithets of reality, the *ultimate truth* and *suchless.*

Perhaps Vasubandhu's favourite synonym of reality is the exceedingly difficult-to-translate *element of factors* (dharmadhātu).

In two of his independent works, Vasubandhu describes the experience of reality which leads to liberation in terms of the perception of the *element of factors.*[14]

Once again, we have an instance of a single term having meanings in two fields. While Vasubandhu clearly uses the term as an epithet of reality, it has another use in the context of the Abhidhārmika reduction of personal experience. There it means simply the object of mental consciousness.

Perhaps we might leave the last word on the subject of reality to Asaṅga who supplies a list of synonyms of *emptiness.* According to him, the synonyms of *emptiness* include, among others, *thatness,* the *ultimate* and the *element of factors.*

In the texts attributed to Nāgārjuna, many alternative terms appear describing the mental derivatives responsible for the creation of bondage. *Ignorance* is not overlooked by any means. *Ignorance,* according to Nāgārjuna, is responsible for the perception of origination and destruction and the emotional affection that follows from such a perception.[16] He declares that entities are products of *ignorance.*[17]

Craving and the mental derivatives directly associated with it are not given primary importance by Nāgārjuna, but *mental formations* does occur at least once in a position of significance. In an apparent reference to the declaration of the Buddha,[18] Nāgārjuna explains that all *mental formations* are not what they pretend to be and are therefore false. What is it then that pretends? he asks. The foregoing has been said in elucidating *emptiness. Emptiness* is not non-existence.[19]

A term which appears frequently in the texts of Nāgārjuna is *imagination.* The agent of action and action (karma), Nāgārjuna says, are products of *imagination.*[20] *Imagination,* together with another derivative, *fabrications of thought* (prapañca), is held to be responsible for the occurrence of the afflictions and actions.[21] *Imagination* is explicitly charged by Nāgārjuna with the responsibility for the appearance of the whole of phenomenal existence. He asserts that the wheel of existence (bhavacakra) originates from the *impressions of imagination.*[22]

Nāgārjuna acknowledges the priority of the term *ignorance* over the term *imagination* and the term *construction* which appears at least once in his texts. His statements are indications of the ongoing process of proliferation and legitimization of terminology and are important clues to an understanding of the evolution of language within the Buddhist tradition. He declares, "The world has *ignorance* as a precondition, because the Buddhas proclaimed it so. Therefore, why is it not justified that this world be the effect of imagination?"[23] The above clearly indicates that Nāgārjuna regarded *imagination* as intimately related to *ignorance,* but that he preferred, for reasons which were probably the effects of a changing cultural milieu, to adopt the term *imagination.* He establishes a similar relationship in the case of the term *construction.* He declares, "What is extinguished when ignorance is extinguished? How will it not be seen to be the *construction* of *ignorance?"*[24] The appearance of the term *construction* in the stanza cited above is an anticipation of the popularity of the term in the literature or the Yogācāra and the association of the term with *ignorance* constitutes a bridge between the earlier and the later usage.

Like Nāgārjuna, Vasubandhu is also fond of the term *imagination.* It occurs together with *impressions* in his description of the evolution of the eight consciousnesses in terms of *imagination.* The *impressions* contained in consciousness are responsible for the appearance of particular forms of *imagination.* The *impressions* of former actions along with the *impressions* of dualistic pattern of apprehension condition additional retribution.[25] Again, Vasubandhu defines one aspect of the mind in terms of its capacity to accumulate *impressions.*[26]

The entire scope of *imagination,* according to Vasubandhu's thought, emerges in the following passage. The *constructed nature* is the whole gamut of factors that may be *imagined* by *imagination.* The interdependent nature (paratantra svabhāva) on the other hand is none other than conditioned *imagination.*[27]

The real talent for evolutionary innovation of the brothers Asaṅga and Vasubandhu is of course evident in their championship of the terminology of *construction.* In its objectified aspect it is evident in the term *constructed,* or *constructed nature.* On the other hand, its subjective aspect is found in terms like the *construction of the unreal* (abhūtaparikalpa). The latter term is used with great frequency by Asaṅga and it also appears in at least one of the independent works of Vasubandhu. It is said that consciousness is characterized by the *construction of the unreal*, because it is not what it appears to be and yet it is not non-existent.[28] I am tempted to compare this assertion with that made by Nāgārjuna who says that while *mental formations* are not what they pretendto be, they are not non-existent.[29] If my comparison is justified, it would establish a definite relationship between the archaic term *mental formations* and the more recent one *construction of the unreal.*

Asaṅga and Vasubandhu agree that the *construction of the unreal* is accountable for the appearance of the entire world of phenomena. It is, according to them, the mind and the mental derivatives of the triple world (tridhātu).[30] Just as for Nāgārjuna, the wheel of existence originated from the *impressions of imagination,* so for Asaṅga and Vasubandhu everywhere the multiplicity of afflictions that is phenomenal existence originates from the *construction of the unreal.*[31]

In attributing the triple world to the *construction of the unreal,* Asaṅga and Vasubandhu apparently make a statement parallel to those that appear in the *Laṅkāvatāra* and *Daśabhūmika* Sūtras where the triple world is attributed to mind only (cittamātra). Vasubandhu echoes the declarations made above. The triple world, he says, is cognition only (vijñaptimātra).[32] Are we to understand then that cognition only and the *construction of the unreal,* not to maintain mind itself, are virtually synoymous? Perhaps so, because Vasubandhu also affirms the synonymity of the following: *mind* (citta), *intellect* (manas), *consciousness* (vijñāna) and *cognition* (vijñapti) and also indicates that mind implies the mental derivates.[33]

Vasubandhu uses the term the *construction of the unreal* in a manner analogous to his use of the term *imagination.* The *construction of the unreal* is also said to encompass the eight consciousnesses.[34] The foregoing would seem to establish a direct link between the terms *imagination* and the *construction of the unreal.*

Although Vasubandhu uses the term *construction of the unreal,* he has his own term which he seems to prefer. Indeed the *construction of the non-existent* (asatkalpa) seems to be used by Vasubandhu in a manner not different from the *construction of the unreal* used in Asaṅga's texts. Vasubandhu remarks that the *construction of the non-existent* is not what it appears to be and yet it is not altogether non-existent.[35] The conclusion is inescapable. The two are virtually synonymous. That is to say, they have a common field of meaning.

Like Nāgārjuna before him, Vasubandhu is anxious to legitimize the use of new terminology by defining it in terms of accepted linguistic usage. He says that the *construction of the unreal* is nothing other than the *imagination* of subject and object.[36] He thereby establishes the credentials of the newly preferred term the *construction of the unreal* by relating it to an already widely used term *imagination.*

All of the above provides a picture of a great degree of latitude in the choice of terms used to indicate two general concepts which were of primary importance for the Buddhist tradition, i.e., reality and the mental derivatives responsible for bondage. It need hardly be mentioned that the alternative terms examined in the preceding pages are not the only terms having the same or similar fields of meaning. There are numerous other alternatives and the lists presented are not at all exhaustive.

It is not my intention to suggest that all of the alternatives used to indicate reality and the mental derivatives responsible for bondage ought to be rendered by common English terms. Nonetheless, it is clear from the manner of their appearance in the texts studied and from the explicit statements of authoritative masters that the terms share common fields of meaning. The common fields of meaning which the lists of alternative terms share proceed not from the existence of an actual common object, because, as it will presently be shown, no actual object exists or can be admitted from the Buddhist point of view. The common fields of meaning rather proceed from a combination of linguistic and conceptual factors existing interdependently in particular relationships. The community of meaning of a given set of terms, therefore, follows from their contextual situation and the nature of the context follows from a particular cultural milieu. The legitimacy of terms is not guaranteed by any necessary relation to any actual object, but is rather merely the product of the use of a term within the context of a set of other linguistic and conceptual factors conditioned by the convention of the world or cultural milieu. Therefore, terminology can and ought to be creatively evolved in order to render it more effective in performing its pedagogical function.

Liberation and Language

The Mahāyāna Buddhist tradition of India is unanimous and emphatic in declaring that objects of the mind or concepts do not exist in reality. It is in fact this very absence of any object of mind that gives rise to the direct experience of reality, its liberating capacity. The absence of any object of mind in reality, of course, also implies the absence of any apprehending subject. In other words, reality is devoid of subject or object. This is accepted not only by the exponents of the Madhyamaka system but also by the founders of the classical Yogācāra, Asaṅga and Vasubandhu.[37]

Language, however, and more specifically linguistic elements or terms, refer only to other linguistic elements and to the conceptual elements or objects of mind with which they are intentionally associated. Because the existence of objects of the mind is not admitted in reality, no terms can refer directly to reality, and therefore language is not capable of immediately including a direct experience of reality which is followed by liberation. In as much as language only refers to language, or at best to the mental objects that are intentionally associated with terms, it can only provide an indirect and mediate suggestion of reality. Therefore, liberation can never follow directly and immediately from language, but only indirectly and mediately. All that language can accomplish is the gradual negation of objects of mind or concepts in such a way as to prepare the practitioner for an immediate non-linguistic and non-conceptual experience of the real. Liberation follows directly and immediately only upon the direct and immediate experience of reality. Śāntarakṣita says, "By the reason which sunders imputation in that (i.e., reality) and causes one to cognise (the real) he who infers cognises (reality mediately), while the masters of meditators illuminate it directly."[38]

For Nāgārjuna reality is characterized by the absence of objects of mind. He tells us that those whose minds have transcended existence and non-existence perfectly meditate upon the real which is devoid of any object of mind or mental support. The enlightened ones who understand entities to be like a reflection are not trapped in the mire of objects.[39] On the other hand, those who apprehend an object will be affected by the poison of the afflictions. The apprehension of an object is responsible for the distinction between an impassioned subject and one who is free from passion, but the enlightened ones do not fall victim to such dualistic conceptions, because they do not apprehend any object at all.[40]

In as much as reality does not admit of the existence of an object of mind, a conceptual element, so it cannot admit of the reality of a term or linguistic element. Nāgārjuna asks the question, "If when analysed, 'this and that' are not to be apprehended, (then) what wiseman will argue that 'this and that' are true?"[41] The objects of mind that correspond to linguistic elements or terms disappear when they are subjected to the analytical examination that is intended to eventually reveal the unobstructed real. For this part, Nāgārjuna explicitly rules out the acceptance of a thesis or proposition (pratijñā) of affirmation or negation in a situation where no object of mind exists or is apprehended. He declares that he has no proposition of his own whatsoever. No proposition is possible when in reality all entities are empty.[42] Affirmation and negation are not possible when no object exists in reality. He says that if he apprehended anything with the help of perception or any of the other means of cognition, he would either affirm or deny it. However, since he does not apprehend any object whatsoever, he neither affirms nor denies it.[43] There is in reality nothing to affirm or to deny, because all entities are empty.[44] Indeed, when everything is empty and no object really exists, there can be no position or point of view advocated and no verbal argument adduced in support of such a position. Besides, if no position is possible, a counterposition is equally impossible.[45]

It would appear from the foregoing that Nāgārjuna would advocate absolute silence, the very noble silence of the Buddha which was in itself an intimation of the real. However, it is an historical fact that Nāgārjuna did not remain silent, nor did the Buddha for that matter. The opinions expressed by Nāgārjuna in the foregoing paragraph would seem then rather to be intended to emphasize the absence of any necessary relationship between reality and language. Nonetheless, it is not without having recourse to the conventional truth that the ultimate truth is taught.[46] The conventional, to my mind, is none other than the cultural milieu and the linguistic and conceptual context it represents. As far as the ultimate is concerned, it too is really conventional so long as it is expressed in language and participates in a linguistic and conceptual context. Śāntarakṣita declares: "The ultimate is free from all the accumulations of fabrications of thought. Since origination, etc. are non-existent, non-origination, etc. are impossible. Since their actuality is refuted, the sound of the names of these is impossible. The activity of refuting non-existent objects does not truely (exist). (It) depends upon imagination; (it) will be phenomenal (saṃvṛti) but not ultimate."[47] The alternative expressions of the Dharma in language are therefore only vindicated by their efficacy in a particular pedagogical context.

The above would seem to be supported by the relevant texts. Nāgārjuna declares, "There is not anything which corresponds to the expressions: not-self, not not-self, both self and not-self (because) all factors which can be spoken of are—like Nirvāṇa—in their own-being empty."[48] That is to say, not-self and the like are linguistic elements which have no real object, because in reality no objects exist. In the same vein, he declares, "There exists the statement of existence and also the statement of non-existence, and again the statement of existence and non-existence. The intentional proclamations of the Buddhas are not easily penetrated."[49] There are also numerous other references to the idea of the intentional proclamations of the Buddhas: Nāgārjuna remarks in another place that the path of origination and destruction was taught intentionally by the Buddhas.[50] Again he points out that the Buddha intentionally taught "I" and "mine" as well as the aggregates, elements and sense-spheres.[51] The idea of intentional proclamation implies the self-conscious use of language for a pedagogical purpose. Such use does not imply any acceptance of a necessary relationship between language and reality.

However, it may be helpful to take up again the discussion of self, not-self and so on already alluded to in the preceding passages. The eighteenth chapter of the *Mūlamadhyamakakārikā* contains a number of stanzas which appear to be directly relevant to the question of alternative linguistic and conceptual formulations. It is clearly indicated that the presence of alternative formulations of the Dharma follows directly from the absence of any object in reality. Moreover, Candrakīrti's commentary supplies valuable additional clarification of the point under discussion.

Nāgārjuna declares that both self and non-self were taught by the Buddha. However, finally, they taught neither self nor not-self.[52] In his commentary, Candrakīrti explains that the existence of the self was taught by the Buddha to the nihilists to correct their inclination to perform habitually unwholesome actions. The non-existence of the self, on the other hand, was taught to the eternalists to correct their attachment to the self which constituted an impediment to their attainment of liberation. Neither self nor not-self, that is to say, the abandonment of both alternatives was taught by he Buddhas to those who had perfected themselves over the course of many lifetimes.[53] In the above, there is evident an example of the use of language in a clearly calculated pedagogical manner. Moreover, the efficiency of the pedagogy depends directly upon a given context. The teaching of not-self, for instance, would not have been pedagogically effective in the case of the nihilists, just as the teaching of self would not have been pedagogically effective in the case of the eternalists. The context determines the utility of expressions like self and not-self. Neither has any necessary relationship to reality as is clearly shown by the fact that finally the abandonment of both is enjoined.

Nāgārjuna declares that when objects of mind no longer exist, that is to say, when reality is directly apprehended, there is nothing to which language can refer.[54] Candrakīrti explains that if there were indeed any object of mind in reality, then a specific character might be imputed to it and also a term applied to it. In a case like this, language would have a real referential quality. However, in reality no entities are either originated or destroyed. Whatever language would pretend to refer to, in other words, the object of mind which is the conceptual correlative of the linguistic element or term does not exist in emptiness. That is to say, it does not exist in reality. The absence of objects is indeed none other than reality itself.[55] Candrakīrti draws our attention to Nāgārjuna's statement according to which the Buddha never taught any Dharma at all.[56]

In reality, no object of mind exists and therefore no term can be applied to it. Nonetheless, the pedagogical use of language is not only permitted, but necessary in order to lead sentient beings towards liberation. The utterances of the enlightened ones are therefore motivated by compassion. Once again, Nāgārjuna refers to "the real", "the unreal" and so forth and declares them to be the teaching of the Buddha.[57] This stanza demonstrates an obvious similarity with that cited earlier, i.e., "Existence, non-existence..."[58] Candrakīrti explains that everything is taught to be real to the neophyte in order to gain his confidence. This is confirmed by Nāgārjuna elsewhere when he says that first the seeker after reality is told that everything exists.[59] On the other hand, everything is taught to be unreal to the practitioner, because from the point of view of the latter, reality would have to be permanent. This too is confirmed by Nāgārjuna elsewhere. He says that when the neophyte understands the nature of things better, he is told that every thing is vacuous.[60] The combined alternative, i.e., real and unreal, allows for the expressions appropriate to both the neophyte and the practitioner, while the final abandonment of objects of mind and linguistic formulations is signalled by the final alternative, neither real nor unreal.[61] Neither real nor unreal also have to be given up for the noble silence which is truely appropriate to reality.[62] The direct experience of reality which is devoid of any object of mind and of any term or linguistic element can only be achieved gradually, through side roads using language flexibly. Correctly used, linguistic and conceptual activity can eventually reveal their own insubstantiality, and relativity. When conceptual and linguistic activity has reached the end of its domain, the way is open for the extraordinary experience of reality which induces liberation.[63]

Candrakīrti explains that epithets of reality are only obtained by means of superimposition, having had recourse to conventional usage, that is to say, to the current cultural milieu.[64] Among the one mentioned by Nāgārjuna are: peace, beyond fabrications of thought, beyond imagination and invariable.[65] Reality is to be experienced directly according to Candrakīrti. Language is incapable of revealing reality directly. Language is inextricably bound up with objects of mind, but reality is beyond objects of mind and terms. Reality is beyond imagination and the other mental derivatives. Not even knowledge exists in the highest truth.[66]

Indeed, it is clear that even the favourite epithets of reality have no necessary relationship to it. Emptiness, for example, one of Nāgārjuna's favourite epithets of reality, is "an approximate thought construction for the reciprocity of existence."[67] Again Nāgārjuna says that empty, non-empty... are not predicates of reality, but instances of linguistic formulations used for pedagogical purposes.[68] Indeed, Nāgārjuna specifically states that emptiness or insubstantiality is reality. He says that if there were something not empty of existence, there might be something empty of existence, but in so far as there is nothing not empty of existence there can be nothing empty of existence,[69]

Emptiness and other epithets of reality participate in a pedagogical procedure conducive to an eventual direct experience of the real and the liberation which is the effect of such an experience. However, they participate too in the interdependent world of linguistic and conceptual activity, and consequently belong to the level of conventional usage or a given cultural milieu. They are not actually part of reality. Therefore, even emptiness cannot post any claim to absolute truth. As Nāgārjuna declares: "Emptiness is the end of all views. Those who adhere to emptiness as a view are said to be incurable."[70]

The paradigm for this pedagogical use of language, which, nonetheless, presupposes the fact that language refers directly only to other linguistic elements applied to objects of mind within a conceptual context, is supplied by Nāgārjuna in the *Vigrahavyāvartanī*.[71] Once again, the issue at stake is the provisional description of reality, emptiness. Nāgārjuna's realists opponent has called into question his declaration that all entities are empty. The opponent objects that, if all entities are indeed empty, then the statement, "all entities are empty", must necessarily include the statement itself; consequently, the statement must be ineffectual, that is, incapable of refuting the independent existence of entities. Nāgārjuna accepts the emptiness of the statement, but maintains that it is, nonetheless, capable of refuting the independent existence of entities which is after all nothing more than an object in the mind of the opponent.

Nāgārjuna offers the analogy of a man created by the magical powers (māyāpuruṣa). The phenomenon is well documented in Buddhist lore, and the analogy also occurs in at least two other places in the texts of Nāgārjuna,[72] where it is used to illustrate the nature of the agent and action. Nāgārjuna likens the operation of the statement, "all entities are empty", to the activity of an artificial man or a man created by magical powers. An artificial man created by the magical powers of the Tathāgata or by a disciple prevents in another man the false notion that an artificial woman for whom the latter has developed an infatuation, is in fact a real woman. Although the text does not explicitly say so, we can assume that in this magical play, the other man, to whom Nāgārjuna refers, is equally artificial. After all, are not the agents of action, i.e., all sentient beings, likened to the artificial creations of magical powers? The statements of reality, the use of language in general is like the activity of an artificial man, a man created by magical powers. It refers to and may refute other linguistic and conceptual phantoms, but language has no necessary or direct relationship with reality.

The conclusion to be drawn from the foregoing is that language and particular linguistic elements or terms have no necessary or direct relation to reality. They exist within a context. That is to say, they participate in an interdependent complex together with other linguistic elements, all of which are applied to objects of mind or concepts. Only in so far as language contributes to the eventual elimination of objects of mind which, as we have seen, are inimical to reality and impediments to liberation is it liberating. Therefore, language which liberates is the language which eventually contributes to the elimination of linguistic and conceptual elements, that is, to terms and concepts. In the mean time, that is to say, so long as reality is not directly experienced and liberation not attained, language in general and terminology in particular derive their value from their function. They acquire their field of meaning only within a linguistic and conceptual context. The linguistic and conceptual context is none other than conventional usage or the current cultural milieu. The cultural milieu is by its very nature bound to change from time to time and from place to place. Therefore, it is imperative that for language to achieve its greatest liberating potential, it may be free from artificial constraints. This, however, can only be guaranteed if the primary aim of the Buddhist tradition, that is liberation, is not lost sight of or ignored. Language, therefore, ought to be used in such a manner as to contribute to the eventual elimination of entanglement in linguistic and conceptual elements, that is to say, terms and objects of mind.

The Buddha-dharma in Translation

In the introduction, I suggested that the process of translation of the Buddha-dharma occurs both intraculturally and interculturally. The process occurs intraculturally, because of the dynamic nature of culture which does not remain fixed, but evolves from generation to generation over the course of time. The evolution of terminology examined in the first part of this paper may be said to reflect this kind of intracultural translation. Gradually, over the course of time, terminology evolved to better conform to the needs of an evolving cultural milieu. Consequently, terminology which at an earlier time was not popularly used came to be emphasized and generally employed. Other forms of expression which were once dominant at an earlier period, although they usually did not disappear altogether, occurred less frequently and all but vanished into the background. It is a case of language changing to fit the contemporary usage of a given period.

Because language is a product of culture and not of the absolute or reality, continuous changes in the use of language are natural and to be expected. In the case of intracultural translation, that is to say, the reinterpretation of old terms and the creation of new ones, the process is relatively conservative. I have shown that Nāgārjuna and Vasubandhu were careful to define the new terms they pushed to the forefront of the contemporary expression of the Buddhist truths in terms of older and more established terminology. In this way, they created a linguistic and conceptual context within which the newly popularized terms were intended to operate. The latter made it possible to identify the field of meaning of the new terms.

In the case of intercultural translation however the process is bound to be revolutionary, involving occasionally entire redefinitions of the linguistic and conceptual context of a particular term and consequently of entirely new field of meaning. Nonetheless, even in such cases, the process of translation, however radical, is natural and necessary. Language in the Buddhist tradition serves the purposes of liberation, and therefore must be made to do liberation's work, notwithstanding the transformations sometimes effected upon it. After all, language in so far as it is what it is merely because of its participation in linguistic and conceptual contexts exists interdependently and relatively. The latter of course is equivalent to saying that language is empty which is another way of saying that language has no necessary relation to reality.

In the discourses of the Buddha and in the teaching of the immediate disciples of the Enlightened One, a process of translation of the Buddha-dharma is evident. The process appears to me to be revolutionary rather than conservative in their case. The latter fact would seem to suggest that although the teaching of the Dharma by the Buddha and his disciples took place through a common or nearly common linguistic medium, it was still, nonetheless, an intercultural translation of the Buddha-dharma. This was in fact the case because, although the people of the so called Madhyadeśa shared common linguistic conventions by the sixth century B.C., there did exist two alternative and competing cultural patterns. The first was the Śramanical culture which had been characteristic of the Indus valley civilization, while the second was the Brahmanical culture typical of the Aryan civilization. Although the two cultural patterns had existed side by side from the middle of the second millennium B.C. when the Aryan people had appeared in India, they had not really begun to interact significantly until the time of the Buddha. It suffices to say that the two cultural patterns differed greatly as it has been noted by a number of eminent scholars.[73] The difference between the two cultures, Śramanical and Brahmanical, is vividly reflected in the radical and revolutionary translation of terms accomplished by the Buddha and his disciples. In their hands many of the key concepts and terms of Brahmanical culture received new and entirely different fields of meaning and this was achieved exclusively through redefining them in terms of a new linguistic and conceptual context, by substituting a new cultural milieu, a Buddhist cultural milieu for the established Brahmanical one. The Buddha and his disciples radically redefined such terms as "ārya", "yajña", "brāhmaṇa", and many others, which had all been key terms belonging to the dominant non-Buddhist culture and they had particular fields of meaning therein.

Before the time of the Buddha the term "ārya" meant simply those people whose origins might be traced to the steppes of Euro-Asia. The Buddha radically reinterpreted it. What previously ethnic affiliation was, now came to have the highest religious significance. Aryan society had regarded the preservation and prolongation of one's own life, marriage, offspring and wealth as the highest goals of existence, but in the discourses of the Buddha, such mundane aspirations are regarded as ignoble. They are ignoble because they are liable to birth, old-age, illness and death. On the other hand, the truly noble "ārya" quest is the quest for the unborn, unageing, unailing and deathless Nirvāṇa.[74] The noble is, therefore, according to the Buddha, the very opposite of what it had been for the representatives of established Aryan society. It is none other than the supramundane. The term then regularly found its way into expressions like the Four Noble Truths, the Noble Persons (āryapudgala) and the like. The term thereby came to be associated with the supramundane religious ideals of Śramanical and Buddhist culture.

Yet another key element of Brahmanical culture was radically reinterpreted by the Buddhist tradition. The institution of the sacrifice (yajña) was the chief vehicle of religious expression in early Aryan civilisation. Through the sacrifice, the Aryans hoped to achieve longevity and other important goals of their value system, but the term sacrifice was given a new field of meaning within the Buddhist tradition. The term was reinterpreted in social and ethical rather than in ritual terms.

The Buddha explained to the Brahmaṇa Kūṭadanta that the best forms of sacrifice were the following: The first of the forms of sacrifice recommended by the Buddha was the offering of alms to recluses. It was followed by the taking of refuge in the Buddha, dharma and Sangha and the observation of the five precepts, viz. abstinence from destroying life and the rest. Finally, the supramundane attainments of the life of renunciation are also counted among supreme sacrificial acts.[75] Therefore, according to the Buddha the sacrifice of the Brahmanical tradition is subordinated to a new interpretation of its meaning, an interpretation which all but obliterates the established significance and replaces it with a new and characteristically Buddhist import.

The Buddha reinterpreted even the meaning of the primary figure of Brahmanical society, the figure of the priest or "brāhmaṇa". The priest, for Aryan civilization, was invested with his sacred role as custodian of the sacrifice and conserver of the Vedic lore by virtue of the place of his birth within the caste system. For the Buddha, however, the status of a priest with all its associations with excellence and privilege[76] is accorded to him, not by virtue of the place of his birth, but rather by virture of his worth. The privileged status of the priest, therefore, is not vouchsafed by one's position within the structure of Brahmanical society, but rather by one's moral and intellectual qualities. A priest is one who has abandoned the objects of desire. He is accomplished in tranquillity and insight. Again, a priest is one who has discarded evil and the like.[77] Once again an important element of Brahmanical culture had been radically reinterpreted by the Buddha in such a way as to give it a whole new field of meaning.

There are numerous other examples of such radical reinterpretations of Brahmanical values. Fire, the principal instrument of the sacrifice and a vestige of primordial religious consciousness, is also divested of its sacred character and associated with the consuming effects of the afflictions, greed, anger and delusion in the Buddha's classical inversion of the significance of symbols to be found in his discourse to the Kāśyapa brothers, the erstwhile fire worshippers.[78] Even the time-honoured practice of bowing to the six directions is given a totally new field of meaning by the Buddha.[79] The practice really implies, according to him, fulfilling one's responsibilities within the network of social relationships. Once again, a ritual act—part of the established religious culture—is redefined in a new way and is given a new ethical and social meaning.

This process of radical reinterpretation was clearly undertaken by the Buddha in a situation where, as I have pointed out, there was a common linguistic heritage even if there was complete homogeneity of culture. Similar processes were of necessity undertaken in the case of the transmission of Buddha-dharma to new lands such as those of south-east, east and central Asia where neither language nor culture had any common base. Can we assume, for example, that Chinese of the first century C.E. had any idea of what was meant by Nirvāṇa, suchless, the real, emptiness and the like before the on-going process of education had familiarized them with the new Buddhist culture? Such terms and concepts could make sense only within a particular linguistic and conceptual context and they could not possibly make sense without it. The same, I am sure, can also be said of the situation in Tibet immediately following upon the first introduction of Buddhist thought there. In all such cases, an appropriate field of meaning for concepts and terms could have been determined within a linguistic and conceptual context that had to be deliberately evolved to suit the needs of the new Buddhist cultural milieu.

Conclusion

In the foregoing pages, I have tried to show that although, within the Buddhist tradition, we use language indirectly in order to eventually induce a direct experience of reality whose consequence is liberation, language itself has no direct relation to the real. Language is rather part of an interdependent complex of elements, linguistic and conceptual. This interdependent complex of elements, the linguistic and conceptual context constitutes what in Buddhist terms is called conventional usage and what otherwise might be called the current cultural milieu.

The fields of meaning of terms are determined by their place within the linguistic and conceptual context, that is to say, within the cultural milieu. This has to be the case, because no real object exists to which terms might otherwise apply directly. Objects disappear, as it were, when subjected to analysis. Reality is therefore devoid of real objects and of concepts. Moreover, if this were not so, it would not have its liberating potential.

In so far as terms acquire their fields of meaning only from a linguistic and conceptual context, it is imperative that an appropriate cultural milieu be created if terms are to perform their intended function within the Buddhist project of liberation. The creation of an appropriate cultural milieu, within which selected terms used in the translation of the Buddha-dharma can acquire proper fields of meaning, is only possible through comprehensive Buddhist education. Therefore, I would urge in the strongest possible terms that, while the task of identifying the best of many possible English translations of key Buddhist terms ought not to be neglected, even the most meticulous selection of terms can have no hope of success without the support of an appropriate cultural milieu. Conversely, if an appropriate cultural milieu can be created by means of a comprehensive programme of Buddhist education, then the selection of terms becomes, almost but not quite, insignificant. This is true because, if an appropriate linguistic and conceptual context is in place, the selected term will naturally acquire the field of meaning wanted by virtue of its position within the cultural milieu.

ABBREVIATIONS

MAK	Madhyamakālaṅkārakārikā
MMK	Mūlamadhyamakakārikā
MV	Madhyāntavibhaṇga
MVB	Madhyāntavibhaṇabhāṣya
PP	Prasannapadā
PSHV	Pratītyasamutpādahṛdayavyākhyāna
ŚS	Śūnyatāsaptati
TK	Triṃśikākārikā
TSN	Trisvabhāvanirdeśa
VV	Vigrahavyāvartanī
VK	Viṃśatikākārikā
YṢ	Yuktiṣaṣṭikā

Notes

1. Suhṛllekha, 105.
2. YṢ 35 & Majjhima Nikāya III. Dialogue 140.
3. ŚṢ 24 & 25 & MMK XXV.
4. YṢ 5.
5. ŚS 3.
6. MMK XXIV 18 & 19.
7. YṢ 30 & 31.
8. MMK XXIV 8 - 10.
9. ŚṢ 1, 70 & 71.
10. ibid. 39.
11. MV & MVB I. 1 & TK 23.
12. TSN 32.
13. TK 25.
14. ibid. 30 & TSN 37.
15. MV I. 14.
16. YṢ 10, 16 & 29.
17. ibid. 26.
18. Majjhima Nikāya III. Dialogue 140.
19. MMK XIII. 1 & 2.
20. ŚṢ 34 & 41.
21. MMK XVIII. 5.
22. PSHV 3.
23. YṢ 37.
24. ibid. 38.
25. TK 17 - 19.
26. TSN 7.
27. TK 20 & 21.
28. MV & MVB I.4.
29. MMK XIII. 2.
30. MV & MVB I. 8.
31. ibid. I, 11.
32. VK I & commentary.
33. ibid.
34. TSN 8.
35. ibid. 8 & 29.
36. MVB I. 1.
37. MV & MVB I. 3 & TSN 36 & VK 27 etc.
38. MAK 75.
39. YṢ 1 & 54.
40. ibid. 52 & 58.
41. ibid. 42.

42. VV 29 & commentary.
43. ibid. 30 & commentary.
44. ibid. 63 & commentary.
45. YS 50.
46. MMK XXIV. 10.
47. MAK 70 - 72.
48. ŚS 2.
49. ibid. 44.
50. YṢ 21.
51. *ibid.* 23.
52. MMK XVIII. 6.
53. PP XVIII. 6.
54. MMK XVIII. 7.
55. PP. XVIII. 7.
56. MMK XXV. 24.
57. ibid. XVIII. 8.
58. ŚS 44.
59. PP. XVIII. 8 & YS 30 a.
60. PP. XVIII. 8 & YS 30 b.
61. PP XVIII. 8.
62. MMK XXV. 15 & 16.
63. PP XVIII. 8.
64. ibid. 8 & 9.
65. MMK XVIII. 9.
66. PP XVIII. 9.
67. MMK XXIV. 18.
68. ibid. XXII. 11.
69. ibid. XIII. 7.
70. ibid. 8.
71. VV 23 & 24 & 27 & 28 & commentary .
72. MMK. XVII. 31 & 32 & SS 40 - 42.
73. G.C. Pande. *Studies in the Origins of Buddhism,* Motilal Banarsidass, Delhi, 1983 & L.M. Joshi, *Brahmanism, Buddhism and Hinduism,* Buddhist Publication Society, Kandy, 1973.
74. Ariyapariyesana Sutta, Dīgha Nikāya.
75. Kūṭadanta Sutta, Majjhima Nikāya I, 163.
76. We need only remember that in the primordial sacrifice, the Brāhmaṇa was fashiond from the head of "puruṣa."
77. Dhammapada, Brāhmaṇavaggo.
78. Ādittapariyāya Sutta.
79. Sigālovāda Sutta, Dīgha Nikāya.

Lost Buddhist Texts: The Rationale of Their Reconstruction in Sanskrit

Mangla Chinchore

In this paper* I intend to spell out the rationale of reconstructing in Sanskrit those philosophical and other Buddhist texts which are not, unfortunately, available in that language, in which they were originally written. However, Tibetan or Chinese translations of many of them are fortunately extant. We do not here wish to go into the tricky question as to how far such Tibetan or Chinese translations are reliable. Instead, presuming that by and large they are, we wish to concentrate on the problem of the necessity of their reconstruction in Sanskrit.

The present paper has three sections. In the first, an attempt is made to outline the contours of the diversified culture within the framework of the broadly monolithic civilization that flourished in this subcontinent. We shall also attempt to sketch some salient features of that civilization. In the second, importance of Sanskrit is taken into account as a common medium of intellectual exchange. We shall consider the importance of this sort of medium which contributed to the widening and deepening of the vistas of comprehension through feedback—both positive and negative—without insulating and isolating one trend of thought from the others. In the last section, we hope to highlight some important aspects of the necessity of reconstruction in Sanskrit of those Buddhist texts which are unfortunately not available in it. This we intend to do in a two-fold way. On the one hand, we hope to bring to the surface some important points of strength of such a venture which are decisive from the points of view of the history and growth of intellectual enterprise in this subcontinent. On the other hand, we also intend to show that the path of reconstructing in Sanskrit those Buddhist works which are not available in it is more likely to save us from succumbing to those modes of weakness and vulnerability which other avenues of articulating the content, if not of reconstruction, of the concerned Buddhist texts from their Tibetan or Chinese translations seem perhaps to be inherently open.

I
INCLUSIVE FRAMEWORK OF THE MONOLITHIC CIVILIZATION AND VARIED CULTURAL STRANDS IN IT

It is pointless to harp upon the superficial similarity between animal and human modes of life. Nor is there any point in subscribing to the view that both animal and human lives are equally mechanical and passive in character. It is a fact that human life is markedly different from animal life in certain respects. One such distinguishing aspect of human life is that overall it is consciously purposive in character. Right from the ancient times human life is seen to be geared towards the realization of certain goals and aspirations. Their plurality has been held to be necessary for taking into account human life in its richness, variety and complexity. Unitary conception of human aspiration is held to be too simplistic in character. Consequently, it does not seem to be taken seriously, especially because it is unable to give satisfactory account of human life in its complexity. Man's initial conception of human aspiration might have been ambiguous and fraught with certain difficulties. But in course of time man's conception of legitimate goals and aspirations of human life began to crystallize gradually and eventually different conceptions of legitimate goals and aspirations of human life surfaced on the horizon and began engaging the attention of the concerned. As we shall soon see, such a conception of legitimate goals and aspirations of human life is an important aspect of a civilization.

The most ancient and the oldest concern of man must obviously have been satiation of needs. This sort of concern must have, as is evident, made man basically confine himself to the present—neither much bothering about the past (except in the sense of learning from the immediate and proximate past) nor about the distant future (except perhaps the immediate one.) In course of time, however, the unitary aspiration of satiation of needs, geared basically towards the problems of survival and procreation, came to be replaced, in this subcontinent as also perhaps elsewhere, by a pluralistic conception of legitimate human aspirations.

A civilization must bring forth consideration of three important aspects of it—(a) the sort of legitimate aspirations and goals of human life it accepts, (b) the sort of orientation towards them that it adopts, and (c) the mode/s of realization of such goals in human life which it makes available, so that they do not remain merely utopian in character. In addition, there is one more consideration also which is at stake in appropriate conception of a civilization. However, to avoid digression at the present juncture of our argument, we shall return to it at a later stage.

We said above that every civilization, including the one which flourished in this subcontinent, must bring forth a certain pluralistic conception of legitimate human aspirations. Even restricting to the civilization which flourished in this subcontinent in ancient times, we do not wish to go into the details of two questions in this paper. They are: whether (a) the same pluralistic conception of legitimate human aspirations—say the *Puruṣārthas*[1]—was accepted by various adherents of different trends of thought which flourished in this subcontinent, and whether (b) the same pattern of interrelationship among them too was accepted by all of them. Leaving aside such issues of historically intricate concern, we may proceed to highlight three salient features[2] of the sort of monolithic civilization that flourished in this subcontinent and within the general framework of which alone perhaps the whole exercise of the reconstruction of the lost Buddhist texts in Sanskrit could make some satisfactory sense.

(A) *Article/s of Faith and Belief not Falling outside the Jurisdiction of Bhāratavarṣa*[3]

In this subcontinent, before the advent of any people reared, nurtured and brought up in a different mould of civilization, three principal groups of people with differential cultural perspectives seem to have flourished. They are: (i) those who owed allegiance to the *Brāhmaṇical* tradition of some form or other; (ii) those who owed allegiance to what is known as *Śrāmaṇic* tradition, within which two important strands are discernible, viz. the *Bauddha* and the *Jaina*; and (iii) those who owed allegiance to neither of these two perspectives. This third group of people seem to fall into two main sub-groups: (a) the independents like *Cārvākas* and (b) the tribals and aboriginals. In spite of such differences, all of them seem to have subscribed to one commitment. And that is this that none of them ever accepted any article of faith and belief which did not fall within the jurisdiction of what may be called *Bhāratavarṣa* in the most inclusive and extended sense of that term.[4] Further, the article of faith under consideration may be abstract or concrete, proximate or remote, external or internal. That one subscribed to such an article of faith was considered to be a mark of identification, re-identification and recognition of anyone in this subcontinent to be belonging to Indian civilization. This sort of broad and flexible spectrum was sufficiently strong to provide a sort of unifying tie to the diversity of cultural and intellectual strands which flourished in this sub-continent. One could call it a sort of civilizational *svadeśī*.[5] It is this tie that seems to have ensured non-alienation of any group or cultural strand, no matter whether central or peripheral, *tāntric* or religiously sectarian, operative in mountains or plains, in the north or south, east or west. Today we fail to realize the significance and importance of this kind of unifying tie—although in a sense negative in character—especially because we seem to have lost the sensitivity to, and the power of discrimination of, what is native to our civilization and what is foreign to it. This point has a number of implications. However, to avoid digression we do not wish to pursue it here further.

(B) *Satisfaction as General Orientation to Life*

Various trends of thought and culture—no matter whether *Brāhmaṇical, Śrāmaṇic* or *Tribal*—that flourished in this subcontinent seem to be civilizationally united in yet another respect. That consists in holding that, instead of mere survival or competition—and in the process outrunning the competitor by hook or by crook—satisfaction should be the general unifying orientation to life. This seems to have been accepted by all people who flourished and operated within the framework of what could be held to be Indian civilization. It consisted basically in holding that so long as the possibility—proximate or remote—of deriving happiness in human life—individual or social—has not been obliterated there is a charm in living and continuation. Deriving this sort of satisfaction was never considered to be governed by or dependent upon material affluence. Rather an excessive devotion to that end was considered to be detrimental and antithetical to satisfaction orientation. This belief is reflected, in varying intensity, in various philosophical utterances touching human life. This sort of satisfaction-orientation seems to have prevented both alienation and undue exploitation. Whether we are talking of collective or individual exploitation here. In the collective aspect, it may mean exploitation of one group by another, while in the individual aspect, it may mean one aspect of one's personality exploiting the other aspects. That is why such so-called trait of what is considered to be a mark of excellence, as figuring one's name in the *Guiness Book of Records,* had almost no value in the eyes of people who flourished within the framework of what could be called Indian civilization. This salient feature of Indian civilization can be said to indicate the climate of civilization within which legitimate human aspirations could be allowed to be realized. It needs to be understood that this sort of satisfaction-orientation remaind decisively important with various cultural and intellectual trends which flourished in this subcontinent in ancient times, especially before the advent in it of any persons or groups brought up, reared and nurtured in a different civilization framework. This unifying feature of Indian civilization is intimately connected with yet another such feature somewhat similar to this. And it is to a brief consideration of that that we now turn.

(c) *Moral Consideration of any Aspect of Life*

Various groups of people and different cultural strands that flourished in this subcontinent were civilizationally united on yet another count. It consists basically in holding that any aspect of human life—individual or collective—must at least be moral to be considered for acceptance. In other words, the most important distinguishing mark of human life, apart from its being purposive in character, was considered to be its moral aspect. Accordingly, this unifying trait has two important implicatoins: (a) with regard to satisfaction-orientation concerning life it amounts to subscribing to the view that even if one may not be able to create satisfaction in someone else's life, one has no business to put obstacles in the path of someone's driving satisfaction in life. (b) Similarly, with regard to the realization of legitimate goals and aspirations of human life this view has an important implication. It assumes that even if we are not in a position to help someone in the realization of legitimate goals and aspirations in his life, we must not interfere with or put obstacles in the way of his doing so. In the same vein, it also abhored the tendency of using someone else as a means of realizing one's legitimate ends. The question of the realization of illegitimate ends with fair means or foul did not simply arise, since no illegitimate ends were worthy of being realized. Thus, if satisfaction-orientation could be said to be spelling out civilizational ecology, then moral judgement of human life in all its aspects could be said to be the touchstone or the acid test on the basis of which all human aspirations—'individual or collective—could be valued as worthy of being realized or not. In all this the moral consideration was, thus, the most important factor.

Judging by the three above-mentioned major civilizational features there is not much variation regarding the central conception of each of them among various cultural and intellectual strands which flourished in this subcontinent. This is not to underestimate or deny altogether variations in their cultural expressions. However, such variations in expression do not seem to undermine or obliterate their decisively unificatory features. There is, nonetheless, one more civilizational feature and we had said earlier that we would take it into account later. This seems to consist in holding, on the one hand, that human life—individual or collective—is constituted basically of three principal kinds of relations: (a) our relation to ourselves—both individually and collectively: (b) our relation with others—humans as well as non-humans—and that too both individually and collectively; and (c) our relation with the world around us at large.[6] On the other hand, it also amounts to subscribing to the view that for living the life worthy of human beings three conceptions matter quite decisively: (a) our conception about overselves, (b) our conception of others, and (c) our conception of the world.[7] As is obvious, these two above-mentioned aspects of the fourth salient civilizational feature are intimately and intricately interrelated.[8]

But on the background of this kind of general agreement concerning the fourth salient civilizational feature, different cultural and intellectual variations sprang up. For example, four major variational strands could easily be mentioned on this count, viz. *Brāhmaṇical, Śrāmaṇic, Tāntric* and *Tribal.* Within each of these strands there were internal variations. Consider, for instance, one example of each of the first three strands that brings forth internal differences among the adherents of the same generic type. Within the *Brāhmaṇical* tradition, such variations as approaches of *Sāṁkhya, Vedānta, Nyāya, Vaiśeṣika, Mīmāṁsā,* etc. are significant. The *Śrāmanic* tradition embraces at least two major variations—the *Jaina* and the *Bauddha*. Within the *Tāntric* tradition, likewise, such variations as *Śaiva-Tantra, Śākta-Tantra,* etc. are noticeable. Again within a given strand further sub-strands of it are also noticeable. For example, in *Vedānta* such variations as *Advaita, Viśiṣṭādvaita, Dvaita,* etc. arose, while in *Buddhism* such variations as *Hīnāyāna* and *Mahāyāna* originated. We don't have to labour on such chains of variations. They are not necessary for our present purpose. The point, however, which needs to be carefully noted is that through such variations differential conceptions concerning ourselves, others as well as the world at large also came to be put forth. In this way, within the framework of certain generic civilizationally salient features, arose quite a large cultural and intellectual variety. This sort of variety also found differential expression through such culturally significant avenues as literature, music, dance, painting, architecture, etc. However, this sort of variety was bound up within the compass and jurisdiction of the unitary civilizational framework and its cementing salient features.

One more consideration also seems to have given rise to some important variations. It was generally accepted that human life—both individual and collective—aims at realization of certain legitimate goals and aspirations. It was also generally accepted that for this sort of realization one has to strive and that human life is required to be planned to ensure that other things remaining the same the possibility of the realization of legitimate goals and aspirations in it does not come to be obliterated.

But even when this is granted by way of general consensus, there emerges a question: whether individual and collective modes of human life are irreducible to each other or not, although the same legitimate goals and aspirations are to be realized in them. In answer to this question the *Brāhmaṇical* and the *Śrāmaṇic* traditions seem to differ from each other very decisively. The *Brāhmaṇical* tradition generally holds that individual and collective modes of human life are irreducibly different from each other. Even if the same goals and aspirations are to be realized in both of them, this cannot be done in the same way. This is not to say that there are no points of convergence between individual and collective modes of human life. They, nonetheless, are not so decisive as to rule out any difference between them. Rather, the points of divergence between them are more decisive than those of convergence. For instance, in a given society some individuals—both men and women—can abstain from procreation. But this cannot be generalized, for otherwise continuity of human race itself would be endangered and jeopardized. And no society can adopt such a suicidal move. Therefore, the adherents of the *Brāhmaṇical* tradition held that individual and collective human lives need to be planned and organized differently through *Āśrama-Vyavasthā* and *Varṇa-vyavasthā*[9] respectively to ensure in principle that for any individual or group realization of the legitimate goals and aspirations of human life does not become impossible.

The adherents of the *Śrāmaṇic* tradition do not seem to have taken this view. Nonetheless, their opposition to the view of the Brahmanical tradition itself gave rise to a sort of discord among them.[10] It seems that the Buddhists generally held that individual aspect of human life alone is decisively significant, since a society is after all nothing else but a collection of individuals. Since, in this way, a society or a group is a construct, there is no justifiable reason for holding a society to be as primordial as an individual. For fear of digression we cannot probe deeper into this issue in this paper. The *Jainas,* on the contrary, seem to have held that it is the collective or social aspect of human life that is of primary importance and an individual after all, being subsumable under a group, hardly needs to be considered to be as important as the group. Again for fear of digression we cannot probe deeper into this issue here. Thus, with regard to realizability of legitimate aspirations of human life, three major strands seem to have originated in this subcontinent—one, within the *Brāhmaṇical* tradition, and two, within the *Śrāmaṇic.* This again happened within the framework of the same unitary general civilizational concern.

If the argument sketched above is generally right, then, on the basis of it, we can see that within the framework of the same general unificatory milieu called Indian civilization, there arose various cultural and intellectual strands and they brought forth different philosophical approaches, which were variously articulated by their followers. And not only that such various strands and approaches flourished concurrently, they remained in existence in this sub-continent for centuries. On the level of articulation, explication and elaborate explanation of their respective approaches on the one hand, and on the level of responding to the variant or rival approaches on the other, there emerged another highly intricate situation. It is to the consideration of that that we turn in the next section.

II
SANSKRIT: A UNITARY MEDIUM OF COMMUNICAITON

As stated above, various philosophical, intellectual and cultural strands and approaches emerged in this subcontinent on the general background and within the framework of Indian civilization. They arose side by side and remained in existence for a long time not in isolation from, but rather in intimate contact with, each other. The initial articulation and explication of these views and approaches must have been oral. This is evident from the fact that no book authored by any *Ṛṣī* of the *Upaniṣads, Mahāvīra* or the *Buddha* is known to posterity. It is also quite likely that adherents of different strands and approaches preferred to communicate in a certain language. For instance, by and large, no important work by any significant adherent of the *Brāhmaṇical* tradition is found to have been written in any language other than Sanskrit. Likewise, while the *Jaina* canons were written in Prākṛit/Ardhamāgadhī, those of Buddhism, known as *Tripiṭakas,* were written in Pali. It is not difficult to imagine what factors prompted the choice of a particular language as a means of communication. Among such factors must have been the language of the region, the language in which intellectual communication was undertaken, the sort of persons for whom the works were mainly considered to be important, and the sort of language they understood easily. That is why, roughly, up to the beginning of the Christian era at least three languages—Sanskrit, Prākrit and Pali—remained in vogue in this subcontinent as the media of scholarly and intellectual communication. Sanskrit was accepted by the adherents of *Brāhmaṇical* tradition, Prākrit by the *Jainas* and Pali by the *Buddhists.*

Although the *Brāhmaṇical* and *Śrāmanic* traditions operated concurrently, perhaps there were not frequent occasions of communication among scholars of these two traditions, primarily because the adherents of the wo traditions preferred to communicate in different languages. However infrequent were such communication between the scholars of these two traditions, some among each must have read some works of the other tradition even though written in a language they themselves did not use. Otherwise, it is difficult to make sense of a number of cross references made in the works of one tradition to those of the other. Such references are found in both the *Jaina* and the *Buddhist* canons, even though they are not many. Therefore, they cannot be held to indicate to any decisively general trend. Hence, in spite of the fact that the *Brahmanical* and *Śrāmanic* trends flourished concurrently there does not appear to have been much interchange of thoughts between these traditions; there was little effective communication between the two.

This, however, was necessary to be able to respond to each other's strands, approaches and perspectives. As Sanskrit was adopted by many scholars as effective medium of communication, adherents of the *Śrāmanic* tradition too might have begun to use it as a medium of articulation of their views and formulation of principles. This enabled them to communicate with thinkers in other traditions. What was perhaps initially adopted as a sort of compromise and means of arbitration—to end an impasse of lack of effective inter-traditional or inter-school communication and the resulting isolation from it—may have turned out, in course of time, to be a lasting feature.[11] This can be guessed from the fact that, once the *Śrāmanic* tradition (both the *Jaina* and the *Bauddha*) adopted Sanskrit as an effective means of inter-traditional communication, no adherent of any of these traditions afterwards wrote any worthwhile treatise either in Prakrit or in Pāli. Thus, the break-away from original medium of communication proved to be decisive and complete, and Sanskrit was henceforth used as the only medium of effective communication for both inter-school and intra-school communication. However grudgingly the initial switch over to Sanskrit may have been effected, once this was accomplished, significant communication of all kinds and with all persons were conducted in that language.

Once Sanskrit was adopted as a medium of articulation by both the *Brāhmaṇical* and *Śrāmaṇic* traditions alike, two important consequences followed: (i) it ended the era of isolation and insulation of different cultural and intellectual traditions and strands, and the adherents of both were exposed to the views of their adversaries. Before this, discussions took place only among the adherents of the same tradition, and such discussions must have been quite stale and unexciting for among them there could have been few points of disagreement. Those dialogues must have been either narrative or instructional in character—as is indeed revealed in the *Buddhist* and *Jaina* canonical literature, and in the *Upaniṣads.* (ii) However, with the advent of different philosophical schools and composition of prominent treatises explicating their respective standpoints on the one hand, and the adoption of Sanskrit as a medium of communication even by the adherents of Buddhism and Jainism on the other, a crucially significant phenomenon emerged in this subcontinent. An era began of two major kinds of dialogue, debate and controversy: (*a*) intra-school and (*b*) inter-school. Roughly from the beginning of the Christian era till almost the end of the twelfth century, and major—and also very many minor—work that any adherent of any philosophical school in this subcontinent compiled or wrote attempted to score on two major counts: (1) cognisance was taken of the views of fellow-adherents of a particular trend of thought, bringing to the notice of the concerned whether and to what extent they agreed with one another, and (2) it responded to the views of the adversaries—no matter whether they belonged to the same trend of thought or a decisively differential one. Thus, as there are large number of instances of dialogues and controversies among the adherents, say, of *Nyāya, Mīmāṁsā, Vedānta,* Buddhism and Jainism, so too there are various illustrations of prolonged debates, say, between the adherents of *Nyāya* and *Mīmāṁsā,* Jainism and Buddhism, Buddhism and Sāṁkhya, Buddhism and Mīmāṁsā, Mimāṁsā and Vedānta, Nyāya and Buddhism and other schools.

With such prolonged and intricate controversies the current of Sanskrit as a medium of communication became quite turbulent in character. So much so that no major trend, no significant work or no important philosophy could escape this impact whatever the nature of its contribution. Every issue that was taken up for consideration was always sought to be located into the complex network of the different thought currents operative in the then prevalent intellectual climate. Every treatise that was written was written transparently in response to the urgent demand and pressure of certain issues being considered one way or the other, and also in response to the views of the predecessors and contemporaries, no matter whether they hailed from the same school and trend of thought or otherwise. One can see that many works written by the first-rate philosophers during the period seek to accomplish the twin objective: to expose the weakness and vulnerabilities inherent in the views of some adversaries and to elaborately explain and vindicate one's predecessors' or one's own view or that of the school to which one belonged in the face of objections raised against it. In a situation such as this, discussion of different major issues generated two kinds of feedback—positive and negative. The positive gave confidence to the concerned scholars about the views, doctrines and principles they uphold and defended. The negative, on the contrary, brought to their notice points of weakness and vulnerability in their exposition and explanation. This forced them to be more cautious and careful so that they do not fall a prey to attacks from their adversaries.

Through articulation and presentation of various thought-currents and philosophical approaches and perspectives in Sanskrit in this way, this language served as an effective unitary means of communication. Different trends were exposed—each to the others. Apart from this, it also contributed to the discussion of issues in wider perspective and at their profounder levels. In the face of renewed objections, changed circumstances and situations, and refined modes of bringing to the surface points of weakness and vulnerability implicit in certain trends of thought, doctrine or principle, concerted intellectual efforts were made to purify them of their crudities by bringing out in the process their continued relevance and significance. This led to more respectable interpretations of, or at times exposed more glaringly the weaknesses in them. It thus led to a twofold growth and development of philosophical thought in this subcontinent: chronological over a prolonged period of time and intellectual in the sense of bringing to the notice of the concerned not only the rationale of the acceptance of certain concepts, doctrines and principles, but also the points of their strength and weakness, viability and vulnerability. That is why various issues—philosophical, cultural, civilizational, mundane or esoteric, of commonsense or scientific—are discussed in that language. In short, no significant aspect of human life, no issue of decisive concern which was required to be considered in the then prevalent intellectual climate seems to have been left out on account of either indifference or intellectual indolence. Sanskrit, thus, as a unitary medium of communication in this country contributed in two important respects: widening the vistas of comprehension and deepening our understanding of issues at stake.

Keeping in view the foregoing discussion, we will now look into the rationale of translating into Sanskrit those Buddhist texts—philosophical or otherwise—which are not available in Sanskrit, though originally written in that language, but only in Tibetan or Chinese translations.

III
THE RATIONALE OF SANSKRIT RECONSTRUCTION OF THE LOST BUDDHIST TEXTS

As stated above, accepting Sanskrit as effective unitary means of communication, a number of Buddhist scholars originally wrote valuable treatises in that language on matters of great philosophical concern or otherwise. Though such works were originally written in Sanskrit, many of them are now available only in their Tibetan or Chinese translations. This is unfortunate but certainly not so unfortunate as the complete loss of a number of the Nyāya, Vaiśeṣika, Sāṁkhya, Mīmāṁsā, and Vedānta texts in Sanskrit, for of these not even any translated versions into any other language are available. All we know about these is that they were written, but with regard to some of them we do not even know who their authors were.

Various factors might have contributed to the loss of many Buddhist texts originally written in Sanskrit. Some of these factors can be easily imagined: (1) Since there was no printing, only small numbers of manuscripts of many texts were in circulation at any time. (2) The tropical climatic conditions, the material on which these texts were written, and some neglect in the matter of preservation may have been partially responsible for the loss. (3) Conditions of insecurity and lawlessness that came to prevail in this country on account of external aggressions may have caused the destruction of some, while some were carried along by those persons and scholars who fled from this country to Nepal, Tibet, China, other places. After the texts were translated in Tibetan or Chinese the original Sanskrit texts may have either been eaten away by worms or some may just have totally disintegrated for lack of care, since practically no-one read the language in those areas. (4) After the disappearance of Buddhism from India, for over a period of 700-800 years, probably little care was taken for preserving these texts, and consequently destroyed, knowingly or unknowingly. Whatever be the cause, the fact remains that many valuable Buddhist texts are no longer available as originally written in Sanskrit.

Why should one make any effort at all, it may be asked, to reconstruct such texts in Sanskrit from their Tibetan or Chinese translation? It may be further argued that Sanskrit is no more a living language in the very country where such works originated, and although it does continue to enjoy the status of a respected classical language, yet now-a-days no work of any great significance is written in Sanskrit. In view of this, the argument may continue, even if such Buddhist texts as were originally written in Sanskrit but are no longer available in that language were reconstructed in that language from their Tibetan or Chinese translations, that exercise would be a waste of time, of valuable resources and of energy; for, hardly any one would read such reconstructed texts in Sanskrit. So it would be more rewarding, this argument may further continue, to study such texts in their Tibetan or Chinese translations and present their content in a language which is widely read, such as Japanese, German, English, French or Russian.

Let us examine this argument against the necessity of reconstructing such works in Sanskrit. In a nutshell, it says that trying to achieve such reconstructions are futile and useless; it also pleads that it is preferable and more rewarding to study the contents of such works from Tibetan or Chinese translations as now available rather than from their reconstructed versions in Sanskrit. We shall try to meet these two aspects of the argument in the reverse order.

The preference under consideration may be sought to be understood via either convenience or wider circulation. The convenience and facility may be accounted for in terms of one's proficiency in the language other than Tibetan or Chinese in which the content of the translated text could be presented. The plea under consideration is understandable although methodologically it is vulnerable. Similar is the case about wider circulation. The problem of primary concern is neither merely of articulation of the content of the text under consideration, nor of its wider circulation. Such moves may be important pedagogically, but they hardly increase research potential and pave thereby a way for enhanced intellectual illumination. For, such moves in themselves do not constitute, methodologically speaking, good research. By the same token, consideration of reward cannot be restricted merely to the gain accruing to the person concerned. Such considerations are important but only in the highly restricted sense of the term. They cannot, therefore, be substituted for genuine methodological and proper research-oriented concerns.

It needs to be clearly realized that each one of such texts was written at a particular juncture of time, circumstance, situation and in the intellectual and cultural climate of a particular sort—all of which were deeply anchored in the civilizational framework within which various issues were discussed. Moreover, the issues were not discussed, as argued earlier, in isolation from the adversaries' views about them. Today the texts in Tibetan or Chinese translations are doubly severed; from the contemporary intellectual and cultural civilizational background with which they are inextricably connected when they were originally written in Sanskrit, and also from the intellectual conditions prevalent in Tibet or China when they were introduced there in Tibetan or Chinese translations. The presentation, therefore, of merely their content in a language and conceptual framework which are different from the unrelated to its original background is more likely to bring in distortions, and make many concepts and notions, doctrines and principles sound either hackneyed, outdated or irrelevant altogether. Or else, these concepts and notions may be twisted, in the process, to make them sensible in our own intellectual climate. This may give rise to double errors: anachronism and distortion. Something of this kind has, unfortunately, already happened in an effort to present outlines of different trends of philosophical thought that flourished at one time in this subcontinent. Attempts were made to present such outlines in the language and concepts which only the nineteenth-century theologicians and students of philosophy or indology or those who came under their sway for some reason or the other could understand. And this resulted in much anachronistic confusion and distortion, and we are yet to free ourselves from those impact and influence. Therefore, however attractively the argument in favour of preference, convenience or reward may be presented, the whole project in favour of which it may be presented makes it fraught with many difficulties in face of which it could hardly be said to be warrantable. The question is not so much of spinning an ingenious argument in favour or defence of what we are accustomed to do or are inclined to accept. It is rather of first deciding what is intellectually appropriate to do and explicate methodologically defensible rationale for it. The task we are pleading for may be extremely difficult to accomplish. But the dividends it is likely to pay in the long run should make the burden bearable.

If Buddhist studies are to become intellectually rewarding in a methodologically defensible way not only in India but also elsewhere then the mere articulation of the content of a given text from its Tibetan or Chinese translation will not be enough. Likewise, merely knowing at what historical point of time a given text was composed is scarcely satisfactory. These details are doubtless important. But, at the same time, it is important to realize that this much alone is not enough. A sense of history is undoubtedly important. But what is of utmost importance for genuine research is to reconstruct intellectual history—from the point of view of both chronology as well as growth and development. For reconstructing intellectual history in this way, the issues discussed in different texts and by various philosophers would have to be made available. Their connections along two routes would have to be unearthed: on the one hand, connections of a text or a philosopher with its or his predecessors and successors from the same trend of philosophical thought, and on the other hand, their connections with those from rival trends of thought. Proceeding this way, many contours, curvatures and linkages so crucial to comprehend inter-school and intra-school dialogues and debates would become clear. For this, conceptual framework of the issues discussed in a given text has to be formulated. It has also to be situated into the conceptual framework of the concerned philosopher. Further, philosopher has to be located into the wider framework of the concerns of the school to which he belonged, and lastly this sort of wider framework of the school under consideration would have to be corelated with that of other schools from the same strand of thought as also with the thoughts and conceptual frameworks of philosophers and schools of thought opposed to his own. This is likely to be an extremely complicated task. So, prolonged, concerted, co-operative efforts, involving in some cases even inter-continental research, are required to be made for its accomplishment.

It is important to remember that comprehension of growth and development does not automatically arise through locating points. Ideas, concepts, doctrines, principles are important. But mere typology or narration of them is neither their history nor a methodologically satisfactory account of growth. Comprehension of growth and development seems difficult to make sense of without commensurability or comparability. And such comparability cannot be engineered through an apology, for although an apology has a grammatical form of a descriptive statement, it does not describe any state of affair in the world, past or present.

For this kind of appropriately methodological considerations such Buddhist texts as are available in Tibetan or Chinese translation but not in the original Sanskrit would have first to be reconstructed in that language. This would not only make it possible to situate them into the intellectual and cultural climate in which they were written but would also facilitate the study of the concerned authors' response to their predecessors and contemporaries—both intra-school and inter-school. Likewise, it would also enable to study responses to an author of his intra-school or inter-school successors.

The great doyen of Buddhist studies in India, Mahāpaṇdita Rahul Sankrityayana, had clearly seen the need and necessity of reconstructing in Sanskrit the lost Buddhist texts in the way we are now talking about. For, he had visualized not only the rationale of such enterprise but he had also seen the rich dividends likely to flow from it. That is why he seems to have left no stone unturned in the circumstances he functioned for the accomplishment of the project under consideration. Our plea for such reconstruction is a humble tribute to him and his vision. But it also originates from the need of our being able to reconstruct our intellectual history—both in its width and profundity—chronologically as well as from the point of view of its growth and development. In its absence, we are prone to get wrapped up in indological and philological details and niceties which alone can hardly lead to any worthwhile philosophical or intellectual illumination.

Locating in this way the issues discussed in different Buddhist texts in their historical, cultural and intellectual context, we would be able to understand properly the rationale of considering them.

Thus armed, we would also be able to comprehend their historical significance and intellectual relevance. Starting from this we can also proceed to take into account their contemporary relevance, if any, with or without modification. Unless we do this exercise, our knowledge of Indian intellectual history is very likely to be fragmented and philosophically unilluminative. Hence our strong plea for reconstruction in Sanskrit of such texts as are available only in Tibetan or Chinese translations.

An example will perhaps clarify the point we are labouring to make. Unless we reconstruct the text of Dharmakīrti's *Saṁtānāntarasiddhi* in Sanskrit, we are not in a position to understand what kind of considerations led him to tackle the issues he discusses in response to the views of his predecessors such as Vasubandhu. Likewise, without such a reconstructed text of the work under consideration, we shall be at loss to make satisfactory sense of Ratnakīrti's *Santānāntarasiddhidūṣaṇa*. Various concepts, doctrines, principles contained in the treatise under consideration have not sprung up from nowhere. They are situated in the respective conceptual frameworks which, in turn are anchored in the intellectual, cultural and civilizational climate of the time.

NOTES

* I am indebted to Professor M.P. Marathe for valuable discussion on a number of points considered in this paper. I am also grateful to him for helping me to write this paper at different stages of its completion.

1. It is very difficult, for example, to defend a view that four *Puruṣārthas* were accepted to be legitimate human aspirations in the *Brāhmaṇical* as well as *Śrāmaṇic* traditions right from their inception. The problem of their interrelationship, too, is equally complex. Additional issues, perhaps, would also have to be taken into account if we include the Tāntric and the tribal trends as well within the purview of our consideration.
2. I am grateful to Professor Marathe for bringing these points to my notice.
3. The boundaries of *Bhāratavarṣa* were certainly not co-terminus with the present-day India or *Bhārata*.
4. Perhaps at a later stage of history the term *Mleccha* was sought to be used generically to indicate any person or group whose article of faith and belief fell outside the boundaries of *Bhāratavarṣa*. We need not go into details of this issue here.

5. One wonders whether this feature of civilizational *Swadesi* was later on converted into complacency and in consequence even crossing sea was considered to be indefensible.
6. On this count, again, it seems to have been accepted that, unless our relation with ourselves is all right, our relation with others or with the world at large cannot be all right.
7. Here again it seems to have been held that, unless our conception about ourselves is tenable, our conception about others or concerning the world at large cannot be tenable and coherent with it.
8. Their joint consideration seems to bring forth the problem of *Duḥkhanivṛtti* which engaged attention of the adherents of many philosophical strands, Buddhism not being an exception to it.
9. Here, perhaps, what *Vyavasthā* means is not merely organization but what the Buddhists understood as *Viplava* as well.
10. The situation here seems to be comparable to the opposition of non-Euclidean geometries to the Euclidean geometry. In spite of this sort of common bond between the former, they differ among themselves fundamentally in certain respects.
11. Something of this kind seems to have happened in social sphere later on. In face of external aggression and situation of lawlessness and uncertainty which prevailed as a result of it, requisite modifications in the *Varṇavyavasthā*, in response to the changed circumstances, did not come to be introduced. Serious thinking about this matter had come to a halt. There was hardly any occasion for exchange and clash of different views. In such a circumstance, marks of external discrimination like the sort of dress one wears, the sort of manners and etiquettes one adopts, etc. themselves came to be used as identificatory marks of different groups as a temporary measure. But since the condition of uncertainty did not end in a short span of time such marks of external discrimination themselves lasted as identificatory marks over a prolonged period of time, no one bothering to consider what values one cherishes and how one seeks to realise them in own's life. This is an illustrious example which shows that history continues to repeat with vengeance so long as we stubbornly refuse to learn anything from it.
12. In this context, it would be rewarding to consider Professor M.P. Marathe's article, "Some Perspectives of Research in Indian Philosophy", *Journal of the University of Poona*, Humanities section, vol. 39, 1974, pp. 11-18.

Problems and Suggestions for Making a Tibetan-English Dictionary of Buddhist Terminology

Tsepak Rigzin

These days we are witnessing a considerable increase in the quantity of translations of Tibetan Buddhist literature, primarily into English. While this is most welcome in itself it is astonishing that the English terms employed to translate Tibetan Buddhist terminology currently include a wide variety of renderings, which readers often find confusing. Therefore, many people have expressed a need for a practical Tibetan-English dictionary of Buddhist terminology, if not for the sake of achieving a universal system of standardization, which is difficult at least in order to assist the work of translation. To achieve this goal it will be equally important to establish some type of infrastructure for a network of communication among all those individuals, institutions and centres of study working in this field.

In the past, in Tibet, the religious kings had complete authority to commission the work of standardization, before which a situation must have existed similar to that which we are now facing in translating Tibetan Buddhism into English. But at the present time, who actually wields such authority and anyway would everyone obey him? The lack of any person or body commanding such respect at the international level is unfortunately a great drawback. We are all generally too individualistic and unwilling to defer to each other. Consequently, free translation, diverse translation, and conflicting and confusing usage of terminology pose a serious threat to the transmission of the original religious sources.

If some sort of general agreement cannot be reached among translators, within fifty years the situation will be chaotic. Therefore, the proposal to work systematically towards developing a common dictionary containing various alternative options for translating Buddhist terms, would seem to be the most practical solution. The task is urgent. Some sort of principles and methods, both at the academic and official level, must be worked out quickly. Since no individual is fully capable of carrying out this task, it would probably be wiser if there is some control or guidance through the heads of each of the particular traditions of Tibetan Buddhism, or their appointed representatives, in the hope that their virtuous forces will help unite the various schools and factions for one purpose. With this in mind, I would, therefore, like to discuss some of the problems that are faced by those who may attempt to create such a dictionary. I will approach this under serveral headings: the nature, scope, research, limitations, and methodology of such a dictionary, the coinage of terms and the infrastructure that will be required.

Nature

The nature of a Tibetan-English dictionary of Buddhist terminology can take many forms: it may be analytical, historical, descriptive and explanatory or etymological. Since, it is still too early to conceive of creating all these types of dictionary individually, we are left with no option but to compile the most appropriate Buddhist dictionary for the present transitional period. What we are badly in need of is a dictionary which is something of a combination of common and special technical terms, incorporating some features of the analytical, descriptive and explanatory approaches, appended with an index of sources, and numerical and technical categories. It is impossible to conceive of any dictionary with which we may hope to solve all problems. Absolute reliability and compactness are by no means easy to achieve. All that we can expect of such a dictionary is that it presents relevant information, including terms which a reader may have to study further to acquire a complete understanding. Neither complete accuracy of translation nor consistent standardization can be readily achieved. What is feasible for the dictionary is to give a number of alternatives of English renderings representing different schools of translation. These may or may not require the reader's further investigation, but it will be up to the individual user to use his discretion. The aim of the dictionary should be to help translation, not to serve as a tool for classical language research.

The task is still not easy. When I refer to a dictionary of Tibetan Buddhist terms in English I am referring to translations of whatever terms are to be found in Tibetan Buddhist scriptures. That certainly includes terms that are technical, e.g., *de-bzhin-nyid* (thusness), archaic e.g., *gdos-su che-che* (important), borrowed e.g., rakta (blood), hybrid e.g., pan-zha (a scholar's hat), polysemy words e. g., *phyag-rgya* (seal) and numerical e.g., *rgyus-rig* (skt: hetuḥ/eng:...?) and *rgyus-rig chen-mo* (skt: mahāhetuḥ/eng:...?) etc.[1] besides some words in the Chinese, Mongolian and Zhanzhung languages. In addition, there are hundreds of Tibetanized Sanskrit terms employed in different disciplines within Tibetan Buddhist literature. Because most of these words have different levels of meaning according to the vehicle, school of tenets, form of Buddhism, or tradition within that form, nature of the discipline, sūtra or tantra, or monastic textbook (*yig-cha),* there is considerable difficulty in choosing which level of meaning to describe in a dictionary.

Problems are also faced due to different modes of Tibetan spelling, variations of Tibetan names, real, given, or acquired, of persons and places, and the lack of a common standard for translation, use of terminology, transliteration and diacritical marks in the target language, which here is English. These problems must be taken into account while making a dictionary of Tibetan Buddhist terms. Besides, specific problems with regard to scope, research approach, limitations, methodology, coinage of terms and administrative infrastructures are also present, and, I shall deal them separately with a few humble suggestions in the following passages. Fortunately, many of these technical problems can be solved with the use of modern technology, such as computers.

Scope

The potential scope of a Buddhist dictionary is virtually unlimited, but considering the importance of imposing certain limits, we can restrict it to some extent. With respect to their sources, lexicons can be reduced into three distinct groups: 1) classical terminology selected from Kangyur, Tengyur and Kama and Terma sources; 2) traditional terminology from the commentaries both written and oral studied in the major monastic universities of all the four schools of Tibetan Buddhism; and 3) the Tibetan-Sanskrit, Sanskrit-Tibetan, and Tibetan-Tibetan dictionaries, glossaries and explanatory notes (*brda bkrol*) found in the works of various Tibetan scholars. There are difficulties in using many of these because the styles of their arrangement of different lexicons varies from each other. Which of the sources are to be considered authentic and unmistaken? Who will make the selection of words, because the real value of a dictionary lies in the quality of its selection of words. Since it is impossible to record every term, some kind of arbitrary limitation must be imposed on them.

The decision to limit a dictionary's scope to a given period of time is always attractive and has been followed before, but it is important that an attempt be made to make the dictionary as complete as possible by making optimum use of available resources with an unbiased attitude. Meaning in a strictly etymological sense can be given least importance here, since we are not trying to compile an etymological dictionary but are more concerned with the religious and philosophical implications and meanings of the terms. Duplication of the main entries of selected words must be avoided as far as possible through cross referencing.

Research

Researching the terms require tremendous effort to sift through the sources mentioned above. This will take much of the time of the team of compilers. All the terms selected from the sources mentioned must be first fed into the computer using programmes that will automatically rearrange them in alphabetical or numerical order. After clarifying the status of the terms within the context of Tibetan, such as whether they are archaic, current, belong to local dialects and so on, they can be classified under various subject headings within Buddhism. While compiling a *dharma* dictionary, the *dharma* terminologies in the oral tradition of teachings cannot be ignored. This form of language is very flowery and penetrative to disciples. Use of idiomatic expressions such as *bying-se-nyogs-se* (the lack of clear comprehension and appearance to a mind), and words like *dkar-na-zho dmar-na-khrag* (fully determined/total confidence), etc. are a unique feature of the oral tradition presented by the lamas. This is a problem of a translator, of a dictionary-maker. Should these words be included in a *dharma* dictionary or not? Next follows the analysis of their meanings, which can be based on a careful study of the citations collected at the time of selecting the terms, and naturally they must be arranged with due attention to different interpretations and levels of meaning. At this stage such citations are the primary materials and affixing the meaning is the task of the editors. Clearly, the larger the number of citations the better the result, but the obvious problem this presents is the time required by the compilers of the dictionary. Wherever numerical lists are given , one must research and try to find out all forms of listing under the same numerical data. It is because, to give an example, the 64 arts listed in the *Vinaya, Vajra ḍākinī tantra* and *Mahāvyutpatti* are different.[2] Similarly, the list of 18 sciences as mentioned in Vinayāgama *(dul ba lung), Ko sa la'i rgyan,* auto commentary of Abhidharma, Kālacakra tantra, Jātaka teachings and Lalitavistara are not same.[3]

In order to minimize the overall problems of compiling a dictionary the task of research should be divided amongst a team of experts chosen for their erudition in general and according to specific areas of specialization. Some may be more able in researching the terminology found in the tantras than in Madhyamika philosophy and *vice-versa*. Some principle will have to be worked out and this depends on the editors and experts.

If possible, words that are not included in other dictionaries should be given particular attention in order to enrich the vocabulary in general. This has a significant bearing on the scope of the dictionary. Only when the work of extracting terms is complete can the dictionary-maker concentrate on translating them or compiling their English equivalents. In this process he or she must not forget that this dictionary is not meant to give exhaustive definitions or etymological information about the things represented by the Tibetan words, but to supply the nearest equivalent and a number of alternatives in English, allowing for the minimal description of difficult and ambiguous words.

Giving a description of words is not the same thing as giving the meaning of things, objects, ideas, concepts and so forth, nor is the reverse true. Both approaches do complement each other to some extent but they soon diverge. For instance, to describe bell is not the same as giving the meaning of a bell, nor is the difference between various kinds of bell the topic of our dictionary, even though it may be noted that bell is sometimes identified with wisdom in tāntric practices. We cannot expect our dictionary to cover all these details because we aim at translation and not explanation. That is the job of a scholar doing specialized research only on one topic for a given period of time. Besides, he must be always ready to face a sundry other problems.

There is the question of how to carry out the extraction work. Keeping in mind the aim of including the maximum number of entries, what is indicated in the description of terms, wherever it is necessary, must be kept to a minimum in order to effect the complete extraction of the widest range of sources. The number of entries must be balanced against the frequency of their use and the different ways in which they are used and so on will have to be carefully noted down. It is only in the case of a limited selection of literature and works that any statistical statement can be attempted. All this is not easy.

Limitations

In order that a Tibetan-English dictionary of Buddhist terminology can be completed within a given period of time various limitations must be imposed and observed. Such problems as the lack of a proper network of information on the available source texts, the lack of a compact catalogue of already existent English translations worthy of reference, and lack of general cooperation are unique. Although there is no copyright on the original works found in the Kangyur and Tengyur, or even on the collected works of many early Tibetan masters, their translations into English are subject to copyright, and there is also no centralized source of information on what translation works are currently being carried out in diverse institutions. Overlapping translations, the widening gap in the usage of terminology and lack of a practical translator's dictionary are further expressions of these problems. They can be overcome if we collaborate and assist each other in a true Buddhist fashion.

Another important point is that a translator must exercise his freedom to translate as he thinks fit very cautiously. A limit must be observed. There are many cases where he may make his own choice of translation for no other reason that to be different from everyone else. This is something of an indulgence. In other cases, for instance, words like *rang-byan-chub-pa* which actually means self-knowledge/self-confidence can be hastily recreated as *rang byang-chub-pa* thus meaning self-enlightenment, and *pu-gur-sdod-pa* meaning to stay alone as baby sitting or else as an innocent child. Proper planning of the approach, research, methodology, personnel and so forth is extremely important. With regard to the time limit, nowadays with modern facilities at our disposal, five years is a reasonable limit. Who will draw up and administer this plan? Punctual achievement of the targets can be better planned by employing the talents of a team of experts made up of both Tibetans and Westerners whose responsibility will be to supervise the physical production of the dictionary.

Methodology

Modern methods of creating a properly ordered dictionary are highly reliable, provided more agreeable standard forms of translation can be worked out. Methods for correctly assigning meaning are important. Terms may refer to or literally represent common things, ideas and symbols, or express proper names. Which meanings of a term must be considered for inclusion in the dictionary? For example, the word *mudrā* alone has as many as 139 different symbolic meanings in Vairocanatantra alone.[4] Besides, how could one expect any dictionary to incorporate all these meanings?

With regard to the arrangement of the meanings of words, they could be arranged according to the frequency of their use, beginning with the most frequent and ending with the least frequent meaning. But this will depend on finding a middle way between the order of the dictionary itself and these meanings. Vocabulary may be divided into three categories, technical, semi-technical and non-technical. However, a translator does not have any guideline to depend upon. There is great benefit to be had from illustrating purely technical meanings with the clearest definitions, in order that the English definitions will be translated clearly. But one has also to know that a single definition of any technical term may only be of limited extent. If the terms unique to each school of Tibetan Buddhism are first gathered individually in fascicles, and can be gradually incorporated into a grand Tibetan-English Mahavyutpatti, this method could be extremely helpful, because of its practicality.

Probably, the translators who will work on the dictionary should be foreign scholars and students in collabration with Tibetan lamas, scholars and translators, following the pattern of the early tradition of Indian paṇḍitas guiding Tibetan translators. Since the beneficiaries are those into whose language and cultural context Tibetan Buddhism is to be assimilated, they certainly should take active participation in the work of translation.

Coining of Terms

Coining of new Buddhist terms in English must be done out with care. Terms that were borrowed from Sanskrit and assimilated into at least three or more languages in more or less the same form, should be considered international. For instance, Sanskrit words such as *vajra, karma, dharma, khaṭvāṅga, dhāraṇī, mantra, tantra* and so on can be incorporated into English as they are. Proper names of places and persons should not be translated to avoid confusing the readers. Units of weight and measure, such as *bre, khel, pagtse,* and *doms* and mantric seed syllables for meditative visualisations such as *Hri* ( ) and symbols such as *Nāda* ( ) should be retained, but sufficient definition of these terms must be given along with these words. Some hybrid terms, such as Bodhimind may be preferable instead of "mind of enlightenment," because it is easier to use one word for a given concept than many. Some times it may be advisable to insist on the use of terms like Dharmakāya untranslated because, although "Truth Body" is perhaps the best attempt to translate it so far, it can hardly mean *Chos-sku.* The case is similar with words like *Mahāmudrā, rDzogs-chen, Śūnyata, Samsara,* etc. But, side by side, explanations must be used in order to facilitate the understanding of the import of these words. Although the first generation is always hesitant to accept these loaned terms, the future will gradually accept, because it is through constant use only that technical terms will acquire their full stature and serve to bridge cross-cultures. On the other hand, there are the synonyms, e.g., the word Buddha alone has as many as 79 synonyms listed in Mahavyutpatti. No doubt all these names stand for Buddha, but we must not forget that each has its individual meaning. In order that these meanings are also transferred to the audience, one must not use the word Buddha or the Fully Enlightened. One alone for *de-bzhin gshegs-pa* (Tathāgataḥ), *bde-bar gśegs-pa* (Sugatah), *bcom-ldan-'das* (Bhagavan), *dgra-bcom-pa* (Arhan), or *rig-pa-dang-zhabs-su-ldan-pa* (Vidyā-caraṇa-sampannaḥ) for it would be tantamount to distortion. To illustrate this, the words *bcom-ldan-'das* means: *a*) one who has tamed the four *maras*, viz. that of aggregates, affliction, death and son of a god and; *b*) one who possesses the six marvellous physical features *(gzugs)*, fame (*grags-pa*), power (*dbang-phyug*), glory *(dpal)*, wisdom *(shes-rab)* and effort (*brtson-pa*).[5] Therefore, certainly it does not share the same meaning as the word Buddha has, which means whose mind is fully opened like that of a fully blossomed lotus. In any case, whether terms are created or translated they should be simple, clear and accurate. Long compound words and phrases should be avoided as much as possible. If an international convention for accepting certain terms cannot be adopted, we must make an attempt at formulating maxims of translation at our own institutional level. No doubt the two languages lack affinity in terms of their structures, syntax and so forth but if we extract applicable rules from *sgra-sbyor bam-po gnyis-pa*, and theories of translations and combine them with experiences of the qualified translators through research, we might come up with some valuable guidelines of translating Tibetan Buddhism into English. Adoption of such norms may offer a solution to some problems.

Administrative Structure

Not much can be said here, but in order to evolve a more efficient network of communication for the purpose of creating a dictionary of Buddhist terminology, a proper infrastructure with supervision over the coining of terminology would be very helpful. Just as there is the Standing Commission for Scientific and Technical Terminology of India, we should make an attempt towards forming a similar Commission for Tibetan Buddhist Terminology. In India, institutions like the Libeary of Tibetan Works and Archives in Dharamsala, the Central Institute for Higher Tibetan Studies in Sarnath and Tibet House in New Delhi are ideal places for centralizing and expediting such projects of translation and compilation of dictionaries.

Notes

1. See *Sanskrit-Tibetan-English Vocabulary* by Csoma De Koros. Royal Asiatic Society of Bengal, Vol. IV, No. 3. 1944, pp. 385.

2. See *Collected Works of Longdol Lama*, Part 1, 2, Lokesh Chandra. International Academy of Indian Culture, 1974. pp. 479. Also see Mahāvyutapatti, Tibetan Tripitaka Research Institute, Kyoto, Japan. Sr. No. 4972-5026.
3. See *Collected Works of Longdol Lama*. Part 1, 2. International Academy of Indian Culture. 1974. Lokesh Chandra, pp. 747.
4. See *On the History of the Buddhist Doctrine in India* (written for modern laymen) by Tsultrim Kelsang Khangsar. Tibetan Buddhist Culture Association. Minamid, Japan. 1988. Part II.
5. See *Tibetan-Sanskrit Lexicographical Materials* edited by Sonam Angdu. Bagso Tongspon publication, Leh, Ladakh. 1973, pp. 8.

Problems and Methods in the Translation of Buddhist Texts from Tibetan

Joe Bransford Wilson

The belief in its ability to understand everything from human culture and history, no matter how apparently alien, is itself one of the defining beliefs of the culture of modernity.

—Alasdair MacIntyre on "Tradition and Translation".[1]

An earlier incarnation of this paper was delivered to the International Seminar on Buddhist Translations in New Delhi, in 1990. It was then in a fairly stable form, but has now progressed to a state which anticipates, without having yet arrived at, what will be (for me, at least) a new approach to translation.

This paper does not, for the most part, deal with specific terms and the problems and possibilities of their translation into English.[2] Nor does it deal with Tibetan language at the grammatical, syntactic, or rhetorical levels of structure. It is a reflection on how Tibetan Buddhist texts have been and are to be approached. It began as a response to comments on Buddhology and translation by Paul Griffiths, Matthew Kapstein, Kennard Lipman, and C.W. Huntington. More recently, Susan Bassnet-MacGuire's work in the field of translation studies has been influential, as have been the writings by George Steiner, Walter Benjamin, and Alasdair MacIntyre.

The Task of the Translator

Kumarajīva is reported by Fung Yu-lan to have said about translation that it is "...just like chewing food that is to be fed to others. If one cannot chew the food oneself, one has to be given food that has been already chewed. Such food however is bound to be poorer in taste and flavour than the original."[3]

In a somewhat less dyspeptic vein, Walter Benjamin, in his well known essay, "The Task of the Translator," says: "The task of the translator consists in finding that intended effect upon the language into which he is translating which produces in it the echo of the original."[4]

Whether a translation is to be thought of as pre-chewed food or as a re-creation of the text in a new way, translation has been with us for a long time in both Western and Asian cultures. Some—for example the Tibetan—have glorified their translators. The *lo-tsā-bas* are remembered as culture heroes, as foundational figures. Our own culture has no such exalted attitude towards translators—for example, in an essay entitled "The Silk Purse Business," Gregory Rabassa notes with surprise that *Time* magazine even mentioned his name, as translator, in their review of García Márquez' *One Hundred Years of Solitude.*[5]

In fact, Western intellectual history has debated, since the times of the Roman translations of Greek texts, the role of the translator.[6] Should translators efface themselves, or is their role as creative as the author's role? The emphasis seems clearly on the former—where translation is regarded "a secondary activity, [seen] as a 'mechanical' rather than a 'creative process.'"[7] In this regard, the Western and the Tibetan traditions are somewhat in accord. When modern-day educated Tibetans think about the translation of Tibetan texts into foreign (that is, non-Tibetan) languages, their ideal—which they identify with the origin of their own Buddhist culture—is a set of standardized translation equivalents, allowing a more or less reproduceable translation from the Tibetan. On the other hand, their attitude towards text transmission (within Tibetan) leads them also to insist on translation teams in which one of the members is a Tibetan conversant with the depth and breadth of his own culture.[8] Whereas the former requirement implies a word-for-word literalist approach to translation, the latter one implies that the understanding of a text and, thus its translation, is highly contextual.

The nature of a text and the role of readers and translators are some of the basic issues that translation studies address. Of course, an even more basic issue is: Why translate at all? In his 1981 article "Buddhist Hybrid English," Paul Griffiths wrote that "translation is very frequently not the best way of performing the hermeneutical task, a fact rarely realized by practicing Buddhologists, most of whom stand transfixed in awe of their texts and are concerned largely to transmit them by means of translation regardless of whether or not they have been understood."[9] (Mention must be made here of Professor Griffith's recent publication, with four others, of an extensive translation of the tenth chapter of Asanga's *Mahāyānasangraha* and its Indian commentaries.)[10] However, as I have asked elsewhere,[11] is there no middle way between a Buddhist Studies which seeks merely to translate texts without analyzing the ideas presented in them[12] and another which seeks merely to show how the ideas seen in the texts relate to issues discussed in the history of Western philosophy?[13] In an earlier essay, I suggested that the task set for the academic translator is twofold:[14]

> As *academicians who study religions in an objective fashion,*[15] we must avoid both the reductive and the constructive extremes. We should fall neither to the extreme of reducing Buddhist ideas to those of other cultures nor to that of constructing a theology of our own. However, *as individuals participating in the intellectual histories of our own cultures,* we find that these extremes are not entirely avoidable and even that such avoidance is not entirely desirable. We must make the translation from, for example the worldview of eighteenth century Tibeto-Mongolian Buddhism to that of our own contemporary culture (which is a necessarily reductionist enterprise), while at the same time, constructively, we bring from our own culture(s) a new critique to the Buddhist position and lay the groundwork for a Buddhist critique of our culture(s). The latter task is constructive because it creates something new, something not previously present either in Buddhism or in our own cultures.

Types of Translation: Interpretive and Literal

It will be useful here at the outset to construct a taxonomy of translation methods; I am going to outline four such formulations, all of which present pairs of contrasting methods.

The first framework contrasts one of the ways in which Indian Buddhist texts were translated into Chinese in the way in which they were translated into Tibetan. David Seyfort Ruegg, in his 1962 review of Herbert Guenther's translation of the *Dvags po thar rgyan* (as *The Jewel Ornament of Liberation*) uses this framework to distinguish between the translation methods of Buddhologists such as Lévi, Stcherbatsky, de la Vallée Poussin, Lamotte, and Frauwallner.[16] The early Chinese method was that of *ko-i* or matching terms, where a similarity was sought between an Indian Buddhist terms and an extant Chinese term with a meaning already established in the conceptual vocabulary of Daoism.[17] This is an example of radically interpretive method.

The Tibetan method involved a one-to-one correspondence of terms between the two languages, with the coining of a new terms in Tibetan rather than reliance on an already extant conceptual system. This is an example of a literal method; Ruegg speaks of it as "technical" translation,[18] although it is clearly not a mechanical one in the sense that a Tibetan term would be considered always to equate to a Sanskrit term taking no regard of context.

When adducing Stcherbatsky as an example of a translator using the former method, Ruegg points out that Stcherbatsky's notion of an ideal method was "a double translation, one literal and philological and the other interpretative and philosophical."[19] So here we have two disparate methods and a middle way which instead of compromising between them merely combines both.

This dichotomy will surface again in the third and fourth typologies.

Types of Translation: First Hand Speech and Second-Order Jargon

The second framework, and in fact the remaining three frameworks, for thinking about translation methods are taken from polemical contexts. The first is mentioned by Kennard Lipman in his preface to a collaborative translation of Mañjuśrimitra's *Byang chub kyi sems bsgom pa,* a title I would translate—presumably to Lipman's chagrin—as *Cultivating the Awakened Mind.* The translators, he says, had decided that [20] "...what was needed was a language that "opened out onto" common usage; that is, while a translation from Tibetan dealing with a subject like rDzogs chen cannot really be encompassed within common English usage, this does not mean that it must be presented in a kind of Buddhist tribal language." Lipman goes on to explain what "Buddhist tribal language" means—characterizing as "Jargon" even the translations of *shes rab* and *ye shes* as "wisdom" and of *bdag med* as "no-self".[21] Later, invoking the phenomenologist Merleau-Ponty, he introduces the distinction between (1) authentic, first-hand speech and (2) second-order speech which is "a mere name [or] sign" and "has ceased to be descriptive of its referent".[22] Second-order speech is jargon and includes "translationese".[23] Lipman's optimal method, of course, uses authentic, first-hand speech—the speech, he says, quoting Merleau-Ponty, "of the writer and philosopher who *reawaken primordial experience anterior to all traditions.*"[24]

It goes without saying that to awaken and develop non-conceptual wisdom *is* the point of Buddhism; however, I wonder if non-conceptual wisdom is necessarily directly involved in translating Buddhist texts. What Lipman suggests comes close to requiring that translators translate not from a conceptual knowledge of Tibetan and a conceptual understanding of Buddhism, but must first have realized emptiness.

Buddhologists will be familiar with the four reliances (*rton pa bzhi*—the four *pratisaraṇa*) that are the foundation of Buddhist hermeneutics—to rely on doctrines and not on persons, and—within doctrines—on meaning and not words, and—within meanings—on the definitive in preference to what requires interpretation, and, finally, on non-conceptual wisdom and not conceptual knowledge.[25] These are obviously relevant to the translation process and, in some way, ought to be useful guidelines for translators. However, while the first two—reliance on doctrines and their meanings, rather than on blind faith in authority or on the letter of the text—clearly seem necessary in a good translation, the latter two are not. The first two reliances correspond to the philological and perhaps even the comparative and historical concerns of translation. The third—reliance on the definitive and not on what requires interpretation—is normative and restrictive, reducing what may be a rich ambiguity in the text to merely one among a number of interpretations. Most interpretive translations act as if they were invoking this third reliance, for their translators have gone beyond the words of the text (hallowed as they are to the philologist), transforming them into what is considered to be a more definitive meaning. This problem will appear in the fourth framework, where translation is held to be an act of creation.

The choice of first-hand as opposed to second-order speech acts as if it invokes the fourth reliance, the move to non-dual wisdom (or, avoiding tribal jargon, "ever fresh awareness untainted by concepts").[26] The fourth reliance calls for a move beyond texts—but, if Buddhism is properly understood, not at the very beginning. The traditional Buddhist account of the development of understanding is in three stages: inthe beginning based on reading or being taught, subsequent reflection on what has been studied, and only then the development of a meditative non-rational appreciation.

I have two problems with Lipman's hermeneutic. First, it moves away from the dictum that the words of ordinary language (into which Lipman says he is translating) are not magical, that they do not inhere in their referents, but are rather arbitrary and conventional. In this regard, Lipman's prescription of authentic, first-hand speech calls to mind what Walter Benjamin says, again in "The Task of the Translator":[27] "It is the task of the translator to release in his own language that pure language which is under the spell of another, to liberate the language imprisoned in a work in his recreation of that work."

I will reserve my second argument against this translation theory until after I have presented the other two frameworks for thinking about translation.

Types of Translation: Historico-Philological, Neotraditional, Comparative

The third scheme of translation methods can be introduced with words written in praise of Robert Thurman by Matthew Kapstein. Kapstein speaks of two types of Buddhist Studies and what he perceives as Thurman's attempt to construct a middle way between them:[28] " I am impressed above all by what I take to be Thurman's central concern, namely to provide a viable alternative to philosophically non-reflective, historico-philological 'Buddhology' on the one hand and the intellectual isolation of Buddhist neotraditionalists on the other."

It is unclear to me exactly to whom the description "philosophically non-reflective, historico-philological 'Buddhology'" refers—it would hardly seem to do justice to Buddhologists such as de la Vallée Poussin and Lamotte, and certainly the work of Stcherbatsky, although he was perhaps a little over-zealous in finding Kant prefigured in Buddhist epistemology, cannot be called non-reflective, nor can that of Ruegg and Schmithausen. On the other hand, translators such as Jeffrey Hopkins and those he has trained and is training at Virginia are presumably included under the rubric of "neotraditionalism". Critics of this method often say that it is methodologically naive to employ the oral explanations of modern-day Tibetan scholars in preference to well established scholarly conjectures about what the Sanskrit original of a Tibetan term meant in the fifth century. I am going to assume that this is not, in fact, an enterprise that stands outside contemporary academic Tibetology and Buddhist Studies.

Of course, if we are talking about the translation and study of *Indian* texts either from Tibetan translations or with the use of Tibetan translations of their commentaries, then the matter is somewhat changed. As a rule of thumb, the best scholarly method is to get as close to a text as possible. In the case of Sanskrit texts, philology and a close scrutiny of the historical context in which the text is found in the tradition of Indian Buddhism is essential.[29] However, if we are speaking of the translation of texts written in Tibet, or of the understanding of Indian texts within a Tibetan tradition of scholarship, then our concern must be not only with Sanskrit philology (and I would argue, not primarily with Sanskrit philology), but rather on the meanings and development of the Tibetan technical terms involved and the position in which a text is found in the history of Tibetan literature.[30] And when the text is studied and translated as a part of contemporary Buddhism in Tibet, there is no way to avoid oral commentary, which must itself be approached as a text.[31] Even those who criticize reliance on explanations of Indian texts from within the Tibetan scholarly tradition[32] will also admit that these texts were, in both India and Tibet, used as vehicles for oral explanation.

Types of Translation: Philological or Text-Critical, Proselytic, Textualist

C.W. Huntington, in the introduction to his translation of Chandrakīrti's *Madhyamakāvatāra*, makes an analysis parallel to the one just introduced, distinguishing between (1) translations based on philological or text-critical method and (2) proselytic translations which seek to arrive at an objective traditional understanding of the text.[33] Both are "to some extent anachronistic vestiges of a style of scholarship that has come under fire from a number of quarters outside the province of Asian cultural studies".[34] Huntington here invokes Richard Rorty, calling for[35] "a 'strong textualist' [reading of the text which] asks neither the author nor the text about their intentions but simply beats the text into a shape that will serve his own purpose. The strong textualist 'is in it for what he can get out of it, not for the satisfaction of getting something right'."

Both the philological and the proselytic approaches share two underlying misconceptions, in Huntington's view. They both presuppose an objective tradition in which the text is embedded (that is, a tradition external to the translator); and they both use a methodology to gain access to this tradition.[36]

As regards the first, while it is true that there is no such thing as Buddhism per se, but only many Buddhisms and, in the final event, only the Buddhism of each person who has an understanding of Buddhism, nonetheless it is convenient and useful to speak of "Buddhism" or of traditions within it (such as the Mādhyamika tradition or the tradition of enquiry of Go-mang College within the Tibeto-Mongolian tradition). Huntington's analysis is based on the idea of choosing an approach that does not harm the texts being translated or studied and, especially in the case of Mādhyamika Buddhism, this means one that retains the absence of absolutes invoked in the Mādhyamika doctrine he appropriates as the title of his book, the emptiness of emptiness. However, he is perhaps forgetting that Candrakirti's interpretation of Nāgārjuna emphasizes not just the ultimate truths of emptiness but also the complementary conventional truths which allow for such convenient designations as "traditions." It *is* true that there are no objectively existent, truly separate traditions (or anything else for that matter) in Mahāyāna philosophy. Nonetheless, traditions exist as much anything else does.

Huntington's second criticism is based, he says, on the rejection of the idea of a privileged vocabulary. Here, he seems to agree with Lipman and others about the need to go beyond a Buddhist tribal language. This, then, brings us back to my second argument against the search for translation language that "reawakens primordial experience anterior to all traditions"—the argument I had previously reserved. This idea of a pure language (in Walter Benjamin's sense), a language that evokes pre-intellectual understanding in its audience, ignores what I take to be an unavoidable fact, notably that the translator always translates into two languages—one more general (such as English) and, within that, a technical language—that is, jargon. Translation from Tibetan into a foreign—that is, a non-Tibetan—language is done at two levels, to two depths:

(1) more superficially there is a translation into a foreign language (such as English).
(2). but, more specifically, there is a translation into a technical vocabulary, a conceptual lexicon which is a subset of the foreign language.

English and Japanese and Hindi are languages, but so are the languages of computer science, of analytic philosophy, of Heidegger, of Jungian or Freudian analysis and so on.

Let me try to put this in context—and, by the way, respond to Huntington's views on method—by speaking of translation in the broadest possible way.

Buddhism is, in this most fundamental sense, translation.[37] It is no great insight to universalize this and argue that all religions are translation schemes in that all propose ways of translating our normal view of things into one that more closely harmonizes with the way things really are. In one way or another, to be religious is to say that there is something wrong with the human condition as we find it, and that the root of this wrongness is our absorption in a superficial reading of what actually is—an absorption in appearances and an ignoring of reality. Thus, to use the translation terminology of Mādhyamika Buddhism, when an ordinary person says or thinks "I exist" that person means not so much "I exist" as "I inherently exist". The phrase "inherently exist" is the Mādhyamika translation of what appears (wrongly) to be mere existence. Thus, it is ordinary language that Buddhism sees as misleading, as disguising pathological cognitive processes that are not recognized as such by the person who has them. All forms of Buddhism say in their various ways that ordinary perception is mistaken and that it needs to be transformed; they all provide *technical languages* for speaking clearly about this mistakenness and for clarifying the distinction between appearances and reality. Thus, what Buddhism seeks is to present alternative languages—languages that speak more clearly about mental processes and ontology. Here I think Lipman and I agree.

What should this suggest to one who translates from Tibetan into a Western language or into Hindi or Japanese? For one thing, that ordinary language is not the desideratum. Given that Buddhists have worked very hard, first in India and then throughout south, east, and central Asia to produce and refine alternate vocabularies, we should not put off the process of creating an alternate vocabulary in English. However, this process will be a lengthy one, and therefore the development of a more specialized alternate vocabulary must begin with ordinary language. Let me illustrate this by presenting two translation strategies that exemplify what I am saying might be avoided:

(1) the first may be seen in the mixing of translation and comparative philosophy;
(2) the second may be seen in highly interpretive translations that explicitly draw translation terms from Western philosophies.

Proponents of the first approach include scholars such as Kapstein, Griffiths, and Huntington. There is, of course, nothing intrinsically wrong with this undertaking. In the long run, it can only have the effect of enriching the Western understanding of the depth and complexity of Buddhist philosophies. And one can only applaud their efforts to clarify translation terminology and to broaden the horizons of both Western and Buddhist philosophy towards a future global philosophy. Nor do I wish to argue that Buddhist and analytic philosophies are incommensurable, at least not that they are radically so.

What I do wish to argue is based on the notion that translation of a Tibetan Buddhist text into English involves translation into not only English but into some chosen conceptual vocabulary within English as well. The vocabulary chosen ought to depend on the audience addressed. Translation is a variety of text transmission, and—if communication of ideas is at stake—the transmitter of the text must speak in terms his or her audience is able to understand. This, in fact, argues *for* the task that Kapstein, Griffiths, and Huntington have set for themselves, the translation of Buddhist philosophical text with ongoing analysis of how these fit into not merely readable English but into the concerns of a philosophy native to the language into which the translation is made—in their case, American and British analytic philosophy. However, I have two reservations about this. The first is general and brief: this is not merely translation, it is analysis and comparative philosophy. Analysis (philological, historical, and philosophical) is needed in translation, but it should be relegated to the introduction, to the footnotes, or perhaps to annotations.

The second reservation is that whereas the concerns that have prompted examination and analysis of the broad issues of being and knowing in the Western tradition are doubtless the same as those that have prompted such examinations by Indians and Tibetans, the contexts in which narrower examinations of individual topics are done are not necessarily similar. A good example is a topic in which Kapstein, Griffiths, and I all have an interest, that of the person and, especially, personal identity.[38] The roots of the philosophical examination of the person in modern Western philosophy are in the writing of John Locke; for Locke, the concept of personal identity is rooted in legal responsibility; it is posited for the sake of having someone to reward or to punish. A person chooses and acts, and so is legally actionable. It goes without saying that Buddhists are persons who act and are morally responsible, but this is not the context in which we find the examination of the person in Buddhism. In fact, the more usual context is not that of the person itself but rather of the non-existence of the normal sense of how a person exists, that is, the context is *gang zag gi bdag med (pudgalanairātmāya*—personal selflessness) and nor merely *gang zag,* the person. We have to search a bit to find examinations of how the person does exist rather than of how it does not. And these examinations are not ones primarily made in the context of moral action, but rather of ontology.[39]

Of course it is possible to take a Tibetan or Sanskrit text, or a range of texts, and engage in a study of them with Western ideas in mind, examining the idea of persons as moral agents, for example. Kapstein has written on Derek Parfit's 1984 book, *Reasons and Persons,* which has, as Kapstein himself acknowledges, "two major, ultimately intertwined, themes, namely, our reasons for adopting given actions, and out nature as persons, that is, as those who act."[40] I have no argument against the legitimacy of such a study; translators should consult such studies. My point is that it ought to be on the basis of translations that comparative philosophy is done, not *primarily* in the context of a comparative philosophy whose agenda are provincially Western that translations ought to be done.

A final reservation is that a translation embedded in a philosophical commentary that takes some aspect of Western philosophical discourse as normative is one that may not speak very well to a future generation. When a translator places a Tibetan or Indian text in the context of the contemporary concerns of a non-Tibetan or non–Indian culture, binding the understanding of the text to the relevance of those concerns, it seems likely that if those concerns and arguments turn out to be relatively ephemeral, so will the translation. This argument, in turn, relates to a more basic issue, whether a translation ought to stand, as much as it can, by itself or should be done as part of an on going dialogue between two cultures.[41] Clearly, if a translated text engages its readers, as it should, then dialogue has been initiated with those readers (not between the translator and the readers, but between the text and the readers), and that is a dialogue between two cultures. But if the translation is overly couched in the terms and concerns of, in the presents example, Western analytical philosophy, then the outcome is more an understanding of new possibilities within that (Western) system than a dialogue between cultures. This is legitimate, but it is not translation. On the other hand, if a translation is presented in a conceptual system intellectually isolated from *any* of the concerns of the culture to which it is presented, dialogue again will fail to be joined and the translation will not be accessible to its audience. We have again come up against the notion of jargon, introduced above by Lipman (as "tribal language"). I agree with Kapstein (and Steven Collins, whom he is reviewing) about the idea of raising a challenge to "the inbred perspective of the English-speaking philosophical tribe."[42] The question becomes one of skilful means—how to engage the trained philosopher, who is trained of necessity in jargon, the Buddhologist, who has learned to think in his own jargon, and the ordinary educated person, who will not recognize the jargon of either group as what it is, shorthand for complex ideas and arguments that cannot be explicitly addressed every time they arise.[43]

The second type of avoidable translation strategy is less conceptual than aesthetic. Those who have sought to create a Buddhist English as one would a work of art, out of the depths of their own non-conceptual reaction to the text being translated, have sometimes given us translations that are in fact like works of art in that they are fully accessible only to the artist. That they communicate something is indisputable, but precisely what they are communicating is sometimes difficult to fathom.[44] A good example of this is the translation by Namkhai Norbu, Lipman, and Simmons of the Tibetan phrase *byang chub kyi sems sgom pa* as "cultivating the primordial state of pure and total presence."[45] *Byang chub* (Sanskrit *bodhi*) is at least recognizable in its translation as "pure and total presence" (with reservations concerning "presence"), but there seems no reason for translating *sems* (Sanskrit *citta*) as "primordial state" or even "state". However, the term may be used in this special context of Dzok-chen(*rdzogs chen*) thought, *sems* is a very common word that in the broader context always refers in some way to mind or perception or consciousness.[46]

A more general example of this translation strategy is the work of Herbert Guenther. On the positive side, Guenther and those who follow his approach are obviously conscious of the need to engage in the task of creating in English an alternate vocabulary in which it is possible to translate ordinary experiences so that they may be examined more clearly. In some of these translations, however, the alternate vocabulary has become so complex and so metaphoric that one needs to memorize it before one can read the book. Now, in one sense, this is a natural outcome of the nature of Indian and Tibetan religious and philosophical texts—they are not meant to be accessible to an ordinary educated reader unless that reader had already had some instruction in the technical vocabulary of the particular text. Moreover, exotic vocabularies can be very powerful symbolically. Among Western Buddhists, there are many attracted to the richly poetic, imaginative vocabulary of such translations and, it might be noted, the *Rdzogs-chen* texts, in which Guenther has concentrated, are written in just such a richly poetic and emotive vocabulary, unlike, for example, the works of *mtshan nyid* (literally, "definitions," but meaning philosophy). Even when Tantra is analyzed in the Gélukba tradition, the language is more restrained and unlike that seen in Nyingma Tantra. So, from the view point of genre or style, the argument can be made that a more poetic and emotive vocabulary may be more appropriate in the cases in which Guenther has used it.

On the other side of the ledger are arguments that relate not to what is being communicated poetically but what is being communicated conceptually. First, even in the early works such as *Jewel Ornament of Liberation*—as Ruegg has pointed out—the translation is "interpretive," done in the *ko-i* style rather than the more philologically precise style typical of the Tibetan translators.[47] Instead of the Daoist terms beloved of the Han translators, Guenther uses terms (for example, "facticity" for *ngo bo* and "noetic" for *shes pa)* taken from Existentialist philosophy and Phenomenology.[48] Such interpretations introduce a conceptual language that is clearly absent in both the Indian text and the Tibetan commentarial tradition. Philosophers in Western traditions are responding in their thinking, as I have noted, to their own cultural situation and, most importantly, to the concerns defined by the Western philosophers who preceded them. Thus, the language they use is language that invokes *specific* issues and assumptions foreign to the Indian and Tibetan traditions. Guenther recognizes this; in *Buddhist Philosophy in Theory and Practice he says:*[49] "'Existential' Buddhism is therefore totally different from the various forms of Western existentialism which is purely anthropocentric and ego-centric ... 'Existential' Buddhism, claimed to be the climax of the philosophical quest, is concerned with Being, not with an ego..."

It seems to me paradoxical to have first to learn what terminology such as "being-as-an-ens" and "facticity" mean, and then to have to consciously dissociate the meanings of these terms from their source. However, when such a method is used—that is, deriving translation vocabulary from a non-Buddhist conceptual system that has non-Buddhist concerns, non-Buddhist goals, and non-Buddhist assumptions—the translator must make it clear to his audience exactly in what ways the vocabulary is being used and in what ways it is not.

The other argument against such translation can be seen by looking at the previously mentioned Namkhai Norbu/Kennard Lipman/Barrie Simmons translation of Mañjuśrimitra's *Byang chub kyi sems sgom pa*. Here the source of the vocabulary is more obscure to me, but seems at least to be inspired by continental philosophy. One phrase from this translation exemplifies well the dangers of this method of translation which, to repeat, is a poetic and affective approach to the subject matter.[50] Where the Tibetan reads *bdag med gnyis*— the two selflessnesses—the translators have "there is nothing that makes both (persons and phenomena) what they are". This is not what selflessness (or no-self, if you prefer) means. There are many things that make persons and phenomena what they are—their causes and conditions, the aggregation of their parts, and the perception of them which imputes them to be persons and other phenomena. Presumably what is meant is that things are what they are and not what they appear to be to a delusive or ignorant mind (*ma rig pa*). It strikes me that such "common language" translations may, without meaning to, obscure more than they clarify.

Postscript

The translation methods presented up to this point share a common assumption, that Buddhist texts in Tibetan or Sanskrit are in fact translatable. That is to say, the assumption is made that whatever is said in the source language (Tibetan or Sanskrit) can be re-expressed in the target language (for me late twentieth-century English). No one today argues that this re-expression ought to be a one-to-one correspondence; Huntington even calls it a misreading (in the context that all translations are misreadings).

In this regard the remarks Alasdair MacIntyre makes about traditional cultures and their languages are instructive:[51]

"... there can be no language as English-as-such or Hebrew-as-such or Latin-as-such. There are not even, it must seem, such languages as classical Latin or early modern Irish. There is only Latin-as-written-and-spoken-in-the Rome-of-Cicero and Irish-as written-and spoken-in-sixteenth-century-Ulster. The boundaries of a language are the boundaries of some linguistic community which is also a social community... But there is, for better or worse, late twentieth-century English, an internationalized language, which ... has been developed so as apparently to become potentially available to anyone and everyone ...."

MacIntyre advances two examples of languages "moving toward" internationalized language: versions of high medieval Latin and medieval Arabic, which were used by people from a variety of backgrounds and differing local cultures. I would suggest that some versions of Tibetan—for example, the Tibetan of monastic textbooks, the sub-commentaries used to study the Indian *śastras,* might qualify as such a semi-internationalized language. Students from a great many local backgrounds came from regions as far away as Mongolia to study the Buddhism which was their great tradition religion, reading, discussing, and debating philosophical issues in this language.[52] The case might also be made that the antecedent of this later religious language, that is, the Tibetan of the Gangyur (*bka' 'gyur*) and Dengyur (*bstan 'gyur*), is also just such a semi-internationalized language. (Much other literary Tibetan—for instance, that dealing with meditative experience, the lives of saints, and so on—is much more clearly of the tradition-constituted and tradition-constitutive variety, to use MacIntyre's terminology.)

This notwithstanding, it is clear that in translating from Tibetan into English, we are, on MacIntyre's model, translating from a tradition-constituted and tradition-constitutive language to an internationalized language. And this means that such a translation is "turned into a text which is no longer the author's, nor such as would be recognized by the audience to whom it is addressed."[53] The position against which MacIntyre is arguing is the one that I believe Huntington has appropriated—that "[t] he understanding of the text is not controlled by authorial intention or by any relationship to an audience with specific shared beliefs, for it is outside context except the context of interpretation."[54]

Notes

1. Chapter XIX, *Whose Justice? Which Rationality?* (Notre Dame: University of Notre Dame Press, 1988), p. 385.
2. I have addressed psychological and epistemological terminology elsewhere: "Translation of Buddhist Psychological and Epistemological Terms from Tibetan," being edited for publication in a volume on translation of Buddhist texts (New Delhi: Tibet House, 1991 ?)
3. Cited by Edward L. Keenan at the beginning of "Some Logical Problems in Translation" in *Meaning and Translation, Philosophical and Linguistic Approaches,* edited by F. Guenther and M. Guenther-Reutter (London: Duckworth, 1978), p. 157.
4. Walter Benjamin, "The Task of the Translator" (pp. 69-82 in *Illuminations,* edited and with an introduction by Hannah Arendt, New York: Schocken, 1969), p. 76.

5. "The Silk Purse Business: A Translator's Conflicting Responsiblities" (pp. 35-40 in *Translation. Literary, Linguistic, and Philosophical Perspectives,* edited by William Frawley [Newark: University of Delaware Press, 1984]), p. 39.
6. This may, perhaps, overstate the case—see Bassnett-McGuire, pp. 43-44.
7. Susan Bassnett-McGuire, *Translation Studies* (London and New York: Methuen & Co., 1980), p. 2.
8. This was the consensus of the first annual International Seminar on Buddhist Translations, held in New Delhi in 1990.
9. "Buddhist Hybrid English: Some Notes on Philology and Hermeneutics for Buddhologists" (pp. 17-32 in *Journal of the International Association of Buddhist Studies* 4/2 [1981]), p. 20.
10. Asanga, *The Realm of Awakening,* introduction by John P. Keenan; translation and notes by Paul J. Griffiths et al. (New York: Oxford University Press, 1989).
11. See my "Pudgalavāda in Tibet? Assertions of Substantially Existent Selves in the Writings of Dzong-ka-ba and His followers" (*Journal of the International Association of Buddhist Studies* 14/1, Summer 1991).
12. See C.W. Huntington, *The Emptiness of Emptiness* (Honolulu: The University of Hawaii Press 1989), pp. 5-6.
13. The former extreme may be seen in many translations published by Western centres of Tibetan Buddhism whereas the latter is seen in Kapstein's article "Śāntarakṣita on the Fallacies of Personalistic Vitalism."
14. "Pudgalavāda in Tibet?"—see note 11.
15. Objective study seems to me not to be a self-contradictory idea. The next revision of this paper will deal explicitly with this issue.
16. David Seyfort Ruegg, " A Propos of a Recent Contribution to Tibetan and Buddhist Studies" (*Journal of the American Oriental Society* 82/3, July-September 1962), pp. 325-326.
17. For some example of this style Kenneth Ch'en, *Buddhism in China. A Historical Survey* (Princeton: Princeton University Press, 1964), p. 372. Ch'en also gives examples from other translation methods. See also Paul Demiéville, "La pénétration du Bouddhisme dans la tradition philosophique Chinoise" (pp. 1-38 in *Choix d' Études Bouddhiques,* Leiden: E.J. Brill, 1973).
18. Ruegg, " A Propos", p. 326.
19. Ibid., p. 325.
20. Mañjuśrīmitra, *Primordial Experience: An Introduction to rDzogs-chen Meditation*— translated by Namkhai Norbu and Kennard Lipman in collaboration with Barrie Simmons. (Boston and

London: Shambhala, 1987), page xvii.
21. Ibid., pages xx and xviii, respectively.
22. Pages xxi, xxii.
23. Page xxii.
24. M. Merleau-Ponty, *The Phenomenology of Perception* (London: Routledge and Kegan Paul, 1978), p. 179, note 1—quoted in *Primordial Experience,* p. xxi.
25. The most well-known presentation is by Robert Thurman: "Buddhist Hermeneutics," pp. 19-39 in *Journal of the American Academy of Religion* (XL VI/1). See also Jeffrey Hopkins, *Meditation on Emptiness* (London: Wisdom Publications, 1983), p. 425, and Robert A.F. Thurman, *Tsong Khapa's Speech of Gold in the Essence of True Eloquence* (Princeton : Princeton University Press, 1984), pp. 113ff.
26. *Primordial Exprerience, p xvii.*
27. Walter Benjamin, "The Task of the Translator" (pp. 69-82 in *Illuminations,* edited and with and introduction by Hannah Arendt [New York: Schocken, 1969]), p. 80
28. Matthew Kapstein, [review of] Thurman, Robert A.F., *Tsong Khapa's Speech of Gold in the Essence of True Eloquence; Philosophy East and West* 36/2 (1986): 186.
29. See, for example, Lambert Schmithausen, *Ālayavijñāna: On the Origin and Early Development of a Central Concept of Yogācāra Philosophy* (Studia Philologica Buddhica, monograph series IV a-b—Tokyo: International Institute for Buddhist Studies, 1987).
30. An example of a study which combines both is David Seyfort Ruegg *La théorie du tathāgatagarbha et du gotra, études sur la Sotériologie et la Gnoséologie du Bouddhisme* (Paris: École Française d'Extrêeme Orient, 1969).
31. Anne Klein presents here use of this method in "Direct Perception (*Pratyakṣa*) in dGe-lugs-pa Interpretations of Sautrāntika" (*Journal of the International Association of Buddhist Studies* 8/1 [1985]), pp. 50-52.
32. See Paul J. Griffiths, *On Being Mindless. Buddhist Meditation and the Mind-Body Problem* (La Salle, IL: Open Court, 1986), p. 165, note 10.
33. Huntington, *The Emptiness of Emptiness* (Honolulu: University of Hawaii Press, 1989), pp. 5ff.
34. Ibid., p. 5.
35. Ibid., p. 8. The material in quotes is from Rorty *Consequences of Pragmatism,* pp. 151 and 152.
36. Ibid ., p. 7.
37. This, as far as I know, is my own interpretation. However, see also

Paul J. Griffiths, *On Being Mindless. Buddhist Meditation and the Mind-Body Problem* (La Salle, IL: Open Court, 1986), p. 51. Griffiths is speaking of the Vaibhāṣika analysis of experience and says, "it can be viewed as an attempt at consistent, coherent, and complete translation of all conventional discourse into dharma-discourse." This he says is reductionist. It seems hard to fault that *particular* claim, but I am not sure that all such translation work (for example, as done by Asaṅga and Candrakīrti) would necessarily be an abstraction from experience.

38. See Matthew Kapstein, "Collins, Parfit, and the problem of personal identity in two philosophical traditions—A review of *Selfless Persons* by Steven Collins and *Reasons and Persons* by Derek Parfit" (*Philosophy East and West* 36/3 [1986: 289-298); Kapstein, "Śāntarakṣita on the Fallacies of Personalistic Vitalism" (*Journal of Indian Philosophy* 17 [1989]: 43-59); Paul J. Griffiths, *On Being Mindless. Buddhist Meditation and the Mind-Body Problem* (La Salle, IL: Open Court, 1986).
39. See my "Pudgalavāda in Tibet? Assertions of Substantially Existent Selves in the Writings of Dzong-ka-ba and His Followers," (*Journal of the International Association of Buddhist Studies* 14/1 (Summer 1991). The concerns of these writers are those of the ontological and epistemological status of the person.
40. Kapstein (1986), p. 289. This is obvious from the layout of the book as well; Parfit begins with an examination of moral actions and moves on from there.
41. The idea of translation as dialogue and encounter may be seen in Whalen Lai, "The Early Chinese Buddhist Understanding of the Psyche: Chen Hui's Commentary on the *Yin Chih Ju Ching*" (*Journal of the International Association of Buddhist Studies* 19/1 [1986]), p. 85.
42. Kapstein (1986), p. 296.
43. The argument may be made that all philosophical discourse (in whatever culture) is jargon. When an analytical philosopher uses the term 'mind' he means one thing; when a phenomenologist uses that term, he means another. Both speak within a broader conceptual world in which, for example, the difference between and relation of mind and body are fundamental. Buddhism, of course, has something to say about this, but the issue is not a fundamental one. (See Griffiths, *On Being Mindless,* p. 56.)
44. An example is the *Primordial Experience* translation to which reference has already been made. It ought to be noted that is a very well arranged book; it is thoughtful and insightful, and, although I cite it mainly as a foil for my own ideas, it has much to

recommend it. My own critical reaction to it owes much to the review by Lou Nordstrom in *Philosophy East and West* 39/3 (1989): 355-57.

45. Ibid., pp. 55 and 115.
46. The meaning of *sems* as consciousness may be paradoxical—as in the standard Cittamātra identification of *sems* and *kun gzhi rnam par shes pa*.
47. Ruegg, "A Propos," p. 326.
48. On Heidegger's use of terms such as 'facticity' see Marjorie Grene, "Martin Heidegger" in Paul Edwards, *The Encyclopedia of Philosophy* (New York: Macmillan Publishing Co., 1967), vol. 3, pp. 459ff. For Guenther's blend of continental philosophy and Nyingma, see, for example, Herbert V. Guenther, "Some Aspects of Tibetan Religious Thought" (*History of Religions* 6/1 [August 1966], pp. 70-87), especially p. 76 and the references to John Wild's *Challenge of Existentialism*, and "The Philosophical Background of Buddhist Tantrism" (*Journal of Oriental Studies* [Hong Kong], vol. 5 [1959-60], pp. 45-64.
49. Herbert V. Guenther, *Buddhist Philosophy in Theory and Practice* (Baltimore: Penguin Books, 1971), pp. 22-23.
50. *Primordial Experience*, p. 55 (English) and p. 115 (Tibetan). I am indebted to Lou Nordstrom's insightful review in *Philosophy East and* West 39/3 (1989), pp. 355-57 for this example; my analysis of it differs slightly, however.
51. Alasdair MacIntyre, *Whose Justice? Which Rationality?* (Notre Dame: University of Notre Dame Press, 1988), p. 373.
52. The Mongolians and their philosophical-religious ties to Tibet are apparently well known in linguistic circles. George Steiner cites eighteenth-century Mongolia as a famous example of a culture in which diffemt groups and levels within one society used different languages (*After Babel* [London: Oxford University Press, 1975], p. 31): "The religious language was Tibetan; the language of the government was Manchu; merchants spoke Chinese; classical Mongolian was the literary idom; and the vernacular was the Khalka dialect of Mongol."
53. MacIntyre, p. 385.
54. Ibid., p. 386.

Upon Translating Philosophical Terminology

Georges Dreyfus

This paper reflects my experience as a scholar whose work primarily involves translation into English of Buddhist concepts rather than whole texts. Since this is a form of translation I hope that the few remarks I present will be relevant to the general discussion.

This essay is organized around the study of two cases of translation. It is primarily practical aiming at suggesting a few methodological conclusions rather than developing a theoretical approach to translation. I explore some of the problems involved in the translation of specifically philosophical terms into modern English. Since my remarks will only concern a particular genre of literature, namely, the technical texts encountered in the study of Buddhist philosophy, the processes useful to translation suggested here may not apply to other translation situations.

I restrict my analysis to terms taken from the logico-epistemological tradition of Dharmakīrti and his followers. These are examples of what I call the technical and philosophical type of literature. I would like to note a clear distinction between these texts, which are overtly philosophical, from the other less technical texts such as practice-oriented texts, poetry, biographies which often relate less to philosophy.

My way of proceeding is quite simple. I take two examples which I have come across and explain the problems they have raised. I start by examining the problem of translating the term *don gcig*[1] and then move on to the more difficult problem created by the terms *spyi bye brag*. Both cases provide some perspective leading to the conclusion, a plea for a contextual view of translation. That means a translation that remains sensitive to the multiple contexts related to a term or idea involving the traditions of both languages. Since my remarks reflect only my very limited experience in the field of translation, there is no need to say that they will be partial and preliminary.

My first study case is an occasion for making a few remarks on the respective advantages and disadvantages of literal translation (*tshig gyur)* versus translation from the meaning of the term (*don gyur*). It will show the importance of knowing and using Western philosophical vocabulary.

As regards the latter, the importance of the correct use of Western philosophical terms can be understood in relation to several concerns. The usage of Western philosophical vocabulary in the translation of Buddhist philosophy stems from a more general problem: how the translations of Buddhist texts are relevant to Western culture. Translation in the large sense of the term must aim at integrating the texts and ideas of the tradition it translates into the cultural conversation of the language into which it is translated.

The use of philosophical terminology is not, however, only dictated by the necessity to make our works relevant. It is also dictated by the philosophical nature of the texts we translate.

Don Gcig

The first study case concerns the term *don gcig,* which is taken from the *bsdus grwa* or *Collected Topics* type of literature. Two properties such as being impermanent and being produced are said to be *don gcig* if, and only if, they satisfy an eightfold pervasion (*khyab pa sgo brgyad*). A common way of translating *don gcig* is "synonymous". I will argue that this translation is inadequate because *don gcig* does not correspond to "synonymous" as used within Western philosophical traditions.

The question of synonymity is certainly one of the most difficult within the framework of Western philosophy. The consensus is that nobody has succeeded in constructing strict criteria for synonymity. There is common agreement, however, that synonymity should be understood to imply a relation between two terms that is stronger than the mere equivalence of the phenomena they denote. Two phenomena, or rather two propositions, are logically equivalent if, and only if, one is the sufficient and necessary condition of the other and vice versa. For example, the two properties of being impermanent and being produced are logically equivalent because any phenomenon that is impermanent must necessarily be produced and vice versa. Moreover, a thing's being produced is sufficient to establish it as being impermanent. A thing's being understood as being produced, however, is not sufficient to make it understood as being impermanent. Being produced is, therefore, not cognitively equivalent to being impermanent.

Logical equivalence of the phenomena expressed by two terms is a necessary condition for the synonymity of these two terms but not a sufficient one. Two expressions are synonymous if, and only if, in addition to the phenomena they refer to being logically equivalent, they are cognitively equivalent. That is to say, that the knowledge of one must imply knowledge of the other. This is certainly not the implication of *don gcig,* for this relation holds between phenomena whose cognitive meaning is different, as for example, being impermanent and being produced.

I would like to argue that the translation of *don gcig* as synonymous is erroneous and I attempt to draw some conclusions from this failure. One may wonder what is wrong with translating *don gcig* as synonymous?

To translate *don gcig* as synonymous creates confusion about the meaning of both terms. Whereas synonymity implies a cognitive equivalence between terms, *don gcig* does not. The possibility of a relation of cognitive equivalence, contrasted with one of logical equivalence, between two phenomema such as being produced and being impermanent is explicitly denied by Dharmakīrti (VII A.D.) and his commentators. Rgyal-tshab (1364-1432), for example, explains that the words "sound is produced" state the fact that sound is produced and not other facts such as sound being impermanent because each such fact is realized differently from the other. Since their cognitive meaning is different they cannot be synonymous.[2] It is therefore not accurate to translate *don gcig* as synomymous.

There does not seem to be any backing in the Buddhist philosophical tradition for such a translation. Moreover, it is extremely unlikely that one could find support in the Western tradition for the radical reinterpretation that the translation of *don gcig* by synonymous would necessitate.

The word synonymous should be reserved for translating *rnam grangs pa (paryāya,* when referring to words). This word used in Sanskrit poetics carries the sense of synonymous. Patañjali (Ist.

century B.C.) has drawn attention to the fact that there are different words with the same sense as well as similar words that have different senses. The latter ones are called *nānārthaśabda* and are an important topic in the grammatical theories. The former are called *paryāyaśabda* and are not considered a major problem by grammarians.[3] As Renou says, this expression is equivalent to synonymous.[4]

My proposition for the translation of *don gcig* is equivalent, but my point here is not just to suggest such a translation. I would also like to draw our attention to the fact that a literal translation does not guarantee the correctness and reliability of the translation of a given term. Literal translation is a necessary starting point but cannot be taken as normative.

The translation of *don gcig* as synonymous is the result of a misplaced effort to use mere literal translation. The idea is that the word *don* means "meaning" and *gcig* means "same". So we have "same meaning," which is then transformed into "synonymous." Let us first notice that the problems raised by such a translation could have been avoided if one had paid greater attention to the Sanskrit of the term *don, artha,* which more often than not means "object", or "thing." So a good literal translation of *don gcig* should be "same thing," a rather unsuggestive translation. Even if we adopt the correct literal translation, which is not "synonymous" but "sameness of object" (to be understood in terms of reference), our translation will still be lacking.

In this case, the successful translation of *don gcig* is greatly helped by diverse factors such as knowledge of Sanskrit and acquaintance with the Western philosophical background of the terminology. A purely lexicological and literal approach is not enough for a good translation of *don gcig.* This case shows that we cannot rely solely on a lexicon but must engage the meaning of the terms we translate as well as the sense of their translation.

Universals and Particulars

The second case raises different and in fact more complicated questions. The translation of the terms *spyi bye brag* reveals other problems posed by the translation of technical terms. I will not consider the problems raised by the translation of the term *spyi* (*sāmānya*), which can be translated quite safely as universal. The word *bye brag' (viśeṣa)* is more complicated. The first temptation could be to refer to a lexicon and translate such a term on the sole basis of the definition we find there. The *Collected Topics* literature offers such a definition, which might tempt translators in believing that their tasks are over. Although this lexicological procedure can be successful, it presents some dangers which I will attempt to illustrate here.

Phur bu mchog 'byams pa rgya mtsho's (1825-1901) *Collected Topics* defines *bye brag* as "that phenomenon which is subsumed by its type (*rang gi rigs yod pa can gyi chos*)," a rather circular definition. It further explains the notion of *bye brag* by elaborating criteria of particularity (*bye brag yin pa'i 'gro tshul*) to formulate an explanation that does not refer back to universals. Following this type of literature, we would translate this word as particular. I am arguing that this translation cannot be adopted unproblematically because it fails to capture an understanding of the word *bye brag* which is important for the Buddhist logico-epistemological tradition.

I will first consider the ideas of Sakya-mchog-ldan (1428-1507) on this topic, showing their relevance to the understanding of *bye brag*. One may wonder why the conflicting understandings found among Tibetan thinkers should be taken into considration by a translator. I am not arguing that the the translator must always take into account all the interpretations of a given concept, for that would be quite difficult and at times uselessly complicated. Not every difference among Tibetan thinkers is equally important. Often, however, these differences are useful, for they alert us to difficulties found in the original sources. Let us examine one case where such conflicting Tibetan views alert a reader to the varied senses of a term in a single text.

Sakya-mchog-ldan on Bye brag

Śakya-machog-ldan's anti-realism is not limited to *spyi* (universals) but also concerns *bye brag*. For him the distinction between these two concepts does not concern reality but relates only to concepts. Universals, it follows, are not properties instantiated by their particulars but unreal conceptual distinctions. It is impossible, then, to describe *bye brag* as real things that instantiate universal properties, as they are understood by dGe-lugs-pa thinkers.

Sakya-mchog-ldan defines *bye brag* as "that assemblage of two differentials that are not only different from their discordant types but also from their concordant type."[6] An example is the conceptual distinction that we make when we think of a particular cow as being both a bovine and an animal, thereby particularizing the cow among other animals. A *bye brag, moreover,* is to be understood as common locus (*gzhi mthun*) between two differentials (*ldog pa, vyāvṛtti*). It differs from a *spyi* (universal in that, whereas the latter appears to thought as a single differential, the former appears as the common locus of several differentials.[7] It is not to be confused with the real things that it differentiates. It is clear that for Śakya-mchog-ldan *spyi* as well as *bye brag* can only be conceptual entities.

Sakya-mchog-ldan does not deny that the word *bye brag* is sometimes applied to the individuals that are differentiated by a differential.[8] He also concedes that Dharmakīrti sometimes uses the word *viśeṣa (bye brag)* in this sense. He maintains, however, that such a description, when applied to an individual, can only be a loose way of talking (as when we say "a particular cow"). This common usage is not the philosophical concept of *bye brag*. For Sakya-mchog-ldan, philosophical understanding, however, cannot be satisfied by the usual practical understanding of *bye brag*. For when pointing at a pot we say "this golden pot is a pot," the real subject of predication, this golden pot, is not the real golden pot but the conceptual distinction of such a pot as opposed to other kinds of pot. Therefore, *bye brag* characterized as the subject of predication of a *spyi* (universal) cannot be the real thing instantiating a general property as common folk and realists assume.

How does the view of the Sa-skya master compare with its Indian source on this subject? My answer to this question will be tentative and nuanced, for only an exhaustive analysis of Dharmakīrti's work can decide the meaning of *viśeṣa (bye brag)*.

Dharmakīrti's use of the concept of *viśeṣa* is far from systematic. Depending on the context, he means different things by the same word. Sometimes it means a conceptual distinction and is then the equivalent of *bedha* (*khyad par*). The Tibetan translation is not very helpful, for that also is not systematic. The *viśeṣa* and *bedha* seem to be indiscriminately translated by either *bye brag* or *khyad par* regardless of the original Sanskrit or the word's contextual meaning. At this stage, my clearest conclusion, which is not entirely trivial, is that both meanings (conceptual distinction and particular thing) are found in Dharmakīrti's works. Let us briefly examine two cases in which the different senses of *viśeṣa* are fairly clear.

Viśeṣa sometimes refers to different substances. For example, when describing differences in the way sense consciousness and thought refer to real individuals Dharmakīrti says:

> Because *viśeṣa* (particulars) do not conflate, conventional appellations do not apply to real things as does perception.[9]

Here the word *viśeṣa* applies to particular and discrete things which have been artificially synthesized by thought into unitary concepts.

There are other cases in which the same word refers to conceptual distinctions rather than real things. In discussing Dignāga's presentation of the nature of a thesis (*pakṣa, phyogs*) Dharmakīrti thus responds to the Sāṃkhya view:

> Depending on the way of stating the argument, the reason is stated as a *viśeṣa* (conceptual distinction) of the subject or the predicate.[10]

Here *viśeṣa* refers to a conceptual distinction made in reference to the subject of predication. This meaning of *viśeṣa* is quite similar to what Sakya-mchog-ldan means by *bye brag.*

My object here is not to analyze whether Sakya-mchog-ldan is right or wrong, but to appreciate the conclusions that we can reach on the basis of his remarks. My analysis has shown, I believe, that his understanding corresponds to at least some of the uses of the word *viśeṣa* in Dharmakīrti. This in itself is enough to demonstrate the difficulties involved in translating *viśeṣa* as particular. For, in certain cases the word means more "particularizer" than particular. Since this understanding is found not only in Sakya-mchog-ldan but in Dharmakīrti himself, the translator might be well advised not to ignore the existence of two quite different understandings of *bye brag.*

The first question raised by my analysis is bound to be: what is the translation? I have to confess my embarrassment, for I do not have a ready-made translation that would cover both meanings of *bye brag.* I wonder even if there is such a translation (my secret hope is that somebody will jump up and say: "this is it, you dullard!") In the absence of a clear candidate, what can we do? We can use the Sanskrit word (viśeṣa) or the Tibetan *bye brag* and leave it untranslated. We can use different translations for the two understandings of the word, such as particular and "particularizer". Or we can use the word particular as applying to both, thereby redefining it to encompass both meanings. Whatsoever the solution we adopt, it is clear that the definition given by the *Collected Topics* cannot be used without addenda. I am here suggesting the difficulties of the definitional approach, but also the necessity of paying attention to the larger range of contexts in which concepts are used. This example taken from the literature of the logico-epistemological tradition shows the help available from various schools within the Tibetan tradition. The translator of Tibetan texts dealing with logic and epistemology might benefit from several traditions, presenting a richer and more accurate picture of Buddhist logic and epistemology. The example of *bye brag* has shown that the difference between Sakya-mchog-ldan and dGe-lugs pa authors is not just a result of the idiosyncracies of these thinkers but reflect some of the difficulties found in Dharmakīrti himself.

Conclusions

These two case studies are quite different. In the first case, there is a relatively clear answer to the question of the translation of the technical term *don gcig*. In the second case, such a clear solution is more difficult. In the first case, the resolution of our problem came from the knowledge of diverse contexts such as Western philosophy, Sanskrit poetics, etc. In the second case, knowledge of different Tibetan views on the topic was helpful for at least pointing out the problems involved in translating *bye brag*. Knowing the history of this word in the Vaiśeṣika school would also be helpful in this case, since the genealogy of the concept may suggest a translation or shades or meaning.

The conclusion from my very sketchy analysis is that translation should not proceed in a purely lexicographical way. The development of ever better lexicopgraphical tools is certainly important in the work of translation. However, a purely literal or definitional approach is simply not enough to determine accurate translations. We also need to be attentive to the varied contexts to which our translation relates which differ from case to case. This, however, is also insufficient. We need to consider how the term is understood in other relevant traditions. For example, in our second case the study of Sakya-mchog-ldan's views reveals important meanings of the notion of *bye brag* otherwise potentially unnoticed.

From this discussion, there does not appear any definitive rules informing us as to which contexts are relevant to our work. All that we can hope for are guidelines that contribute to an ever increasing awareness of the historical and, therefore, necessarily limited nature of the task of translation.

Notes

1. Since this essay examines problems of translation, it does not investigate the differences between the way in which *don gcig* is used within the dGe-lugs-pa school and its understanding in other segments of the logico-epistemological tradition. Rather, assuming the dGe-lugs-pa understanding of the concept, I examine whether its translation as synonymous is possible or not.
2. Rgyal-tshab, *tshad ma rnam' grel gyi tshig le'ur byas pa'i rnam bshad thar lam phyin ci ma log par gsal bar byed pa* (Varanasi: Press of Elegant Sayings, 1974-5), 81.4-82.16.
3. K.K. Raja, *Indian Theories of Meaning* (Madras: Adyar Library, 1963), p. 32.
4. L. Renou, *Terminologie Grammaticale du Sanskrit* (Paris: Champion, 1942), p. 202.
5. Phur bu mchog 'byams pa rgya mtsho, *Tshad ma'i gzhung don 'byed pa'i bsdus grwa rnam par bshad pa rigs lam 'phrul gyi lde mig las rigs lam che ba rtags rigs kyi skor* (Bylakuppe, India: Sera Jay's Library: block), 21.a.1.
6. rang gi rigs mi mthun pa las log cing rang dang rigs mthun pa nang las kyang ldog pa'i ldog pa gnyis tshogs/Śākya mchog ldan, *Tshad ma rigs gter gyi dgongs rgyan rigs pa'i khor los lugs ngan pham byed* (Collected Works X. Thimphu [Bhutan]: Kunzang Tobgey, 1975), II.118.14.
7. Śākya mchog ldan, *Pham byed,* II.119.5.
8. Śākya mchog ldan, Pham byed II.215.3. A smilar view is expressed by Go rams pa bsod nams sen ge, *Tshad ma'i rigs gter gyi dka' gnas rnam par bahad pa sde bdun rab gsal,* in the Complete Works of the Great Masters of the Sa sKya Sect. Tokyo: Toyo Bunko, 1968, XII.1.1.1-167.3.3 *Ga,* 1.a-334.a., 43.b.1-2.
9. ananvayād viśeṣāṇāṃ saṃketasyāpravṛttitaḥ/ (khyad par rjes 'gro med pas na / brda ' jug pa ni med phyir ro/.Y. Miyasaka ed., *Pramāṇavārttika-Kārikā* (Tokyo: Acta Indologica, 1971-2), III.128.ab. I am here giving the order of chapters in accordance with Steinkellner's *Verse-Index of Dharmakīrti's Works.*
10. viśeṣas tadvyapekṣātaḥ kathito dharmadharmiṇoḥ/ (de ni ltos nas chos dag dang chos can khyad par yin par brod). Miyasaka ed., *Pramāṇavārttika,* IV.31.ab

An Opinion on Translating Buddhist Terminologies

(Focusing on the Term *Pratītyasamutpāda*)

Chogkhan Thubten Tandhar

Gyaltsab Chosje Dharma Rinchen has said in his famous commentary[1] on Ācārya Dharmakīrti's *Pramāṇavārtika* that, "without depending on the teachings of Buddha, if no one can even speculate on subtle impermanence, selflessness, and so forth, how can anyone understand them."[2] As the Dharma is a very uncommon teaching, it requires uncommon terms to express it.

Pratītyasamutpāda is the key[3] to the treasure of the fully enlightened teacher's dispensation as well as the essence of that treasure.[4] All the great Indian and Tibetan followers of Śākyamuni in the past were of the view that this is the basic tenet that differentiates Buddhist philosophy and the Buddha, from other philosophies and teachers.[5]

The different Buddhist schools of thought evolved mainly through their different interpretations of this fundamental philosophy of *pratītya samutpāda* (Pali, *paṭicca samappāda;* Tibetan, *rTen Cing hBrel hByung;* English, personally, I prefer 'dependantly relatedly origination'). *Pratītyasamutpāda* is, undoubtedly, one of the most important terms in the Buddhist lexicon. However, different Buddhist schools propound different explanations and interpretations of it in accordance with the profundity of their understanding. The "second Buddha," Ācārya Nāgārjuna, commenced his greatest philosophical work, *Mūlamadhyamakakārikā* with a praise to the Buddha, for his teaching of *pratītyasamutpāda.*

When we translate such exclusive terms into other languages, we should put all our efforts into producing terminologies which are both exclusively Buddhist[6] and at the same time potentially acceptable to all Buddhist schools. And it is very important that these terms also convey, as far as possible in the translated languages, all the subtle implications that the original Sanskrit or Tibetan conveys.

A great many number of scholars use "causality" to translate *pratītyasamutpāda*. This term may find support with the "Realist" schools of the Vaibhāṣikas, Sautrāntikas and Cittamātras. They accept only the *pratītyasamutpāda* of cause and effect. To the followers of Nāgārjuna and his Madhyāmika, the term "causality" appears to be very limited, which fails to convey the two higher levels of meaning that the original term does, that is, the *pratītyasamutpāda* of the part and whole, and the *pratītyasamutpāda* of the imputation and the basis of imputation.[7] Both the Svātantrika Mādhyāmikas and Prāsaṅgika Madhyāmikas propound that all phenomena do "dependantly relatedly originate" from their parts. Moreover, the Prāsaṅgikas maintain that all existences, including permanent phenomena, "dependantly relatedly originate" from the conception too. No Mādhyamika accepts the eastern part of the sky as a cause of the sky or the conception that conceives sky as its cause. As the other Buddhist schools, they do not propound the tenet of causality of permanent phenomena. Hence, the sky is asserted to be *pratītyasamutpāda* though it is devoid of causality. Any phenomenon which has cause and effect is necessarily an impermanent phenomenon.

Sāṃkhya, Vaiśeṣika, Naiyāyika, Nirgrantha, and many other ancient *darśanas* accept the system of cause and effect as well as a karmic linkage.[8] But these non-Buddhist schools reject the exclusive philosophy of *pratītyasamutpāda*.[9] Is their non-acceptance of this philosophy a consequence of their belief in the permanent and absolute person-ātman?

We come across a number of works which have made use of other terms for *pratītyasamutpāda*, such as," relativity," "conditioned co-production", "the chain of conditioned arising," "causal genesis," "dependant arising," and so forth. Each of these terms may have their specific merits; for instance, the term, "relativity" may attract admirers of Einstein and so on.

However, the usual and common meanings of these expressions may be misleading to the readers, making them misunderstand the exclusive Buddhist philosophy for common philosophy of Buddhists and non-Buddhists. The great Tibetan scholar, Tsonkhapa, has emphasized the importance of Ācārya Nāgārjuna's praises of the Buddha's authoritative and independant exposition of *pratityasamutpāda*.[10]

The power of intellect should, of course, flow freely to fathom various meanings of the different levels of these subtle and profound terms. But when we take the extreme unnecessary liberty of translating a single Sanskrit or Tibetan term in a dozen different ways, we are, I think, contributing more to confusion than to clarity.

It would be an excellent idea to form a group of distinguished scholars, under the guidance of the universally respected scholar, His Holiness the Dalai Lama has a plan to develop an English Bye Brag rTog Byed Chen Mo (Mahāvyutpatti).[11] This, I feel, will go a long way towards solving the confusion often created by using in translation a variety of expressions for a single term in the original that has some precise meaning. This will then help in presenting the Dharma and Buddhist studies in a better focus for those who study these subjects through English.

Notes

1. Gyaltsab Je's rNam ḥGrel Thar Lam gSal ḥByed is the main commentarial source for the famous annual studies on Pramānavartika called Jang Gunchos.
2. Ibid. (Sarnath, 1986), p. 228.
3. Alagsha Ngawang Tandhar, rThen Brel bStood Paḥi bKah ḥGrel Rin Chen Phreng Wa (Geshe Yeshe Tobden, ?), p. 10.
4. Acharya Nāgārjuna, Suḥrllekha, 111.
5. Acharya Tsonkhapa, Drang-Nges Legs Shed sÑing Po (Mani Printing Press, Kalimpong), pp. 118-20.
6. Even in the Tibetan Buddhist tradition, though there is no basic difference in the ultimate philosophy among the four major sects, the "tainting" of each other's exclusive terms of different traditional teaching lineages was strongly objected to. His Holiness the Dalai Lama always emphasizes that the practice of Sre Lhad Med Pa (pure and untainted) does not mean an individual not practicing various traditions, but it means that particular tradition's exclusive vocabulary should not mixed with that of another. Refer to lTa ḥkhrid Yid Kyi Mun Sel by Khedub Chosje Gelek Palsangpo.
7. lChang kya Rolpaḥi rDorje, gGrub Tha Thub bsTan Lhun Poi mZes rGyan (Namgyal Monastery, 1984), pp. 487-93.

8. Jamyang Zhepai Dorje, gGrub Tha ḥKhrul sPong gDong lNgaḥi sGra dByangs (Tibetan Cultural Printing Press, Dharamsala), pp. 3-12.
9. Acharya Tsonkhapa, Drang Nges Legs bShad sÑying Po (Mani Printing Press, Kalimpong), pp. 119-20.
10. Ibid., p. 114.
11. The standardized Tibetan-Sanskrit dictionary compiled by lotsāwas and panditas including the three famous translators—Ska ba dpal brtseg, Cog ro kluḥi rgyal mtsan and Zhang Aeshe in the eigth century during the time of King Khri srong.

On the Usages of the Pronoun "Khyod"

Shunzo Onoda (Kyoto, Japan)

The pronoun "khyod" originally and normally means "you" as the second person pronoun in the daily usage of ordinary Tibetan, but in terminology at monastic debate it has a special usage as a variable logical operator as in the following:

> *khyod dmar po ma yin pa dang dmar po khyod yin pa gnyis kyi gzhi mthun gzhog* (Show a common instance of "*khyod* is/are not red [colour]" and 'red is *khyod*"!)

In this case, *khyod* is a variable. In other words, the opponent can apply any word to this unknown item *khyod*. For example, the opponent can substitute "existence (*yod pa*)" for the variable. "Existence" itself cannot be said to be red, and therefore we can say that "existence is not red (*yod pa dmar po ma yin*)." We also say "red [colour] is [an] existence (*dmar po yod pa yin*)." The opponent can reply that "*yod pa*" is a common instance of "*khyod dmar po ma yin*" and "*dmar po khyod yin.*"

If the opponent would like to present as a correct solution "yod pa", he states "*yod pa chos can*! (lit. [when you adopt] *yod pa* as the subject [the formula is correct])." This "chos can (subject)" here does not mean *dharmin* as in Indian logic. It signifies what is to be substituted for "khyod". The "chos can" which the opponent presents corresponds to the topic of the proposition, and the proposition can then be reconstituted as "*yod pa., chos can/khyod dmar po ma yin/dmar po khyod yin* (lit. yod pa. the topic, *x* is not red, [and] red is x)". It can be translated as follows : "If you substitute *yod pa* for the function *x, x* is not red and red is *x*." In other words, we have here what can be expressed in mathematical terms as a solution for the unknown *x*. Whatever is denoted by "chos can" can be substituted for the variable "khyod". This principle applies whether the contents of "chos can" are words, sentences, or even phrases which alone do not make logical sense.

Using "khyod" we can make various types of statement such as:

sgra chos can/khyod mi rtag pa yin ([when you substitute] "sound" for the *khyod* [as the variable *x*], [it can be said that] *x* [i.e. "sound,"] is impermanent)

The item "khyod" can also be used as the predicate of a statement:

yod pa chos can/bum pa khyod yin ([when you substitute] "existence" for the *khyod* [as the variable x], [it can be said that] vases are x [i.e. vases are "existents"])

yod pa chos can/ bum pa khyod kyi bye brag yin ([when you substitute] "existence" for the *khyod* [as the variable *x*], [it can be said that] vases are a species of *x* [i.e. a particular instance of "existents"])

In the latter case, "khyod" is used as a part of the predicate of the statement.

One can use many "khyod" or variables within a single statement:

bum pa chos can/ khyod khyod dang gcig yin ([when you substitute] the "vase" for the *khyod* [as the variable *x*], [it can be said that] *x* is identical to *x* [itself]

Statements which point out the relationship of "pervasion" also become a stage for the application of "khyod":

bum pa chos can/ khyod yin na yod pa yin pas khyab ([when you substitute] the "vase" for the *khyod* [as the variable *x*]. [it can be said that] whatever is *x* must be an existence)

In logical consequences also, this relation between "khyod" and "chos can" is maintained:

bum pa chos can/ khyod khyod dang gcig yin te/khyod yod pa'i phyir ([when you substitute] the "vase" for the *khyod* [as the variable *x*], *x* is identical to *x* itself because *x* exists)

Various techniques of logical "tricks" which are usually deployed in oral debating have been invented on this principle. For example:

dkar po'ang khyod yin, dmar po'ang khyod yin na, dkar dmar gnyis ka khyod yin pas a khyab (If both white and red as well are *x*, then are the pair white and red necessarily *x*?)

Given this question, the opponent tries to find a counter example (ma khyab pa'i mu) which proves that the antecedent is not pervaded by the consequent. In this case, the antecedent is the condition that white is "khyod" and red is also "khyod", and the consequent is the condition that the pair white and red are "khyod". A counter example should be something which fulfils the antecedent but contradicts the consequent when the "khyod' is substituted by the same single term or sentence.

The correct solution for this question is "ma khyab (unpervaded= not necessarily)" and a counter example is "gcig (singular)". When we substitute "gcig" for "khyod", the antecedent would be:

> *gcig chos can/ dkar po'ang khyod yin, dmar po' ang khyod yin* ([when you substitute] "singular" for the *khyod* [as the variable *x*], both white and red as well are *x*)

The consequent, however, would then be:

> *gcig chos can/ dkar dmar gnyis ka khyod ma yin* ([when you substitute] "singular" for the *khyod* [as the variable *x*], the pair white and red are not x)

One cannot say that the pair, white and red, are singular. Thus when one uses "khyod" for a variable, and moreover uses the *khyod* as a sentential predicate, it becomes sometimes quite complicated and may create knotty puzzles for the beginning students.

One principle of verbal art in Tibetan monastic debate is the use of phrases open to various interpretations, or misinterpretations, through which the debater, as it were, fools his opponent into selecting the wrong meaning for a statement. For example, hearing a verbal question like the following.

> *ri bong khyod kyi mgo la rwa yod na/ ba glang khyod kyi mgo la rwa yod pas a khyab/*

the opponent probably thinks that the question means: "if there are horns on the head of a rabbit, then must there be horns on the head of a cow also." Now, there can never be a horn on a rabbit. Since the principle is that "if one assumes something is the horn of rabbit, then it can be anything imaginable (*ri bong rwa yin na, gang dran dran yin pas khyab*)," it seems as if the necessity of a rabbit having horns follows from the fact of a cow having horns. However, when one substitutes a phrase like "ma yin par gyur pa'i ba glang dkar po" for the content of "khyod", then the construction of this sentence will be changed as follows:

> *ri bong <ma yin par gyur pa'i ba glang dkar po>'i mgo la rwa yod na, ba glang <ma yin par gyur pa'i ba glang dkar po>'i mgo la rwa yod pas a khyab* (if there are horns on the head of a white cow which has not been a rabbit, then there must be horns on the head of a white cow which has not been a cow?)

This consequent is internally inconsistent; therefore, the logical necessity cannot be established. In this case, the meaning of *<ma yin par gyur pa>* by itself is "that which has become *ma yin pa* [as one of the two divisions of ways of existence: *yin pa* and *ma yin pa*]". But when the phrase is used as a predicate to a sentence such as *ri bong ma yin par gyur pa,* it means only "that which has not been a rabbit", so the construction of the sentence is completely changed.

The construction can also be radically changed when the conjunction "dang" or a genitive case particle is used before or after the "khyod". For example:

> *kha dog dang khyod kyi gzhi mthun yod na, mdog tu rung ba dang khyod kyi gzhi mthun yod pas a khyab* (if there exist common instances of "colour" and "khyod", then there must exist common instances of the "what is considered to be colour" and "khyod".

"What is considered to be colour (*mdog tu rung ba*)" is the definition of "colour (*kha dog*)". The definition and its definiendum are in a relation of mutual pervasion (*yin khyab mnym*). Therefore, it seems as if this pervasion is established. But when one substitutes "gcig dang mtshon bya gnyis (the pair, singular and definiendum)" for the variable "khyod", the antecedent will become as follows:

> *"kha dog dang <gcig" dang "mtshon bya" gnyis> kyi gzhi mthun yod* (there are common instances of the pair consisted of what is identical with colour and definienda)

However, the consequent will be as follows:

> *"mdog tu rung ba dang<gcig" dang "mtshon bya" gnyis> kyi gzhi mthun med* (there is no common instance of the pair that is identical with what is considered to be colour and a *definiendum*)

and the pervasion cannot be established.

The "tricky question" above is formed by skilfully using two meanings of the conjunction "dang". The conjunction "dang" works not only to connect two nouns but also as the case particle which indicates a starting point of meeting and parting, i.e. "from" or "with" in Enghlish. In this case. "... dang gcig" means "identical with ...".

The genitive case particles used before or after by "khyod" are also able to change their function:

> *kha dog khyod kyi mtshon bya yin na/ khyod kha dog gi mtshan nyid yin pas a khyab* (if "colour" is the definiendum of "khyod", then "khyod" must be the definition of colour.)

In this case a "ma khyab pa'i mu (counter example)" is *"rtag pa ma yin par gyur pa"*. The term by itself means " that which is not permanent". Taking this as a *chos can,* and substituting that for "khyod", we have the following antecedent:

> *kha dog <rtag pa ma yin par gyur pa>'i mtshon bya yin* ("colour" is a definiendum which is not permanent)

But the consequent will be:

> *<rtag pa ma yin par gyur pa> kha dog gi mtshan nyid ma yin* ("that which is not permanent" is not the definition of colour")

The antecedent can be established but not consequent; therefore, the pervasion cannot be established.

The variable "khyod" possesses such ambiguities as those mentioned above; on the other hand, in the monastic disputations, it gave rise to a number of creative and unrestricted ideas. In the Tibetan logical tradition, every term denotes its contents or referent (the normal meaning of the term) and it also means "itself (*khyod rang,* the quotative mention of the term)." Sometimes these two aspects create conflict between them.

The consideration of the concepts "yin pa srid pa" and "yin pa mi srid pa" depends mostly on the usage of this "khyod". "Yin pa srid pa" means "what possiblly exists". This term is used together with other concepts such as "yin pa srid pa'i shes bya (existence that possiblly exists)." The definition of "yin pa srid pa'i shes bya" is *"shes bya yin pa gang zhig/ khyod kyi yin pa yod pa* (1) what is an existence, and (2) there is something that it is)". An example is "bum pa (vase)". A vase is an existence, and a "gser bum (gold vase)" is a vase. Compared to this, there is also a "yin pa mi srid pa'i shes bya (existence which cannot possiblly exist)". The definition is "*shes bya yin pa gang zhig/khyod kyi yin pa med pa*". An example is "ka bum gnyis (both a pillar and a vase)". Both the pillar and the vase are existences, but there is no thing which is both a pillar and a vase simultaneously. So it exists nominally, but there is no instance of something that it is.

The examination of whether something is self-descriptive (homological) or not (heterological) was also one of the early philosophical distinctions made in Tibet. According to the later descriptions of *bsdus grwa* literature, *Phya pa Chos kyi* seng ge was one who brought this way of examination into the presentation of "rdsas chos (substantial phenomena)" and ldog chos (conceptual phenomena)". Phya pa defined "rdzas chos" as:

> *khyod khyod rang yin/ khyod ma yin pa khyod ma yin* ([substantial phenomena are] those in which *x* is *x* is itself, and in which what is not *x* is not *x*)

For example, "the vase" is:

> *bum pa chos can/ khyod khyod rang yin/ khyod ma yin pa khyod ma yin* ([when you substitute] the "vase" for the *khyod* [as the variable x], [it can be said that } *x* is *x* itself, and what is not *x* is not *x*)

Whereas, "ldog chos (conceptual phenomena)" is defined as following :

> *khyod khyod rang ma yin pa' am/ khyod ma yin de khyod yin pa gang rung yin pa* ([conceptual phenomena are] those in which either *x* is not *x*, or in which what is not *x* is x)

Conceptual phenomena are, therefore, non-self-descriptive (heterological) either negatively or positively. The former is called "rang yin pa'i ldog chos (homological [predictable] conceptual phenomena)" and the latter is called "rang ma yin pa'i ldog chos (heterological [non-predictable] conceptual phenomena)". For example, the conceptual phenomena "metaphysical" is metaphysical, and "non-metaphysical" is also metaphysical. Therefore, the conceptual phenomena "metaphysical" can be called a "homological conceptual phenomena (rang yin pa'i ldog chos)". An example of the latter is "concrete". The conceptual phenomena "concrete" itself is not concrete, and "non-concrete" is also non-concrete. Therefore, the conceptual phenomena "concrete" is a heterological [non-predictable] conceptual phenomena.

We do not yet know where "khyod" was invented and since when it has been in use, nor by whom such concepts as "rang ma yin pa" or "yin pa mi srid pa" were invented. Hopefully, future research will clarify some of these points.

My Experience as a Translator

Karma Monlam

Namomañjuśrīghoṣāya

Translation from one language to another has taken place since early times in almost every part of the world, although the translation of literature began at a later stage. In Tibet it became prevalent from the sixth century A.D. onwards.[1]

Translation has made a significant contribution to the transmission of knowledge from one part of the globe to another, and thus has encouraged cross-cultural relations. This is because translation of every single foreign word or term is accompanied by a concept—the idea conveyed by that term— and it is through such processes that Eastern ways of thinking have travelled to the West and vice versa. Most of the translations I am referring to are free and personal, except in case of some religious texts.[2]

However, the process of translating Buddhist scriptures from Sanskrit into Tibetan was well organized, systematic, scientific and disciplined. This was achieved under the patronage of the Tibetan Dharmarājas, with the supervision and guidance of Indian paṇḍitas, in conjunction with the Tibetan *Lotsāwa* or translators' profound knowledge of their subject and linguistic ability. Much could be said about this, but I will only deal with it briefly towards the end of this paper.

Problems

1. Linguistic problems are the main obstacles faced by every translator and they are the main cause of the loss of the aesthetic appeal, rhythm and rhyme, and even the meaning and intent of a piece of writing. We can find examples of this in the Tibetan translation of Ācārya Daṇḍi's *Kāvyādarśa,* especially the *Śabda-alaṅkāra.* Literal transla-

tion of the source language does not make any comprehensible sense. Therefore, the translator has tried hard to convey the meaning in his translation. In so doing, the play of words, which is the essence of *Śabda-alaṅkāra,* is lost and identification of the *Alaṅkāra* in the target language becomes impossible.[1]

2. The cultural background is also a major cause of problems in translation. Take, for instance, the poetic conventions relating to natural and universal phenomena, which are interpreted variously according to different cultural perceptions. In eastern culture expressions concerning the full moon are favoured, while in the literature of western culture the crescent moon finds a more prominent place. The same can be said about creatures such as the peacock, nightingale, crane, raven, elephant, snow-lion, camel, etc.

   Due to cultural differences, literary themes and modes of expression differ so much that a translation is often unable to convey the essential meaning contained in the source language. Rabindranath Tagore himself translated *Raktokarabi* into English in 1923, but they are not exactly identical.[4]
3. Geographical factors also have a role in creating translation problems. A native born and bred in a given geographical environment has certain conceptual tendencies which may not permit the easy accommodation of foreign concepts.

Necessary Qualifications of a Competent Translator

(a) Linguistic competence
(b) Creativity
(c) Understanding of the conceptions involved
(d) Honesty and accuracy
(e) Sympathy towards the author
(f) Knowledge of the cultural background, etc.

Requirements of a Good Translation

(a) It should be done directly from the source language[5]
(b) It should be authentic
(c) It should be faithful to the original
(d) It should retain the flavour of the original

I have tried to raise some of the major points of translation, and since my purpose in attending this seminar is to learn from other scholars attending it, I do not wish to be longwinded.

As the theme of the seminar is Buddhist translations and even that is focused on translation from Tibetan language into other languages, I take the liberty of mentioning that Tibet has one of the richest treasure troves of translation. It was started in the sixth-seventh century. Considering the period of time and manpower involved in this undertaking, no other country or nation has achieved as much in any similar field as this systematic, co-ordinated and disciplined translation of Buddha's teachings[6] and the later works of renowned Indian Ācāryas.[7] If we go through the introductory part of *sGra-sbyor bam-po gnyis-pa,* we will find that the rules established by the paṇḍitas and *Lotsāwa* under the patronage of the kings to ensure the authenticity, uniformity and sincerity of the translation remain practical guidelines for a translator.

But, the problems that confront us today are the opposite of those faced by the *Lotsāwa* of old, for we are translating from, rather than into, Tibetan. Keeping our discussion centred on the translation of Tibetan Buddhist texts especially into English and other western languages, it is obvious that the intercourse between these languages and the Tibetan language is very recent, raw and immature as compared with the relation between Sanskrit and Tibetan. Today, we are not short of manpower and facilities, but we are hampered by an excess of freedom, lack of co-ordination and superimposition of personal notions based on our different cultural and philosophical backgrounds. Therefore, I have a very strong feeling based on my experience as a translator as well as a lexicographer that there should be some kind of central body to co-ordinate the flood of ever increasing translations of Buddhist texts. I do not favour the imposition of an impractical system of standardization, but rather some practical working guidelines which could arrive at consensus on standardization over a period of time.

Notes

1. The translation of the Greek epics and dramas under the orders of the Greek slave-masters to entertain the Roman soldiers was the beginning of Latin literature.
2. (a) At the instance of the emperor Akbar, Abul Fazl, a great Persian prose-writer, revised *Anwar-i- Supayli* and produced Iyar -i-Danish.

(b) The *Holy Bible,* King James version and the *Quran.*

3. Skt., Manen manen sahki ... etc.
   Tib., Grogmo mza-bo-i-skye-bo-la...etc.
4. The principal reason being the differing cultural backgrounds of the two languages.
5. Translation of material already translated from another source is but an imitation of an imitation and should never be encouraged. For instance, the word *artificial* was translated into Chinese as *man-made (ren-zao),* since the Chinese do not have such a concept. Subsequently, it has been translated into Tibetan as *mis-bzos,* despite the existence of *bchos-ma,* meaning artificial.
6. *bKa'-'gyur* 108 volumes consisting of around 1100 titles.
7. *bsTan-'qyur* over 200 volumes comprising approximately 4000 titles.

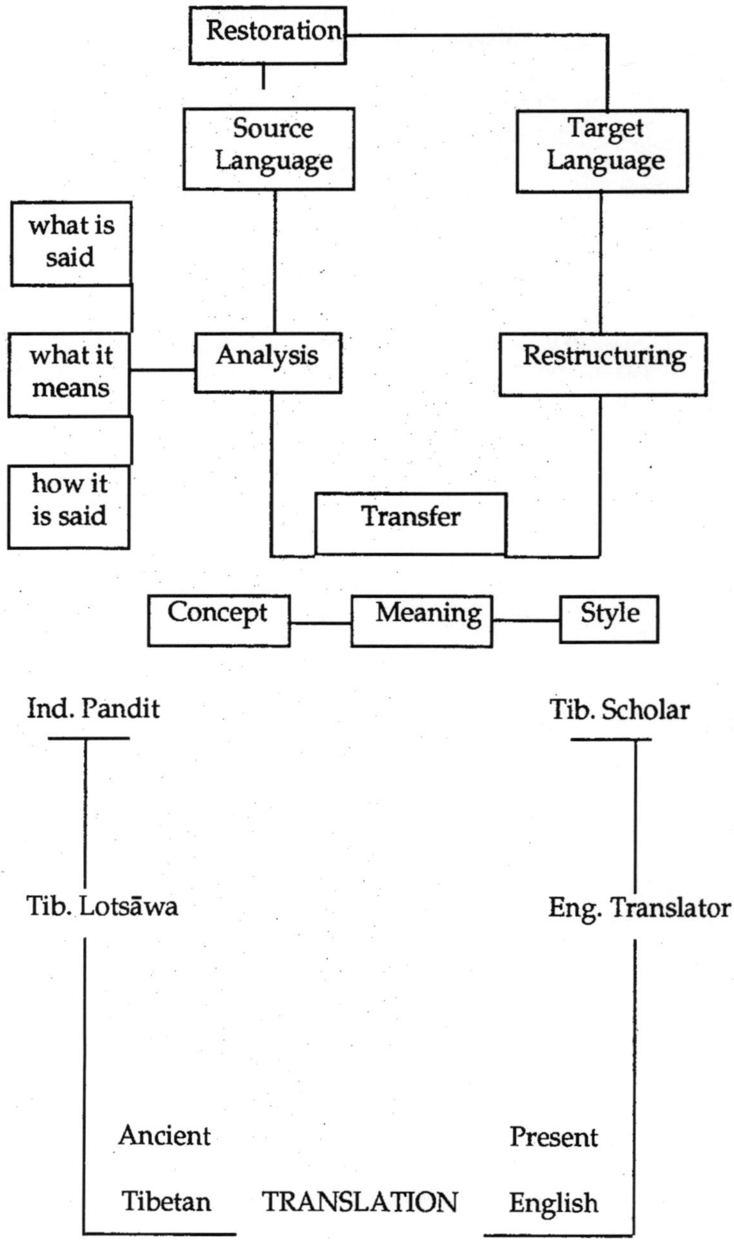
Restoration
Source Language
Target Language
what is said
what it means
how it is said
Analysis
Restructuring
Transfer
Concept
Meaning
Style
Ind. Pandit
Tib. Scholar
Tib. Lotsāwa
Eng. Translator
Ancient
Tibetan
TRANSLATION
Present
English

Editors and Readers

Christian Lindtner

As I received the programme for this seminar on Buddhist translations: Problems and Perspectives, it occurred to me that we might expect to hear a good deal about various theories, problems and experiences pertaining to translation from a Buddhist language (esp. Tibetan) into a modern one (esp. English). There would presumably be a considerable risk of too much repetition, or redundancy.

And so I thought that it would not be a bad idea to say a few words not so much about the tasks of the translator, but rather about the persons upon whose labours and expectations the translator has to rely, namely the *editor* of the texts, and the *readers* of the translation.

The editor is, among other things, a sort of textual detective. Yesterday Dr Samtani and Dr Saito gave us some fascinating glimpses into this workshop.

What we are talking about is Buddhist philology. The Buddhist philologist works, or ought to work, in exactly the same way that, for instance, a classical philologist works. Only their objects, or areas of study, differ, not their methods.

Traditionally, and very reasonably too, philological inquiry is divided into three stages: (1) textual criticism, (2) higher criticism (i.e. questions having to do with authenticity, date, etc. of texts), and (3) interpretation (or hermeneutics).

A Buddhist philologist is not a theologian, nor is he a missionary. His deepest wish is not to defend or propagate Buddhism. His highest authority ought to be reason and common sense. He is willing to go wherever these authorities intend to lead him. He wants to study ideas and their development in a given context from a historical point of view. His personal belief about the absolute value of these ideas is irrelevant to his professional work. He wants to recreate an image, a living image, of the development and the struggle of the idea and actions of creative and original individuals. It goes without saying that a Buddhist philologist would never even dream of reading feminist or other modern ideas into his text.

A Buddhist philologist, doing editorial work performs textual criticism. As an editor, his highest goal is to present before the public (including the translator) a given text in the form (or *almost* in the form, he may modernize punctuation, etc.) he believes it to have left the hands either of (1) the original author, or (2) the previous editors (redactors), or (3) the translators.

The materials on which he must work are texts as transmitted in manuscripts, or even in print when manuscripts are no more available. Comparing, or collating, the available evidence, his first task is to eliminate those witnesses whose testimony is dependent, or secondary, being merely a copy based on another, more original source.

To take an example. When speaking of Tibetan xylographs we thus usually say that Chone depends on Derge, and Peking on Narthang. This, true enough, is often the case, and would imply that we could eliminate C and P from the apparatus of our critical edition—otherwise it would only burden it. But there are several known exceptions to this rule. This means that whenever editors prepare critical editions of such Tibetan texts in the future—here, of course, I am speaking of canonical texts translated from an Indian language, e.g. Sanskrit — they must in each case try to look upon C, D, P and N with fresh and unbiased eyes. Only if the general rule proves to apply without exception, the editor is permitted, indeed obliged, to eliminate the secondary evidence, as it lacks independent value.

But this primary material is seldom sufficient for the editor to reach his goal, which, as already said, is to establish a given text in the form he believes it to have left the hands of its author, editor, or translator. There is also what we might call external, or supplementary materials. This concept covers a wide and varied ground. Here I need not speak of the value of quotations, "para-canonical" versions, etc. But let me give you a few samples from my own experience as an editor of Buddhist texts. When editing the *Pañcaskandhaprakaraṇa* of Candrakīrti—an Abhidharma treatise from the Madhyamaka point of view—it proved possible to make several corrections (emendations) in the Tibetan translation—our primary textual evidence—by comparing parallel passages in other Abhidharma texts and in other works written by the same author. In other words, it would have been impossible to edit this Tibetan text properly without the help of sources in Sanskrit and Chinese.

Let me give you a specific example. When working on some Nāgārjuna's works it soon became clear that in several cases the available primary material in Sanskrit or Tibetan would not be sufficient for establishing a text that, for various reasons, could be assumed to be more or less identical with the text that the author himself wrote. Thus, for instance, in verse 17 of the celebrated *Suhṛllekha,* the Tibetan version has the word *sems, i.e.* mind or *citta.* All modern translators that I know of as well as later Tibetan commentators have understood it like that. And it makes good sense. But it is wrong. It can, in fact, be shown that Nāgārjuna here is referring to a canonical passage (AN I, p. 283 in the Pāli, see my *Nāgārjuniana,* p. 220). This passage, which Nāgārjuna clearly has in mind, speaks not of mind but of human beings (*puggala*). In other words, *sems* in Tibetan is an abbreviated form, *metri causa,* for *sems can,* living being. Without an awareness of the author's background we would never have known this.

Another interesting case is the same author's *Ratnāvalī* V. 26a. The Sanskrit text (ed. M. Hahn, Bonn 1982) reads *anuvijñaptisaṃyukto.* This reading is confirmed by the Tibetan version: *rjes rnam rig dan ldan rtog.* But it does not make very much sense in the context given. From the context it is clear that Nāgārjuna is referring to an old list of "minor faults" (*kṣudravastuka*). Similar lists are found in several Abhidharma works in Pāli and Chinese, and the corresponding term in Pāli is invariably *anavaññatti,* meaning "freedom from disregard." The Pali reading is not *anuviññatti.* So it is quite certain that Nāgārjuna did not write *anuvijñapti-, but anavajñapti-.* The correct reading is, incidentally, confirmed by the Chinese rendering (*shun jué jué*), and by Nāgārjuna's own subsequent definition. And, naturally, it is the only one that makes sense. How the mistake came about—it must have come about rather early—is easy to account for provided one has some experience with Sanskrit manuscripts. Often the indication of vowels is irregular, *a*-s and *i*-s are confounded. And this, then, is how we end up with the meaningless *anuvijñapti-* (translated by e.g. Hopkins:

"making understood") for a meaningful, historically correct *ana-vajñapti-*, "not to despise...." Again, without a knowledge of Nāgārjuna's sources we would never have known. Even our most learned Tibetan friends would not have been able to save us here.

Let me give you a further example: this time from Āryadeva's *Catuḥśataka* VIII.19 (ed. K. Lang, Copenhagen 1986). It runs:

nānyayā bhāṣayā mlecchaḥ śakyo grāhayituṃ yathā/
na laukikam ṛte lokaḥ śakyo grāhayituṃ tathā//

This celebrated verse, often cited in Tibetan scholastic literature, is rendered as follows by Karen Lang: "Just as it is impossible to make a barbarian understand in a foreign language, it is impossible to make people of this world understand [the truth] without reference to worldly things." In his impressive, but utterly unphilological boom, *Meditation on Emptiness,* London 1983, p. 837, Hopkins translates: "Just as a barbarian cannot be/ Approached without another language/ So the world cannot be approached/ Except with the worldly."—whatever that is supposed to mean!—What interests me here is the reading *nānyayā bhāṣayā,* a foreign, or another language. To be sure, the reading is supported by the Tibetan *skad gzan gyis,* and also by Candrakīrti's commentary. But it is quite wrong.

I am quite convinced that Āryadeva wrote, not *nānyayā bhāṣayā,* but *nāryayā bhāṣayā,*"not in the Aryan language". Students of Sanskrit literature often come across the distinction between the unintelligible language of the *mleccha*-s as opposed to that of the *ārya*-s i.e. Sanskrit. (Some references in my *Nagarjuniana, p. 279.)* So what Āryadeva did was to repeat an old and well-known dictum to the effect that you cannot use the noble Sanskrit language (in which his own *Catuḥśataka* is written!) to teach "barbarians." Quite true too! Again, anyone familiar with Sanskrit manuscripts knows that *n*-s and *r*-s are often written by scribes so as to be indistinguishable. So, without a general knowledge in Sanskrit we would not have known this.

Similar experience could easily be multiplied, but these examples will suffice to establish my point. Before we translate Buddhist texts we must have good and reliable critical editions of the texts we translate. We cannot just go ahead and translate, say from a Tibetan xylograph. A text-critical edition is the first desideratum. The editor of a Buddhist text has a rather heavy burden to shoulder. He must know the main Buddhist languages (esp. Pāli, Sanskrit and Tibetan) very well. He must also have a good general knowledge of all sorts of Buddhist literature, and also of Sanskrit literature in general. He should know some Prakrit, and he should be able to read Sanskrit manuscripts. He must be able to distinguish the various scripts that are and have been used in order to spot out mistakes due to misreadings. And, most of all, nature must have given him the gift of being able to combine, at the right time, the right things in the right place. An editor of works translated form Sanskrit into Tibetan may certainly benefit from consulting his learned Tibetan friends, but their help will seldom be sufficient.

I have now spoken of the first stage of philological inquiry, i.e. textual criticism. But I have not touched upon *all* aspects of editorial work. I have said nothing about lexicography, I have said nothing about punctuation. A minor matter, perhaps, but nevertheless. It would often be wrong simply to "normalize" punctuation found in xylographs, or manuscripts, according to the "rules" of grammarians. Sometimes, I think we face "irregularities" that seem to make some sort of sense. I suggest that we in such cases speak of "pause-commas." It also needs to be considered, especially when one is editing Buddhist texts in Sanskrit prose, to what extent the rules of *saṃdhi* were observed. It seems to me that the rules of orthography and euphony were occasionally and deliberately violated, for instance, for the sake of emphasis, or "punctuation." This is a rather complicated issue because it may well be assumed that scribes—not to speak of modern editors—have often tacitly "normalized" such irregularities. The usage of *saṃdhi* in Pāli, I can assure you, can often give a modern editor a real headache. Even *A Critical Pāli Dictionary*, though in most ways setting the standard, is not consistent in this regard. That the problem is really an old one may be seen from various ancient works on *śabdaśuddhi,* such as the *Mukhabhūṣaṇam* (ed. K.K. Raja, Adyar 1973), or the *Sāhityakaṇṭakoddhāra* (ed. T. Venkatacharya, Delhi 1980). The ideal, however, remains quite clear and beyond question: The editor must try to present his text in the form it is assumed to have left the hands of its author, editor or translator.

There is an exception to this rule, however. Obviously the ancient authors could not be as helpful to their readers as a modern editor can. To facilitate the task of the reader the modern editor should not hesitate to introduce page-numbers, paragraphs, different types, punctuation marks, etc.—even though all these devices were unknown to the ancients themselves. But otherwise the modern editor should not interfere with the old documents.

Most of what I have said till now will not come as a surprise to a Classical philologist. On the other hand, experience shows that not all editors of Buddhist texts are aware of how much they still can learn from their colleagues in the classics.

I need not now waste many a word about the second stage of philological inquiry, i.e. problems having to do with authenticity, authorship, chronology, etc. It goes without saying that such questions must be taken very seriously. Without an understanding of the historical development of Buddhism, we shall end up in a mess that might satisfy mystics and missionaries of Buddhism but by no means scholars.

This finally brings me to the third stage of philological inquiry, interpretation, or hermeneutics. The endeavours of the translator falls into this category. We all know how difficult it is to translate the technical terms in which Buddhist texts abound. Just think of such terms as *dharma, svabhāva, artha, satya, ākāra,* etc., etc.

When I speak of interpretation I do not wish to be misunderstood. I do not mean that we should look upon the old texts through the dim and coloured glasses of, say, Marx, Freud, Adler, Jung, Wittgenstein, Adorno, Chomsky, Niels Bohr, Lévi-Strauss, or other neo-intellectuals whose rather peculiar way of thinking has had, in my opinion, a most obnoxious impact upon modern academic life, especially after World War II. Nor will it do just to understand an ancient text in the light of an ancient commentary. The ancient commentators seldom took a historical approach towards the basic text. Mostly they lacked a sense of history and development of ideas.

Let me just give you one good example of this. All of you are familiar with the final verse of Nāgārjuna's *Mūlamadhyamakārikā* XVIII. 12:

saṃbuddhānām anutpāde śrāvakāṇāṃ punaḥ kṣaye/
jñānaṃ pratyekabuddhānām asaṃsargāt pravartate//

Basically all the ancient commentaries, be they in Sanskrit, Chinese or Tibetan, are in agreement about the interpretation of this celebrated verse: Pratyekabuddhas are able to obtain *jñāna* even though there are no Buddhas or Śrāvakas present. And yet

Nāgārjuna's point was no doubt quite different. He is speaking of three kinds of *jñāna:* the first has to do with *anutpāda,* the second with *kṣaya,* and the third, a result of *asaṃsarga*. Had the ancient commentators taken a philological approach to Nāgārjuna's text they would have asked for his sources. This would have enabled them to point out that Nāgārjuna is here referring to an old canonical distinction between *anutpāde jñāna* and *kṣaye jñāna* (see e.g. DN III, p. 214). This is also the case in *Ratnāvalī* IV. 86 ab:

anutpādo mahāyāne pareṣāṃ śūnyatā kṣayaḥ /

As a rule, then, the best commentary to a given text will not be a later commentator (or a modern thinker), but parallel or related passages in the author's own works, or in works known to him. As a rule, the original (basic) text and its commentaries are two entirely different things. (This does not, of course, mean that one should not read the commentaries; one should, but one should also maintain a *docta ignorantia* about them when trying to understand the basic text on its own merits.)

Before he tackles these problems the translator will do well to think about his audience, his readers. Who reads Buddhist texts in translation now-a-days anyhow? There are, perhaps, three groups: The scholars, the not-so-scholarly, and what we might call the educated lay reader. Their demands and expectations are by no means the same. What sort of work the scholar expects from the translator is clear to all of us. This type of work has a long tradition, especially in Europe. It is characterized by Sanskrit terms being given in brackets, by heavy annotation, a close adherence to the words of the text, etc. It is seldom very philosophical, but very useful for those who are able to read the Buddhist texts in the original language. Often more respect is paid to the words of the text than to the sense of the text. This sort of work, surely, addresses itself to a small group of insiders. If done well it will retain its value for a long while.

Then there is the less scholarly reader. This is really a mixed group, a *mixtum genus* as Cicero would say. It comprises (esp. in the US) dharma-practitioners, young and old people interested in mysticism, and what not. Many of these people, according to my experience, lack elementary knowledge of their own background, have a poor education, but, on the other hand, often have a lot of personal problems. It is a question how much a translator of

Buddhist texts can do for such people even though they may be among his most avid readers. Mr Singh in his paper has provided us with some perceptive remarks about Westerners turning their backs to their own cultural tradition.

The third group in my opinion is the most interesting one. Buddhism, or Buddhist studies, is not just here for the sake of the scholar, or for "dharma-freaks," or believers. This group is probably a rather small one, the educated reader. What is worse, it is constantly getting smaller and smaller. Philology, as I said, is a historical science. Historians believe in the development of ideas. History is not just the past, but also the present. We study it, not for entertainment but for edification. There is a lot of good observation and sound reasoning to be found in many Buddhist texts. But there is also a lot of erroneous and naive ideas in the old texts, e.g. with regard to cosmology. Reason should be the highest judge in sorting and shifting all this.

To be fruitful not just to his own ambitions as an academic, the work of the Buddhist philologist must somehow reach the educated reader. When we translate very technical texts we should probably try to come up with fairly literal translations, but when we translate genuine pieces of literature this will not do. In this connection I may be permitted to quote Mogens Boisen, who has translated more than 700 books—of all sorts—into the Danish language: "The translator—he or she—must possess the ability to *live* him- or hereself *into* the way other people think and feel, just as an actor must be able to, and the actor even has the advantage that he usually only has to play *one* role in a play whereas the translator has to "play" *all* the roles in the book.... The translator of such demanding literature must therefore have experienced life and listened to the many tones on its gamut. This does not necessarily mean that the translator must be an elderly person, but an intensive relationship to life and his fellow human beings is certainly a must for him to be able to fulfil the task. Sorrow and happiness, love and hatred, sex, despair, ecstasy—all have their own language, their own words and phrases. The author has weighed them on an invisible golden scale of inspiration or intuition, and there is a demand on the translator for recreation that rings true, and to be able to do that he need to experience again all that the original author experienced—horror, compassion, or whatever the intention of the author may have been. Here clichés are the translator's worst enemy...."

Please permit me, in this connection, briefly to draw your attention to a fruitful but rather neglected field of comparative studies, viz. translation techniques from Greek into Latin versus translation from Sanskrit into Tibetan (and Chinese). In both cases, we deal mostly with translation of philosophical or religious texts.

How did Cicero translate when he translated from the Greek? In his *De optimo genere dicendi* 14 he says: *non verba adnumerare lectori putavi oportere, sed tamquam adpendere*, i.e. Cicero is not in favour of a literal translation; what is important is an elegant translation that brings out the sense clearly in a natural Latin. Likewise in *De finibus* 3,15: *nec tamen exprimi verbum e verbo necesse est, ut interpretes indiserti solent.* In *Acad. post.* 1,10 Cicero praises the Roman poets Ennius, Pacuvius and Accius for rendering the sense, not the words of the ancient Greek poets: *non verba, sed vim Graecorum poetarum.*

Horace is of a similar opinon when, in his *Ars poetica* III, he says: *nec verbo verbum curabis reddere fidus interpres.* And so is Seneca. For instance, in *Epis.* 9, 2 he observes that *impatientia* would be a literal rendering of the Greek απαυε ια. But the term is ambiguous in Latin and so Seneca proposes a paraphrase: *invulnerabilis animus* or *animus extra omnem patientiam positus.*

But the "free translations" of Cicero were criticized by those who favoured a more literal approach. What is interesting to note in this connection is that the novel approach to translation techniques, the respect for the letter, is intimately related with the new religion. i. e. with Christianity. In the Holy Bible, it is said, everything, even the order of the words, is a mystery. Translators with a religious background, rather than those with a liberal one, could subscribe to the celebrated words: *bella e infedele, brutta e fedele.* Cicero, no doubt, would have preferred: *bella e fedele.*

When the Christian writers called for a literal translation—an *absolutissima interpretatio*—of the Bible this meant that the bad translators, Cicero's *interpretes indiserti,* now had things their way. Now all the Christian translators did a bad job, though. For instance, Anastasius, in one of his letters, complains of a translator who *pene per singula relicto utriusque linguae idiomate adeo fuerit verbum e verbo secutus, ut quid in eadem editione intellegatur aut vix aut numquam possit adverti in fastidiumque versa legentum pene ab omninus hac pro causa contemnatur,* i.e. a translator who, by being too literal, does violence to the norms of both languages as well as to the sense.

How the bad translators violated not only the sense but also the dignity of the Latin language comes out clearly in the case of Greek compounds. Thus υε οδε βε δΤαΤο is now rendered verbatim but not very elegantly by *deicolentissimus.* Cicero rendered the word by *quod estad cultum deorum aptissimum.* The literal translation had a dangerous tendency not only to be ugly but also to be unintelligible, neither beautiful nor faithful. Eventually the humanists reacted against literal translations on aesthetic grounds whereas professional scholars reacted against them on scientific grounds.

The superficial, mechanical way of translation, a mode that exempts the reader from finding any sense in the text, is also to be found today in many modern publications on Buddhism.

One could summarize the above to the effect that the veneration for the letter and for a literal translation has its roots in a fundamentally religious attitude towards the scriptures. As opposed to this the respect for the sense of the original and for the norms of the "target language" is ciceronian, or, if you wish, classical. The antagonism between these two approaches persists to this very day. Some translators from the Greek such as Wilamowitz have come very close towards the ideal: a conciliation of both.

Translators of Buddhist texts no doubt could benefit from paying closer attention to the history of translations of the ancient Greek and Roman authors.

At all events, to quote Seneca: *id agendum, ut non verbis serviamus sed sensibus,* i.e. the translator has to pay more attention to the meaning of the words than to the words themselves.

It is quite clear to me that this is an ideal, and a difficult one at that. Truly educated readers, readers with a classical background, are rare these days. Also Buddhist scholars with a classical background are rare.

A few years ago, Allan Bloom, a classical scholar from the US, published a book entitled *The Closing of the American Mind* (New York 1987). It has the subtitle: "How Higher Education has failed Democracy and impoverished the souls of today's students." Bloom's argument is that many of the evils and confusions in modern Western society are due to the fact that our universities have failed to provide the knowledge of Western classics—literature and philosophy—that formely made students aware of the order of nature and of man's place within it as a moral and intellectual creature. Mr. Bloom certainly has a point, and what he has to say applies, *mutatis mutandis,* to the European scene as well. About our own field Mr. Bloom remarks: "The humanities are like the great old Paris Flea Market where, amidst masses of junk, people with a good eye found cast-away treasures..."

If Buddhist studies are to have a future in the West it must be in a sort of dialogue with the best in Western tradition, I mean, of course, the Greek-Roman heritage.

The revival of classical studies, of a humane or liberal education, if you wish, is a prerequisite. Otherwise, and I have no doubts about this, Buddhist studies will just remain an odd treasure in the curiosity-shop of the humanities.

I hope I have made my point clear. Buddhist studies in the universities are, like all the other departments in the humanities, in fear of being isolated. In fact they already are. It may be a splendid isolation, sure, but still an isolaton that eventually will end up in self-sufficiency and self-poisoning. We have seen it happen in the classics in the universities.

You will recall the verse of Āryadeva quoted above to the effect that you cannot communicate with a barbarian in the noble language of Sanskrit. We, too, obviously face a problem of communication. It is certainly not solved by rendering noble ideas into a barbarian language, i.e. by adapting them to an uncivilized or vulgar mind. One of Denmark's great humanists, Vilhelm Thomsen, once published a booklet entitled *Videnskabens Faellessprog,* i.e. *The Common Language of Science.* Such a thing hardly exists any more. It was lost when scholars lost touch with the classical tradition and turned specialists instead. Unless we somehow manage to learn "the common language of scholars" again—in the old days it was Latin, then to some extent, and for a while, it became English—I do not see how we can really hope to communicate again. There must be something fundamentally wrong when, for instance, I myself cannot understand long passages in a modern English rendering of a Buddhist text without consulting the original!

Communication on an academic level—as on all other levels—pre-supposes not just a common jargon but some sort of common and civilized background.

I have much personal sympathy with Dr Lokesh Chandra's fantastic visions about the revival of Sanskrit culture, if I understood him correctly. I myself am a great lover of Sanskrit literature and philosophy. But can this ever become a Western ideal, even if we are prepared to recall and search for our common Indo-European roots?

Dr Cabezón spoke of *upamāna* as a *pramāṇa*. His point is well taken. It has to do with the necessity of recollecting our own background, a sort of Platonic *anamnesis* is required. Dr della Santina spoke of the necessity of a "cultural context" for successful communication. Quite true. And Dr Napper also made some good points about the buzzwords that quickly change, and modern culture in which fads and styles change so quickly.

Co-Translation: Its Value and Problems

Migmar Tsering

Many centuries ago the great Tibetan *lo-tsa-wa* braved all the climatic, geographical and social hazards to travel all the way to the Land of the Āryas and to study Buddhist literature in Sanskrit language. Their Indian gurus and hosts provided them with perfect guidance and kind hospitality. The result is what we now have—the vast collection of the Bka'-'gyur and Bstan-'gyur. The Tibetan translations of the Tripiṭaka, Tantra and the works of Indian Buddhist masters would not have become so accurate and perfect as is tobe now widely acclaimed had it not been for the joint efforts of the admant Tibetan translators and the skilful Indian paṇḍitas. Translators from both sides made it sure that no words or verses were translated without taking into consideration their complete meaning, explicit as well as implicit. It is, therefore, not surprising that many Buddhist Sanskrit scholars of modern times have found that they could grasp the full meaning of several Sanskrit passages only after consulting the Tibetan translations.

The early translators thought it necessary to join two Tibetan words to construct one where one Sanskrit word would render two different meanings. An example is the translation of the term "Buddha," the enlightened one. While the solitary Sanskrit word means both " sangs-pa," i.e. awakened and 'rgyas-pa," i.e. enlightened there is no one Tibetan word which express both these meanings. Hence, it was translated as "sangs-rgyas," the combination of both. There are many words and terms whose translations demand a full understanding of their etymological explanations which may vary according to different schools of thought. While translating such words it would be inappropriate for the translators to give credibility to one particular interpretation. However, it is another matter that when you analyse certain philosophical points to come to one doctrinal conclusion you need to accept one notion and reject all others.

Interestingly, a considerable degree of dependence is noticed between terminologies and philosophical thoughts. In fact, the terms are coined on the basis of certain ideas but sometimes these terms are interpreted otherwise by those who adhere to different ideologies. Take the example of the term "sangs-rgyas-' bring," i.e. mediocre Buddha, indicating Pratyekabuddha in the beginning of Madhyami avatāra. According to Tsongkhapa, the term Tatvabuddha can be applied to all the three Arhats and when Buddha refers to Pratyekabuddha it should be understood and thereby translated as "De-nyid-rtogs-pa" but not as "Sangs-rgyas." Another example is the term "Pāramita." It is translated in Tibetan as "pha-rol-tu-phyin-pa" meaning "gone beyond" and signifies the Buddha's transcendental knowledge, but is also used as imputed for the attributes of the Bodhisattvas, such as giving, morality, etc. Some scholars, however, assert that if "para" meaning "pha-rol" and "ita" meaning "phyin-pa" are left as they are the meaning would be "gone beyond.' On the other hand, when these two words are joined by adding the singular suffix 'am' to 'para' it would mean 'to be gone beyond" and this refers to the attributes of the Bodhisattvas.

Let us also look at one summary verse in Abhisamayālaṁkāra on the topic of Dharmakāya. According to Arya Vimuktisena and his followers, this verse states that the Dharmakāya is characterized by three Kāyas and Buddha's Activity. On the other hand, Haribadra and others interpret that the Resultant Dharmakaya is symbolized by four Kāyas, including the Realization-Dharmakaya. Some Tibetan scholars following the three kaya system argue that if Dharmakāya is one of the symbolizing factors the Tibetan word "dang" but not "ni" should be used between it and Nirmāṇakāya. They think the word "ni" makes all the difference. However, a modern scholar doing research on the Kāyas said that the Sanskrit śloka mentioned neither "ni" nor "dang."

These examples of Sanskrit-Tibetan translation are presented here so that the same errors are not repeated in the translation of Buddhist texts into other languages, notably from Tibetan into English. If there are many chances of making errors while translating from Sanskrit into Tibetan has a similar sentence structure as Sanskrit then there is little doubt that such chances of shortcomings in the translations with respect to other languages are much more Attempts are being made to retranslate several texts from Tibetan into Sanskrit. It is anybody's guess how far these translators are successful in restoring the lost Sanskrit originals but some of their works are admired as quite accurate by Sanskrit scholars. Such accuracy cannot be expected with regard to retranslating from English into Tibetan. Nevertheless, it is not impossible as long as the English translations are done as perfectly as the Tibetan translations. It is saddening to note that even some reputed scholars take for granted the status of English translations. I remember once being advised by a senior scholar who said, "You can translate straight from Tibetan into English as many texts as possible. It is not as difficult as retranslating Tibetan into Sanskrit."

A need is sometimes felt to trace the source of a term to translate it properly. Take the example of the work *Nārāyaṇa*. It was originally translated into Tibetan as "Sred-med-kyi-bu" and is generally accepted as such. Sakya Pandita, however, said in his Mkhas-pa-'jug-pa'i-sgo that it should have been translated as "Mi'i-theg-pa". Another Tibetan scholar is said to have translated it as "Mi-lam-pa". Here I was appalled to hear a modern scholar comment that this is a case of Pandita not remaining absorbed in concentration (Pan-di-ta mnyam-par-ma-bzhag-pa'i-skabs) meanign that Sakya Pandita was wrong. I would rather say that the scholar's comment is a case of jumping too early into conclusion out of cheap excitement. I have asked several Sanskrit scholars about the source and meaning of *Nārāyaṇa*. No one could provide a satisfactory answer except going through various mythical accounts surrounding *Nārāyaṇa*. Such is the profundity and complexity of the term. A similar case is that of the word *Saraswatī*. While others accepted it in Tibetan as "Dbyangs-can-ma", Sakya Pandita translated it as "Mtsho-las-byung-ba" or "Mtsho-byung-ma".

In English translations there are so many confusing words. To give just a couple of examples, there are the words "undergraduate" and "graduate" for slob-pa" and 'mi-slob-pa" respectively and the word "Abbot" for "Mkhan-po." The latter may sound a perfect equivalent of the Tibetan word but at times scholars use it to mean a head of a monastery who is not necessarily a monk. While the head of a monastery can be a Tantric lay Lama the title of "Mkhan-po" is conferred only on a monk. Without this knowledge one may be easily misled by information such as, "In the Red Hat Sect of Tibetan Buddhism a married Lama can become the abbot of a monastery."

These days we come across translators who cannot speak a correct sentence in Tibetan but translate volumes from Tibetan into English. Had they consulted or sought the assistance of some Tibetan-speaking scholars as the early Tibetan *lo-tsā-wa* had done with their Indian counterparts their works would have been much better. The same can be said of those translators who have a reliable knowledge of Tibetan but lack good command of English, but still insist on translating independently. There are of course some exceptional translators who are endowed with the rare combination of perfect knowledge of Tibetan as well as English. Nonetheless, the outcome of the exertion of two intelligent minds is far better than that of one. History is witness to the fact that despite his excellent command of Sanskrit language Sakya Pandita sought the help of Kashmiri Paṇḍita Śākyaśrībadra in retranslating the Pramāṇavārtika. Indeed he said in the Sa-skya-legs-bshad,

> "When two intelligent persons consult,
> Another better intelligence occurs."

The Importance of Team-Work and Consensus on Terminology in Translating Buddhist Texts

Sharpa Tulku, V.

It has been pointed out, again and again, that Buddhism is not a dogmatic religion but a way of life. Our teacher, the great Śākyamuni, was once an ordinary individual, no more unusual or spectacular than any of us. Living an ordinary life, through his own efforts he discovered the cause of sufferings that are no different from those we ourselves go through. He also discovered their antidotes. Through his immaculate compassion, he attained enlightenment, not for his own complacent peace of Nirvāṇa, but for all living beings. So we know that the teachings and practice of Buddhism originated from an ordinary person who became an extraordinary person, and that he has shown us how we, ordinary beings, can and should become like him.

The first sermon preached by Śākyamuni on the four Nobel Truths are the source of Buddhism which continues to play a very important role in the minds of countless millions. Out of these teachings developed the Mahāyāna and Hīnāyāna, the Pāramitāyāna and Vajrayāna and so forth. The benefit of these teachings, as we all know, did not remain restricted to the fortunate few only who lived in India, but spread to the neighbouring countries in south-east Asia and to China, and gradually to Japan, Mongolia, Tibet, and many other lands.

We know that the Dharma first came to Tibet through the kindness of the great king Songtzan Gampo who sent his minister, Thonmi Sambhota, to India, who studied Sanskrit among other subjects, and on his return to Tibet he set the wheels in motion for the spread of Buddhism throughout Tibet. From that time onwards, many Indian paṇḍits came to Tibet, among whom were

Śāntarakshita, Atisha, and Guru Padmasambhava. On the other hand, a countless number of Tibetan *lotsāwa* went to India. In order to pursue their studies with Indian masters, they had to endure great hardships and face dangers of various nature. Many even sacrificed their lives. Later on, these Indian pandits and Tibetan *lo-tsā-wa* worked together on the translations of many Buddhists texts which continue to be an endless source of information and benefit. Among such works are the Kangyur and Tangyur, and a multitude other texts that have been rendered into Tibetan so precisely.

With the spread of Buddhism from India to other countries, when it was brought to Tibet, much of the living tradition of India of the time was adopted and propagated in Tibet. That way Tibet received the complete range of Buddha's speeches. As His Holiness the Dalai Lama explained in a speech given to a distinguished gathering of the Asia Society in New York city on his first tour of the United States, Buddhism in Tibet is the most complete form of Buddhism today, comprising all aspects of Hīnāyāna and Mahāyāna Buddhism. This is attributed mostly to the selfless efforts of the earlier translators who rendered so faithfully the Buddhist canons from Sanskrit into Tibetan.

How did they accomplish this? The rendering of these original texts was so accurate that nowadays, when many of these texts in the original Sanskrit have been lost, efforts are being made at the Central Institute of Higher Tibetan Studies at Sarnath to reconstruct the original texts in Sanskrit from the existing Tibetan, and the result is proving so satisfactory that many eminent Sanskrit scholars of India are much impressed by these re-translations. I feel that the faithful rendering and the excellent quality of these translations are due in part to the standardization of terminology under the guidance of the Tibetan King Triralpachen, and the credit for this must be attributed to the excellent teamwork performed by the translators. For centuries, Tibetan translators and Indian paṇḍits worked together very closely in translating these Buddhist texts.

For a long time, as we know, Tibet remained a very isolated country beyond the mountain wall of the Himalayas. With the exception of a few scholars, not many people outside of Tibet knew much about the complete form of Buddhism as practised and preserved by the Tibetans. While the pioneering efforts of these scholars were an important beginning to the unfolding of the treasures of Tibetan Buddhism and culture, it has been pointed out that they made serious mistakes in the rendering of many crucial words and concepts, because Tibetan masters were not associated with this task.

Let us now look at the positive side of the Chinese invasion of Tibet. After the forceful occupation of Tibet by the Chinese Communists in 1959, tens of thousands of Tibetan refugees, including many lamas and scholars, followed His Holiness into exile in India, and guided by His wisdom they began to re-establish the seats of learning, even under the very difficult circumstances they lived as refugees. Since then, great opportunities have opened up for closer contact of many Tibetan scholars with people of the rest of the world.

As early as 1960, many masters of the Tibetan language—monks as well as lay people—were invited to study and teach in Indian universities and Western countries, and many non-Tibetans became interested in the Tibetan masters' knowledge of Buddhism, and they took this opportunity to learn more about Buddhism. This brought them close to the Tibetan traditions, and they began to work on the production in western languages as much as possible of the essential teachings preserved by the Tibetans.

As late as 1971, when I first started translating at the Library of Tibetan Works and Archives in Dharamsala, and when His Holiness opened the newly-constructed library and initiated the classes on Buddhism for non-Tibetans, many words and concepts were still very new and foreign to them and their translated forms awkward. I was fortunate to have been selected for training in America in the early sixties for the purpose of doing translation work. Living in America and working among the Americans, I have I hope gained sufficient knowledge of English; and later much practice at the library over the years in both oral and written forms of translation gave me valuable experience about team-work. All this has given me a keen appreciation of the necessity for close collaboration between the native speakers of both languages so that a rendering is not just literal, but may also convey the feeling, the literary style and the subtle nuances of the original language, without which much of the intent of the teachings is inevitably lost. Without collaboration of this kind by native speakers of both languages, serious mistakes are likely to occur.

Tremendous progress is being made in the transmission of Buddhism worldwide. Many full-fledged Dharma centres and organizations have sprung up in different parts of the world. Interest in Buddhism is now also growing in many socialist countries. Not only that; many scholars, both Westerners and Tibetans, have produced excellent works of translation. It is evident, however, that when a translation is the product of a team in which native speakers of the concerned languages have collaborated, it has many advantages; fewer mistakes occur and the quality of the original can be better captured.

Translators I feel should not allow themselves to be carried away by the wish to prove their superiority by using exclusive terminology they have coined. We need to work together with other translators for everyone's benefit. If instead a translator is motivated by a wish to dominate the field, the purpose of preserving the vital tradition of Buddhism is likely to be defeated. If one has a desire to fulfil such ambitions, there are other countless fields of knowledge to which one can devote one's creative energies for achieving distinction.

At this point I would like to draw attention to what His Holiness said, in a discourse on 16 January 1990 in New Delhi, about the great importance of co-operation at every sphere of existence and at every aspect of our life. Pointing to the instinctive co-operative spirit and behaviour among what we call lower beings like the bees, ants, and some other social insects, he said that at the human level also our very existence and survival, our society, our family life, the functioning of all great undertakings is based on co-operation.

We should see the great importance of co-operation in the kind of translation work we are discussing. Co-operation does not reduce the status of a translator, nor does it diminish the importance of his role. The translator bears the responsibility of disseminating the right meaning to the reader who depends for his understanding almost entirely on such translation. Therefore, this is not a matter for indulging in misplaced pride or misguided ambition. Co-operative efforts are necessary for translating all treatises on Buddhism in general, but this is even more necessary for translating philosophical and tāntric texts. One must be particularly careful and take all responsibility, to the full extent of one's ability, for the accuracy of the rendering, and no emotion of any kind be allowed to interfere with the appreciation of one's duty to those who will put these words into practice and strive to achieve the intended results.

In trying to follow the excellent example set in the past by the great translators of India and Tibet, it is desirable to reach some consensus on terminology, to find some common ground for co-operation.

Over the years, in countless translations of Buddhist texts, many individual translators have used terminology of their own coinage in preference to the existing and more comprehensible one. This creates much confusion, particularly if a text translated this way were to be translated back into Tibetan. In that case it would be difficult to find the original terms used. As we know, because of the standardization used in the translation from Sanskrit into Tibetan, it is not only possible but relatively easy to translate from Tibetan back into the original Sanskrit. Although English and Tibetan have completely different grammatical structures, we can maintain certain consistency of terminology, even while maintaining a diversity of styles of presentation. This would make it possible to achieve in translation something similar to what the original is designed to convey.

What I am suggesting here is not an artifical standardization, but that, as the conveners of this seminar have envisioned, among other goals, we set guidelines for developing a consensus. One factor that I think is worth considering in setting such guidelines is the intent of any translation of Buddhist scripture, which is to help the reader to learn what the Buddha intended. When choosing an English word, it should be one which both conveys the meaning of the original expression and also one that does not bear a strong connotation that might prejudice the reader's mind. For example, if the word "sin" is used for translating *sdig pa,* then, although literally these two words may be equivalent, "sin" in English carries a wealth of associations with Christian views, as well as all the accompanying emotional significance, of guilt and so forth. In view of this, it is difficult for the Western reader raised in a Christian culture to be able to investigate with an unbiased mind the meaning of a passage bearing such loaded terms. If the purpose of the reader is to determine for themselves what the Buddha meant, the translator can help immeasurably by providing a terminology with the greatest possible precision and a minimum of cultural ambiguity. Again, this requires both a feeling for and a mastery of the nuances of English and an implicit appreciation of the subtleties of expression in the original language. Having lived with, studied under and worked in close association with native English-speaking people for many years with joy and happiness I suppose I am fairly fluent in English. However, I am fully aware of my own limitations. I can never hope to grasp the subtleties of the English language as well as a native-speaker of it. With due respect to the non-Tibetan translators who speak Tibetan fluently, I must say the same is true for them. Therefore, for achieving satisfactory translation there is no substitute for close rapport between the native speakers of the two languages. This has been amply demonstrated by great translators of the past.

I have done a number of translations on my own, but I enjoyed the greatest satisfaction and confidence in being able to convey the meaning to the best of my ability when I worked in a team.

In conclusion, I must say that this seminar on Buddhist translations is very timely, for more and more Buddhist works in many languages are in great demand, and talented translators are emerging continuously. Here is a precious opportunity to bring their problems and perspectives forward for the consideration of all those who are genuinely interested in solving these problems and ensure that the necessary evolution of accurate Buddhist translation may proceed satisfactorily.

The Author Versus the Subject as the Focus in Tibetan Translation

Glenn H. Mullin

Successful translation of any text involves a number of considerations.

The first and most obvious of these, of course, is the literal meaning of the words; and quite appropriately it is the meaning of the Tibetan texts that has acted as the focal point for the attention so far of Western scholars and translators. Tibetology in this sense has largely come to be regarded more as an offshoot of Indology than as a discipline in and of itself, with researchers concentrating on those texts and subjects most closely linked to classical Indian thought, the systems of philosophical giants such as Nāgārjuna, Āryadeva, Asaṅga, Vasubandhu. Dignāga and Dharmakīrti having taken central stage.

As a result, most translations in English have taken a subject-orientation in their presentation, often to the point of overlooking the function played by the Tibetan author in the process and the presence of that author in his work. The emphasis has been to capture the basic statement of the original as precisely as possible, generally to express this meaning within a philosophical or theological context. A minimum amount of energy has been dedicated to discovering the man (or woman) behind the words, the magician within his creation. This is understandable, given the ostensibly religious nature of most Tibetan writing; and also given the disciplines from within which most western translators are working. That is to say, most translators today are academics whose interest lies not in the art of Tibetan literature *per se,* but rather in the thoughts of the Tibetans on subjects such as *madhyamaka, pramāṇa, prajñāpāramitā, abhidharma,* and so forth.

A number of years ago it struck me that it might be useful to approach the writings of some of Tibet's great authors in a somewhat different manner, to take the focus from textual content to the context of the author's presence in his writings; not his presence in the sense of whether he takes Bhāvaviveka's or Buddhapālita's side in a dispute over an interpretation of a particular verse from Nāgārjuna's *Mūlamadhyamakakārikāśāstra,* nor in the sense of whether he takes *ālaya* to refer to emptiness or the foundation consciousness. Rather, I thought that it might be both useful and fun to see if some of the Tibetan material could work simply as good (albeit somewhat spiritual and exotic) literature.

I decided to take as my subjects the writings of the early Dalai Lamas, their importance to the Tibetan literary landscape, and the availability of their *gsung-'bum* or "Collected Works," making them ideal candidates for the experiment.

This paper, then, may be regarded as an informal report on the experiment: firstly, on the process itself; and secondly, on some of the problems involved in looking for style beyond meaning.

The Process

With a view to translating primarily as literature, and not simply as religious or philosophical grist for the mill, at least as much attention must be dedicated to capturing the spirit of a text as to capturing its meaning. For it is the spirit of the expression that brings moist flesh to the dry bones of flat words and pumps warm blood through the cold veins of literal satement.

But spirit in literature is both subtle and elusive. There is no *mTshan-nyid* text in which we can look up the definition of the spirit of the writings of, for example, the Eighth Dalai Lama. Rather, style and spirit is simply an undercurrent running beneath the ice of transparent script; it is something one senses in literature but cannot quite touch, an atmosphere that pervades the contents of a text yet somehow flows more between the lines than within them. It is the art in the science of writing, a component that cannot be articulated in the concrete terms of a strict categorical outline; yet it is as present and important as the paper on which sits the ink.

To uncover an author's style it is always useful to first look into the source of the writing, which is the author himself. To detect the presence of the man in his writings one must first try to understand just what kind of man he was, and then see how this comes to be embodied in what he writes.

The Dalai Lama literature is thus perhaps an easier corpus of textual materials to work with in this way, for we can still find several biographies of each Dalai Lama, as well as of many of their teachers, students and friends. For example, in preparing my work on the First Dalai Lama I was able to locate different biographies of him, each written from a somewhat different perspective; and also biographies of numerous other personalities central to his life. While researching the second Dalai Lama, I located four different biographies, as well as a brief autobiography.

What is of interest in these biographical material is not so much the historical account of the events in the author's life as the clues to personality and character. Was he stern or kindly, serious or good-humoured, meditative or scholarly (or neither or both), and so forth? How did he speak, dream and spend his time? (One of the First Dalai Lama's biographies records several dozen of his dreams.) Also, what is said about the conditions surrounding the composition of his various works? What did he write at the request of others, and why; and what did he write simply because he was inspired to do? All such information can offer hints to the nature of the man as an author, and thus can contribute to the detection of what could constitute elements of literary style.

The next step is to try and read as many of the author's written works as possible, to see how the human being one encounters in the biographical material is reflected in his writings, and where that reflection is most strong. What titles are written with affection, humour, warmth and enthusiasm; and what (if any) are written with a forced and belaboured pen? How does his writing evolve over the years of his life; what in his literary style changes, and what remains constant. The aim here is to attempt to get a grip on his individual sensitivity to language, and thus on what distinguishes him artistically and literarily from other authors.

Generally, at this point it becomes obvious that some of one's subject's writings have a greater literary merit than others, and are more original in both spirit and letter.(I think it is safe to say that there is a lot of "borrowing" in Tibetan writing, sometimes almost to the point of plagiarism, although it is done more as an act of devotion and flattery than of literary theft. Obviously any piece of this nature, although revealing a relevant facet of the author's personality, will not be as characteristic of his style as will a piece written more freely.)

Also, at this point it becomes clear that some titles afford themselves to translation better than do others, and also to being read simply as literature. In the cases of at least the first four Dalai Lamas, all their writings have a strong spiritual perspective: but this in no way makes them any less valid as pieces of literature. However, if they are to work in translation purely as literature (and not just as a kind of religious or philosophical cookbook or auto-repair manual), their literary as well as their spiritual quality must be conveyed.

Finally, when one has settled on what titles can work as representative of the author, it is useful to read each of them several times, at least one of these readings being with a qualified Tibetan scholar, before putting anything down on paper. This is advisable, in order to gain certainty of the literal meaning and also to discern any literary mechanics being employed. And as Tibetan literature is rather *genre*-oriented, it is also useful to read several works of the same *genre* by other authors, which enables one to get a contrast in styles of treatment.

Tibetan authors generally begin their texts by dividing the contents into three phases: the preliminaries, the actual body, and the concluding procedures. In this classical sense, the above stages of research would all fall under the category of the preliminaries. And probably these phases are the most time-consuming in the overall process. When they have been done well, the actual work of translation usually is fairly smooth sailing.

As for concluding procedures, generally I try to pass the final manuscript around to a few fellow translators for their appraisal; and then try to have a few *literateri* friends who know little or nothing about Tibet or Tibetan Buddhism read through the material, to see if it works as literature in the unreal world of the urban concrete jungle.

Problems in Searching for and Translating Style

The main obstacle in capturing and translating style within content arises from the distance between Tibetan and English literary sensitivity, and the different ways in which the two languages work. Firstly, it is not always obvious just what it is that constitutes an individual literary style in Tibetan writing; and then the task of trying to capture that character in translation becomes something of a delicate task.

It seems to me that literary Tibetan is by nature a somewhat modest and understated language, and its emotion much more subtle than that of English, particularly American English, which in comparison is often quite bombastic and flamboyant. The subtlety of this emotion, working within its own milieu, usually stands out well enough; but if not intensified in English translation it is easily lost. In the Tibetan it can be drawn out over half a folio or more, with a single sentence containing half a dozen clauses and subclauses, each having enough words and meanings to form half a dozen sentences in English. To keep all of this in the Tibetan format generally produces a clumsy and ugly wad of gobble-de-gook with little sense and less literary merit. The style itself must be transposed into a rhythm that recognizes the context of normal English usage, and that utilizes the English environment to create something of the same effect as is created by the passage in Tibetan.

This means that a translated passage in English should generate in an educated English reader the same kind of emotional response as the passage in original Tibet would in a Tibetan reader. If this is not the case, then even if the translator gets the intellectual/ conceptual meaning right he has failed in the sense of a wholistic rendering.

And here we begin to walk on delicate ground indeed, for often we encounter images in Tibetan literature that simply do not work in the same way in English. A Tibetan reading the words in his own language will experience a sensation of "ah, how wonderful," whereas a literal rendition of the same words in English will generate the sense of "how wierd" . This is to say that the real meaning of words is not in what they say but in the impact that they have on the mind of the listener and the reader. The translator is here indeed placed in a quandary. Does he bend the words to bridge the cultural gap, or remain literal and completely lose the author's message and art? A small rock on the road may not disturb someone riding along slowly on a yak; but for someone cruising at full speed in a different vehicle it can break an axle. We don't want to lose sight of the forest by focussing too intensely on the trees, nor do we want to miss the trees by swooning in the grand vision of the forest. A "middle way" seems to be the most appropriate approach.

The handling of technical terms is obviously another problem area. If one wants the English to read as literature rather than as a "how-to" manual, some degree of normalcy in expression is necessary. It may be useful here to look at what the Tibetans did when they translated Sanskrit into Tibetan; when they did not like the aesthetics of the Sanskrit etymology, they simply ignored it and used whatever they felt worked best, such as Sangs-rgyas for Buddha, or Chom-ldan-'das for Bhagawan, etc. Simpler and more common terms are often better left in the original Sanskrit; those that are translated should be recognizable as English. As for the talk of standarization of technical translations and terms that in vogue with certain academics these days, my own feeling is that it is premature. The process is still in a pioneer stage, and the experiments and experiences of different translators offer new directions and possibilities as time goes on. Standardization will have to wait for another century or so.

But in terms of the basic approach to language, here the words of Will Durant, in his preface to the 1927 edition of his *The Story of Philosophy,* come to mind, wherein he defends himself for clarifying the thoughts of the great philosophers by using a popular and contemporary language to express their teachings: "Those ... have only themselves to blame if their exclusiveness and their barbarous terminology have led the world to seek ... what they themselves have failed to give."

Conclusion

I would suggest that it is possible to address the style and spirit in Tibetan literature, provided that sufficient effort is first made to appreciate the textual materials within the context of the life of the author and the Tibetan literary environment, and that one chooses to work on subjects wherein the elements of style and spirit stand out in a sufficiently clear relief.

I would also suggest that some Tibetan literature is so highly technical that style is probably the last thing one would want to consider; though for me, texts of that nature are the last things I would want to translate.

Concerning the degree of literalness that translation should take as opposed to the freedom of poetic licence that a translator can reasonably grant himself, I regard the primary purpose of myself as a translator is simply to bring across the meaning, sense, atmosphere and beauty of the original as well as I am able, to present the text for an educated modern audience much in the same way that one friend attempts to present to another in the best possible light. My interest is not anthropological, nor religious, nor philosophical; it is merely to bring the literature of what to me are great Tibetan authors into English in a way that reflects the greatness of their pens and the wit of their spirits.

In terms of my attitudes toward other translators, I believe there is a place for every approach to translation, provided that a market can be found for the final product. No one approach is ultimately correct for everyone, although undoubtedly some are more successful than others.

I would like to close with a comment made by Professor Jeffery Hopkins during a course on Tibetan language, philosophy and translation techniques that he gave to some of us in Dharamsala in 1974, in which he loosely quoted Nāgārjuna as saying, "What is truth? It is that which helps. And conversely, that which helps has the ring of truth." The context was simply that the best way of translating something generally is the way that brings across the highest meaning to the reader, in the sense of the most useful significance of the passage.

In the end I think history appraises the value of a translation in terms of not the reviews it receives in academic journals, nor how literal it is or is not, but simply how much pleasure it brings to its new audience. Some of the best translations in English have received some of the worst reviews, and some of the most literal translations stand amongst the most clumsy testaments to be found in the English language. The professional translator is not merely documenting material from a source to a target language; it is also his function to speak in a tongue that is both relevant and palatable to his designated audience.

Styles and Problem Areas in Translating from Tibetan into English

Tenzin Dorjee

From prerecorded times the art of translation has flourished as a creative media of communication between peoples of diverse languages and cultures. Down the ages scores of scholars the world over have devoted themselves to the task of translation. Their works, notwithstanding the limitations inherent in translation, have enlightened people about the collective culture and civilization all over the world.

In course of time, scholars have developed various styles and techniques in the approach to translation; however, it is evident from the numerous definitions of translation that despite the best efforts it has not been possible to solve certain basic problems inherent in the nature of such work. I would like to speak a few words on the styles or techniques of translating from Tibetan into English. There are many styles, but I would confine myself to only the following: literal style, concept style and thematic style.

I have compared several well-known translations in English with their original Tibetan texts. I appreciate the great efforts put into these translations; I also appreciate the merit of these translations, but when I look at them objectively some considerations arise to which I wish to draw your attention. It may sound unscholarly, but I will refrain from mentioning any names in this discussion, for I don't want to bring in any person in it.

Although much has been said in favour of translating by concept rather than by words, I have observed that a literal trend dominates the style of most translations. The greatest fallacy I see in this approach to translation is the disparity, and sometimes the mismatch, of the literal sense of Tibetan and English words, such as "novice monk" for *dge tshul pha* and "intention" for *sems pa*; the

Tibetan terms carry shades of meaning that are absent in what is taken to be their English equivalent.

In order to overcome the problems of literal translation some scholars have adopted what I call "a concept style." This style of translation overcomes, to some extent, certain problems of literal translation, such as the difficulty or impossibility of sometimes finding literal equivalents in the target language.

However, concept translation also has its special kind of difficulties, which may, in fact, be quite formidable. In the first place, a translator must be sure that he has grasped precisely the original concept; secondly, he has to convey this sense to the reader without distortion. It is not enough for the translator to understand the original concept; he has to actually get it across to the reader. And because of the anisomorphism, i.e. differences between the Tibetan and English languages, as well as of some other reasons, this is often quite difficult, if not impossible, to achieve.

Concept translation also results in the loss of information due to skipping over the etymological background of terminology make-up. Especially, in the context of distinguishing *drang don*, "the implicit meaning," and *nges don*, " the explicit meaning," both the literal and the concept translations have to be done. Also, I have observed many cases where a literal translation would have brought forth a better sense but the translators have not followed that approach. For instance, the Tibetan expression *dal ḥbyor gyi rten* literally means "a life with leisures and endowments"; we often see this important term translated simply as "human life"; not only is this imprecise, it suggests a meaning different from what the Tibetan expression conveys. Such lack of precision leads people to ask questions such as the following. If human life is very rare and hard to obtain, why is the population of the world increasing? Does this mean that sentient beings are observing more ethical conduct and are accumulating more positive actions? And so on. In Tibetan, a big difference is made between the terms *miḥi rten*, or "human life," and *dal ḥbyor gyi rten*, "a human life with leisure and endowments." From this view-point, although the population of the world is increasing there is nothing wrong in saying that it is very rare and hard to find human life with leisure and endowments; not all humans have these freedoms and endowments. Some scholars have done what I call a "thematic translation." By this I mean that they have read a passage and taken its theme as the central focus of their translation. Since there are various Buddhist treatises which deal more or less with the same kind of themes, a style of translation such as this results in overlapping. It also results in the loss of information and of many other subtleties found in the original texts.

At this point I would like to say a few words about my method and strategy of translation. I was trained as a Buddhist monk and as a philosophy student at the Buddhist School of Dialectics (now the Institute of Buddhist Dialectics, Dharamsala). I was not trained professionally to be a translator, but for the last ten years I have been working as a translator, first at the Dialectic School and now for over eight years at the LTWA.

Considering the complex nature of translation I do not favour adopting any one particular style or technique. Problems are many, and no particular style seems to provide an answer to all. Therefore, in my translation work, I follow multiple styles, which minimizes to a great extent many poblems.

The Tibetan *lotsāwas* and Indian abbots of Tibet's classical period worked in Tibet at translations in collaboration with each other. We at the LTWA follow their example. Tibetan and Western scholars collaborate on translation work. We believe that this helps improve the quality of the end-product in terms of accuracy.

It is very hard to achieve both accuracy and stylistic elegance in translation. I am sure that we all strive to accomplish these ends; but, for me, when I have to make a choice between the two I always give preference to accuracy. By accuracy I mean faithfulness to the original. To me, elegance is the literary style of translation. I consider accuracy to be more important, and I do not like to compromise on the content of the original. Stylistic elegance to me is secondary.

I attempt an almost line-by-line translation, and feel that the strategy and style of the translation implicitly speaks of the criteria of the translator. I emulate Professor Jeffrey Hopkin's approach.

Scholars have different opinions with regard to the criteria of a good translation. Some say that if a translation fulfils the purpose for which it is made then it is a good translation. In my view, a good translation is that which is readable, intelligible and conveys the original sense of the source text to the reader. Even if a translation is intelligible and makes sense yet does not convey the sense of the original to the reader, it is then, to my thinking, not a good translation. On the other hand, even if a translation lacks elegance but gives the original sense in the target language it is a good translation. A translation has to be intelligible to the extent that beyond which it amounts to over-simplification of Buddhism. Spoon-feeding is unacceptable.

Nida defines translation as: "Translating consists in producing in the receptor language the closest natural equivalent to the message of the source language, first in meaning and secondly in style." As I mentioned above, numerous definitions and styles of translation indicate certain problems in translating from one language into another. I would focus on a few major problems in translating from Tibetan into English.

The syntax and semantic differences between the Tibetan and English languages are a major problem area, especially in a simultaneous oral translation. This is because in a simultaneous translation one should be able to anticipate verbs which normally appear at the end of a sentence in Tibetan.

Another major problem is how to handle textual ambiguity, a common characteristic of Tibetan writing. In English literature ambiguity is frowned upon, and a single clear meaning is preferred. In translating from Tibetan we come across many ambiguous passages, especially in some of the fundamental philosophical texts, and this ambiguity must be preserved. Often we see that a scholar has interpreted a passage according to a particular commentary and has thus destroyed the ambiguity. Although the rendering is not wrong, the multidimensional quality of the passage is lost. This amounts to a loss of a great deal of meaning. Often in these cases words which are versatile in Tibetan are reduced to single concept words in English.

Yet another major problem is how to give the complete sense of a given Tibetan term. For example, many Tibetan words have the same form both as a noun and a verb. *Zag pa,* for instance, is such a word. When it is translated as "contamination" or "delusion," only its noun-aspect is being addressed, and its verb-aspect is being overlooked. As a verb it means "falling." The combined meaning of its noun and verb aspects gives a profound sense in Tibetan; the sense is that as long as one has delusions, no matter how high one goes in cyclic existence, one will eventually fall down. It may not be possible to give this complete sense of *zag pa* everytime it appears in a text, but I feel one must somehow convey both meanings, even in a footnote if necessary. Likewise in Tibetan there are many terms that have a wide range of meanings. Take *rtog med,* for instance. It could mean "non-conception," "non-examination," "absence of thought," and even "non-perception." It is hard to find an English equivalent that could mean all these. Often such words can be rendered according to the context; however, in certain cases it can mean more than one thing, such as both "non-conceptual" and "non-examination." Tibetan scholars interpret the word in either of these two ways.

I have noticed another problem area. Sometimes even the best English equivalent does not work. For example, *gtsug lag khang* in Tibetan does not simply mean "temple," as it is usually rendered. The syllables *gtsug lag* refers to the *bkah gyur* and *btsan gyur* or the entire Buddhist canons; and *khang* means "house." Therefore, *gtsug lag khang* means a temple that houses the entire Buddhist canons. The simple word "temple" does not convey that sense at all. Translating *chos* as "religion" has similar problems.

As with translating literature from any civilization, we find in Tibetan many culture-bound words such as *bla* and *hgrel gtor.* One cannot gloss over these words; otherwise, we fail in our responsibility to bridge cultural gaps. But it is very difficult to find a precise English equivalent to terms such as these. Sometimes, instead of creating a clumsy equivalent, it may be better simply to retain the Tibetan term and cultivate a direct familiarity with it within the reader, and to explain its use in footnotes.

A major problem arises from "borrowed words." For instance, words like "good", "Centrist," Idealist," and "the existentiality of things," come across heavily loaded. They can confuse the reader by not conveying the sense of the original Tibetan. To adopt them in Buddhist translation not only obscures the original but often give an entirely different idea to the reader, if not a complete misunderstanding.

Besides there is the lack of consistency in rendering Buddhist terminology. The disparity created by the various English words employed by scholars to render the same Tibetan term is certainly confusing. For instance, when *chos rnams kyi gnas lugs* is translated as "the ultimate mode of existence of phenomena" by one scholar and "the existentiality of things" by another, the reader finds it hard to discern that both are talking about the same thing.

Perhaps the greatest problems encountered are in translating works on Buddhist metaphysics and *tantras.* Some scholars have translated works of such nature but I personally feel that English language has to be refined to translate such works which require mathematical accuracy. Otherwise Buddhist metaphysics may not work; and in the case of the *tantras,* such as *Guhyasamāja,* the translation has to be accurate to the extent that it can be elucidated with *mthah drug tshul bshi,* i.e., six ways: *draṅ don, nges don, dgongs pa can, dgong pa can min pa, sgra ji bshin pa,* and *sgra ji bshin pa ma yin pa;* and the four modes: *yig don, spyi don, sbas don,* and *mthar thug gi don.*

The two major obstacles that I see hindering consistent translation efforts are a lack of precise English equivalents for many Tibetan terms; and the lack of any standardization of technical terminologies. Before the efforts of the various translators working with Tibetan literature can be coordinated, these two factors must be resolved.

In early Tibetan history, when the Buddhist texts were translated from Sanskrit under the royal patronage of the great Dharma kings, many new terms were coined to represent certain Sanskrit words. Later, there was a general standardization of technical terminology. In fact, a classical language was created and refined for centuries to translate Sanskrit texts into Tibetan.

I am aware of the various problems that would arise from trying to do the same kind of thing in English. However, there should be a gradual movement in these two directions. We must begin the gigantic task now. I think we can gradually create new terms where necessary and somewhat standardize essential terminology.

On my part I have been working for some years now in regular oral translation at the Library of Tibetan Works and Archives, Dharamsala. Here I have been translating mainly the texts of Indian sages and Gelugpa scholars. To help the movement for a standardization of English terminology I have mainly followed Professor Jeffery Hopkins' terminology. I think scholars translating the works of other Buddhist traditions could do the same thing. This is one possible avenue of working towards a standardization, and of moving towards a refining and increasing precision of Buddhist terms in English.

With regard to the coining of new terms or adopting words from other languages or systems, I must say that we should define such words as precisely as possible in the footnotes, I admire Professor Herbert V. Guenther in this regard, for he mostly provides such wonderful footnotes. When *nyon mongs,* for instance, is translated as "delusion," one should define it according to the Buddhist tradition. This will help the reader to get a better understanding. Ordinary English dictionaries will give a different meaning of "delusion," perhaps not encompassing the Buddhist concept.

I also share the views of my friend and colleague, Mr Tsepak Rigzin, that under the aegis of the institutions such as the Library of Tibetan Works and Archives, Tibet House and the Central Institute of Higher Tibetan Studies, Tibetan and Western scholars should collaborate to establish the needed new words in English, and to standardize technical terminology.

Examples of a Dharma Centre's Contribution in the Field of Translation: Study Programme and Dictionary

Oliver Petersen

I would like to inform you about our dharma centre's experiences and future aims in the field of translation in Tibetan Buddhism. Mainly I would like to speak about our seven-year study programme for lay students and a dictionary project for Tibetan religious terms as interpreted in the Gelukpa Order.

Development and Aims of the Tibetan Centre

Twelve years ago the disciples in Hamburg asked Geshe Rabten, a well-known scholar of Sera Jeh Monastery, later the abbot of Rikon Monastery and Tharpa Chöling Monastery in Switzerland, to send a qualified teacher to Hamburg. Geshe Rabten suggested some Geshes to His Holinesss the Dalai Lama, who selected Geshe Thubten Ngawang, a Lharampa Geshe from Sera. Since then Geshe Thubten has been living in the Tibetan Centre and teaching there. In teaching he followed the long-term vision to establish the complete Buddha-dharma in the West, so that it can have a positive effect on the individual and society. With the well-being of society in mind, he has also made a lot of contributions in the field of dialogues with academic scholars and representatives of other religions.

In this task of transmitting the complete Buddha-dharma, the role of translation is vital. By now several monks and one nun from our centre are qualified to translate from Tibetan, both scriptural sources and oral teachings. Other disciples transcribe oral translations or they translate books from English into German.

Approaches to Translation, Academic and Non-Academic

It is difficult to be sure, but in my opinion the approach to translation may be a little different for translators who are practising Buddhists, especially the ordained ones,from that of the academic scholars who, in most cases, are probably not Buddhists themselves.

The dharma centres have to consider the practical needs of their students. They carry the responsibility for the spiritual development, the personal well-being of those who trust in them. A Buddhist translator looks at the scriptures as medicine to cure the mental diseases of humans, not as a work of mainly historical and philological interest that has its place in the field of knowledge like every other subject. The Buddha himself compared the Dharma to medicine quite frequently. When such a translator chooses the texts he likes to work on, he is inclined to take those texts in the first place that are most needed as a foundation for the path to liberation. His decision does not depend on the curriculum of a university or financial considerations.

At the beginning of every traditional scripture, the following are generally laid out: an overview of the contents (*bjrod bya*); the purpose (*dgos pa*), i.e. the understanding of the path: the ultimate purpose (*nyin dgos*) i.e. the realising of the spiritual path in oneself and ultimately liberation; and finally the relationship (*'brel-pa*) between the contents, purpose and ultimate purpose of the scripture.

I think these criteria should be borne in mind by the translator of a particular scripture especially if he is a Buddhist.

The conditions under which a translator in a dharma centre works are different from those under which a scholar in the academic field works. The former has his place in a certain tradition he believes to have the power to lead to spiritual transformation. Oral commentaries and studies with his Lama play an important role in his striving to understand difficult passages and their relation to other texts. This situation may be comparable to the meeting of the Indian and Tibetan scholars at the time when Sanskrit texts were translated into Tibetan. Apart from using scriptural sources such a translator also relies on the living experience of his teacher and the interpretation of his lineage that has proved its value through the centuries. Partly due to the lack of time that is chronic for someone who works to establish a dharma centre in the West, it may be true that historical studies, philological training in other Buddhist languages, long philological footnotes and the comparative study of different traditions are often set aside. This situation can be irritating for academic scholars or even lead them to disregard works translated in this way.

It is true that, in the case of non-qualified teachers, there is the danger of blind faith and sectarianism. But in the case of a qualified spiritual guide, the above-mentioned approach can also lead to good results. Such translations are often more accessible to the practitioner who does not know Tibetan than the academic translations. Scholastic works sometimes treat points which are more important from a religious point of view with the same care as those that are less important, giving long commentary material, different interpretations, footnotes and references. This often leaves the reader irritated about the ultimate aim of the scripture and confused as to the meaning of the teaching within a particular tradition as a whole. The restriction to one tradition and interpretation is sometimes more useful for the spiritual progress of the practitioner than the mixing of various traditions in one work. Furthermore, a translator who is a practising Buddhist considers his spiritual experience derived from his faithful practice in prayer, meditation and debate as an important condition to complete his understanding of the texts.

In short, I think both approaches, the scholastic and the traditional Buddhist way, are valuable and can support each other fruitfully. In the discussion of our dictionary project I will try to show an example of the possibility of mutual exchange and support between these two traditions with their different backgrounds, aims and self-assessment.

Development of Translation in the Tibetan Centre, Hamburg

In the beginning, the translations done in the centre were mainly of the oral teachings given by Geshe Thubten Ngawang and visiting lamas. The students in the centre not only studied classical Tibetan but considered spoken Tibetan to be very important and as a result learned it quite quickly. This proved to be very useful later, not only for a better contact with the lamas, but for the whole study and teaching programme in the centre. For example, today the advanced classes are held solely in Tibetan and the older students are able to teach classical and colloquial Tibetan logic and debate and lead discussion groups of the seven-year study course which will be explained below.

Scriptural translations first dealt mainly with *pūjas* and texts most needed for the regular services and general teachings. We translated prayers to different Buddhas, the *Guru Pūja (bla ma mchod pa)*, the Guru Yoga of Tsong-kha-pa called *Hundred Deities of Tushita (dga'ldan lha brgya ma)*, the *Fasting-Meditation Rite of Avalokiteśvara (nyung gnas)*, etc. and basic study texts such as short *Lam Rim* texts including the *Thirty-Seven Practices of the Bodhisattvas (rgyal sras lag len so bdun ma)*, the *Three Principal Aspects of the Path (lam gtso rnam gsum)* and also parts of the *Bodhisattvacaryāvatāra*. Later, basic teachings of our teacher and also the talk of the Dalai Lama in Hamburg 1982 were printed. That was most influential for Buddhism in Hamburg.

Systematic Study Programmes

Two long-term study programmes take place in the centre, apart from general teachings on meditation and other seminars. The first started about ten years ago, shortly after Geshe Thubten arrived in Hamburg. The disciples living with him—mostly monks and nuns—are trained in the more profound studies of Buddhist philosophy, together with the practice of debate. The curriculum and texts studied follow the traditional studies of the great monastic universities that end with a geshe (*dge bshes*) degree. There are several classes, the advanced being solely in Tibetan.

Recently Geshela expressed the wish to make such studies, which also include the study of epistemology and logic, available to the lay disciples who do not live in the centre and in most cases do not know Tibetan. Therefore, in September 1988, a second study programme, lasting for seven years, was started for them. The senior students with their more detailed understanding play an important role in this, translating the scriptural sources and leading discussion groups. A similar development of study programmes are found in some other European centres too.

Not only the systematic studies for resident students in the centre, but also the starting of a seven-year study programme for lay students that week by week covers the whole of Buddhist philosophy at least in a gross manner is also in accordance with the wishes of Dalai Lama. He frequently expresses his hope that westerners can take on the burden of teaching Buddhist philosophy to their fellow countrymen in their own language.

In fact, as you all know, for the true establishment of Buddhism it is essential that at least some people gain a deeper analytical understanding of the teachings. Otherwise Buddhism will degenerate and be mixed with less developed systems. The statements of the Buddha have to be interpreted correctly with the help of logic. We should use the opportunity as long as the necessary conditions are present. In Tibet only the monkhood had the time and interest to study these subjects, but in the West with its complex social structure and intellectual background, also the lay community has the wish and capacity to learn from these scriptures and their reasoning. The fact that over eighty participants enrolled in the seven-year study programme makes this evident. Even though most of them have full-time jobs, their enthusiasm in learning and taking part in the weekly teaching and discussion groups is remarkable.

Even if such a study programme will not necessarily make people lamas, it can, on different levels, enable Westerners to discuss questions with new devotees, write articles and act as qualified partners of discussion with scientists and people of different faiths in the dialogue between cultures. It can also enable them to lead meditation sessions, make it easier to translate Buddhist texts and give talks and even conduct basic teachings in an authentic Buddhist way. It has never been the motivation of the Tibetan lamas to make themselves irreplaceable. They only followed the requests for teaching in the West out of compassion, leaving a big gap in their own monsteries and renouncing their own progress in study.

The general programme of meditation courses and seminars beside this seven-year project faces the difficulty of always having to deal with newcomers and people who don't come regularly. So it is normally not possible to go into detailed, gradual studies and deeper discussions of the great scriptures. The same basic teaching has to be given again and again to ripen the minds of the listeners. Now, in this seven-year programme, all the main subjects of the Geshe study programme of the three great monasteries of the Gelukpa tradition are covered systematically, but in a slightly different order. Every teaching takes place in conjunction with a discussion period, led by the senior students. Tests are written every half year, but understanding the true meaning and value for one's personal development is considered to be more important than good marks. Study through tapes and manuscripts is also possible.

Overview of Texts Studied in a Traditional Study Programme in Sera Monastery

I would like to give here an overview of the scriptures that are or will have to be partly translated for these two study programmes and also for the dictionary project discussed later. As I have already mentioned, the curriculum and texts studied by the resident students in the centre follow the traditional studies of the great monastic universities. There they form the main course of education for the young monks and prepare them for the Geshe degree, enabling them to teach every aspect of Buddhism. I think a short overview of the texts studied—following the example of Sera Jeh Monastery—could be interesting for many. In the course of studying these texts the disciple first listens to teachings on them. Afterwards he learns them by heart and contemplates their meaning. Then daily debate plays an important role in deepening his understanding. The mind becomes sharp and flexible through this logical exercise of formalized debate. Apart from intellectual study the monk, keeping ethical conduct, purifies his mind and collects merit with the help of prayer and ritual. On the basis of his deep analytical understanding he enters meditation and eventually experiences a direct perception of the truth. His ultimate aim is to conquer ignorance and understand ultimate truth, namely emptiness, and so attain liberation and Buddhahood for the benefit of other suffering beings.

The gradual studies can be divided into preliminary studies and the advanced studies of the five great scriptures:

A. The Preliminary Studies

1. The *Collected Topics on Valid Cognition (bsdus grwa)* by *Phur bu lcog*

In the course of the preliminary studies a few works of *Phur bu lcog,* the tutor of the 13th Dalai Lama, are studied to present the terminology and categories used in the great scriptures of Buddhist philosophy. Since they have this function, the texts are called the "Collected Topics on Valid Cognition, a Magical Key to the Great Scriptures". These texts are divided into the small, middle and great *Path of Reasoning (rigs lam chung ngu / 'bring/ che ba)* followed by the section on awareness and knowledge (*blo rig*) and on types of logical signs, or reasoning (*rtags rigs*). The content is mainly taken from the Sautrāntika system of tenets, and the system of logic and epistemology primarily follows the system of Dharmakīrti and Dignāga, because it is considered to be an important stepping stone and prerequisite to the understanding of Madhyamaka. The *blo rig* section mainly deals with the mind and its functions, and so presents Buddhist theory of cognition and psychology. The *rtags rigs* section introduces one to the different elements and types of logical proofs.

2. Systems of Tenets (*grub mtha'*) by rJe-btsun Chos-kyi rGyal-mtshan

This section deals with the Buddhist systems of tenets, being Vaibhāṣika, Sautrāntika, Cittamātra and Madhyamaka, thus encompassing both Hīnayāna and Mahāyāna. Presented is an overview of the theories of the basis, paths and fruits of the different systems of Buddhist thought.

3. Spiritual Grounds and Paths (*sa lam*) by rJe-btsun Chos-kyi rGyal-mtshan

This section presents the definitions and divisions of the grounds and paths of spiritual develoment.

4. The Seventy Topics (*don bdun bcu*) by rJe-btsun Chos-kyi rGyal-mtshan

In this section seventy vital points of Mahāyāna Buddhism from the *Abhisamayālaṁkāra* of Maitreya are discussed.

B. The Advanced Studies

Having finished this preparation, the student are trained well enough to study the complex great scriptures of Buddhism directly. The study of the so-called Five Great Works (*gzhung bka'pod lnga*)

is started. These works cover five subjects that encompass the whole of Buddhist philosophy. These subjects are Pramāṇa, Prajñāpāramitā, Madhyamaka, Vinaya and Abhidharma.

Each of these subjects is studied with the help of one main scripture. The so-called ornaments of India, the great teachers of old, most venerated in Tibet, are the authors of these scriptures. They are Nāgārjuna and Āryadeva as teachers of the philosophical view of the Madhyamaka-System, Asaṅga and Vasubandhu as teachers of the conduct of a Bodhisattva and of Abhidharma, Dignāga and Dharmakīrti as teachers of logic and the science of knowledge, and Guṇaprabha and Śākyaprabha as teachers of the monastic discipline. This fact shows that Tibetan Buddhism is completely based on Indian Buddhism and still preserves this ancient tradition. Also the three higher trainings are covered by these main subjects. Vinaya stands for moral discipline, Prajñāpāramitā, and Abhidharma for meditation and Madhyamaka and Pramāṇa for wisdom. These three trainings should never be separated. Nowadays the training in the Vinaya may be difficult for many people.

The five main scriptures are:

1. *Pramāṇavārttika* by Dharmakīrti

This covers the subject of logic and theory of cognition. The second most venerated teacher in this field is Dignāga. Apart from the main text, commentaries by rGyal-tshab-rje, mKhas-grub-rje, Tsong-kha-pa and dGe-'dun-grub are studied.

2. *Abhisamayālaṁkāra*, traditionally ascribed to Maitreya and written down by Asaṅga

This text builds the foundation for the study of the subject of Prajñāpāramitā, the general teachings of Buddhism as implicitly taught in the Sutras on the perfection of wisdom. Commentaries by Haribhadra, Tsong-kha-pa and rGyal-tshab-rje are studied.

3. *Madhyamakāvatāra* by Candrakīrti

With the help of this work the ultimate truth as presented in the Madhyamaka system of tenets, considered to be the highest school of thought, is studied. The works of Nāgārjuna are also studied for this purpose, together with commentaries by Tsong-kha-pa and dGe-'dun-grub.

4. *Vinayasūtra* by Guṇaprabha

By means of studying this text the discipline is studied. Also commentaries by mTso-na-pa Shes-rab-bzang-po and dGe-'dun-grub are studied.

5. *Abhidharmakośa* by Vasubandhu

In this section the phenomenology of Buddhism is studied. Commentaries to this work are written by dGe-'dun-grub and mChim-'jam-dpal-dbyang.

In general the monastery textbooks (*yig cha*) of Se-ra rJe-btsun-pa Chos-kyi rGyal-mtshan are studied to enable one to understand the root texts, and their translation will be important for us. Other monasteries often have their own *yig chas* that vary only little from those of Sera. The whole process in Ganden and Drepung is similar. Please take the exact names of commentaries studied from the appendix. Also studied are the text on the stages of the path (*lam rim*) by Tsong-kha-pa and the *Bodhisattvacaryāvatāra* by Śāntideva.

The study programme can last for more than twenty years until the Geshe degre is gained after rigorous examination. Afterwards many Geshes enter the tantric monasteries to study secret mantra. This system of education proved to be very successful in that it produced real scholars of Buddhism. The future will tell whether it is adaptable to the West and whether the situation in the process of transferring Buddhism from India to Tibet and our present situaton is comparable.

Extracting Main Subjects for the Seven-Year Study Programme

The study programme of our seven-year course of lay people can naturally cover only the main points of the study programme in the monasteries of India. Also the course of study had to be changed. Our study programme is arranged along the four schools of tenets using mainly the *Garland of Tenets (grub-mtha' rin chen phrengba)* by dKon-mchog 'Jigs-med dBamg-po as a guideline, starting with the more gross and easier to grasp Vaibhāṣika school and after that Sautrāntika and so forth.

In the first year, instead of starting with *bsdus-grwa,* which involves debate, students started with important passages from the Abhidharmakośa to get a background on basic phenomenology, like divisions of phenomena into 18 elements or 12 sense-sources, mind and mental factors, different causes and effects, karma and the 12 links of dependent arising. The relevant passages have been translated, mostly together with the commentary of dGe-'dun-grub. Time for debate is much too short; often the time is also short for reading debates with opponents of one's own system, because the students are not living in the centre or a monastery.

In the second year, the system of the Sautrāntikas is studied, using mainly the small, middle and great *Path of Reasoning* (*rigs lam*) from the Collected Topics, including the study of reasoning with different types of consequences (*thal 'gyur*) and proofs (*sgrub byed*), and epistemology from the *rTags-rigs* and *bLo-rig*-sections. Mainly the sections of the presentation of one's own system (*rang lugs*) are already translated and studied.

In the third year, the system of the Cittamātras will be studied, following the *Great Exposition of Tenets* (*grub mtha'chen mo*) by 'Jam-dbyang-bzhad-pa and the second chapter of the *Pramāṇavarttika*.

In the fourth year, the system of the Prāsaṅgika-Mādhyamikas will be studied based on the sixth chapter of *Madhyamakāvatāra* and Tsong-kha-pa's *dGongs-pa-rab-gsal*.

In the fifth year, the Svātantrika-Madhyamaka system will be looked at, and in addition the first and eighth chapter of the *Abhisamayālaṁkāra*, which includes the study of Pāramitā.

In the sixth year, emphasis will be put on meditation, relying on Tsoṅ-kha-pa's *Middle Exposition of the Stages of the Path to Enlightenment* (*Lam rim 'bring*).

The last year will be reserved for special studies like Vinaya for ordained students and an introduction to tantra based on texts written by Paṇ-chen bSod-nams-grags-pa and Bu-ston.

Not the whole scriptures of course but parts of these texts and other related texts and commentaries will be translated and distributed to the students. The lessons by Geshe Thubten Ngawang are regularly transcribed and proof-read; and it is planned to publish these annually together with the translated scriptural passages. We think in this way—parallel to the ongoing study programme—a reasonably complete overview of the different Buddhist systems and vehicles based on ancient Indian Buddhism and its continuation in Tibet will for the first time be presented to the German-speaking reader. Also, the materials collected from the scriptural and oral sources can serve as a good basis for another main project related to the centre: a dictionary of Buddhist terms.

Project of a Dictionary of Buddhist Terms

1. Purpose

The other long-term project that is closely connected to the above-mentioned study programmes is a dictionary of Buddhist terms, called the "Clear Illumination of the Teaching" (*brda dkrol bstan pa'i snang gsal).* The project has been started by the Foundation of Tibetan Buddhist Studies which is recognized by the Hamburg Senate. The members of the advisory committee include the well-known scholars Professor Seyfort-Ruegg and Professor Schmithausen of Hamburg University, scholars from other universities in Germany and also translators from the Tibetan Centre.

This project should fulfil the needs of both practising Buddhists and scholars from the academic field, as I have already mentioned. We think that both feel the need for such a dictionary. The practising Buddhists are interested in an easily accessible glossary of terms which they come across when reading books or listening to teachings, so that they can understand the meaning better. For them such a work should be clear, short and understandable, an authentic background without too much philology and references to different sources.

On the part of the academic users and also the more learned Buddhists and translators there is a feeling that the older dictionaries of Tibetan religious-philosophical terms, like the Jäschke and Chandra Das dictionaries, are somehow incomplete, not fully reliable or precise enough to be of assistance. Other dictionaries only cover the field of spoken Tibetan. The *Bod-rgya Tshig mdzhod Chen-mo,* a Tibetan-Tibetan Chinese dictionary, published in Tibet in 1984, can give us some orientation, but translation into a Western language and reference to sources is lacking. Tzepak Rigzin's *Tibeton-English Dictionary of Buddhist Terminology* is also valuable but there is still room for improvement. For example, the planned work should not only contain the translation and explanations of a certain term, but also references to different sources. Commentary passages should be translated and also be cited in their original language, namely Tibetan. Buddhist translators often do not have the time to look up the relevant passages in the scriptures or to discuss questions in detail with their teachers. Also they are often not completely trained but forced to translate the needed texts. For them such citations would be extremely helpful. Also synonyms and etymology as well as oral commentaries should be included. Even if oral commentaries are never in contradiction to the scriptures, they can show relations and levels of importance and make the studies more lively and understandable for people today. They can sum up points spread all over the different scriptures and bring to light hidden points and meanings, the so-called implicit meaning of a phrase. So, also quotations of oral commentaries should be contained. Having deeper knowledge of the background of a term will make it easier to find suitable equivalents according to different contexts.

2. Creating an entry form to establish a database

Now, how can we fulfil the needs of both of these groups practically? The plan for this work has to be organized very well right from the beginning, because the system must be able to contain a wide range of information but also be reducible to a selection of the most important material for the specific needs of different people, as already mentioned.

Using an electronic database can make such projects possible. A mask for entries has been developed, which I would like to explain. It contains 12 fields and serves as a standard form for entries, which can be done by hand or by computer. It should be noted that it is not a final version, but can be adapted and improved, if necessary.

1. TIB: (dngos po)
2. SKT: bhāva*
3. GER: wirksames Phänomen, Ding
4. ENG: effective phenomenon, thing
5. OTH: -/-
6. SYN: (mi rtag pa/, dus byas/ byas pa/ rang mtshan/, don dam bden pa)
7. S-S: RLChu, 7b.4
8. S-C: (don byed nus pa/) That which is able to perform a function. Effective phenomena are divided into three types: (bem po) matter, (shes pa) consciousness and (ldan min 'du byed) non-associated com-

positional factors.

9. O-S: GTN, from transcript of seven-year study programme, semester III

10. 0-C: The function an effective phenomenon is able to perform is that of creating an effect. According to this system of Sautrāntika, which asserts a truly existent object condition (Æ(dmigs rkyen)) prior to perception, a main function of an effective phenomenon is to act as a cause for the direct perception of itself.

11. RES: CS

12. CHD: OP

1. The first field contains the Tibetan word, written in the transliteration system of T. Wylie. It can later be transformed into Tibetan letters. We ourselves are using the Tibetan-Programme from Boulder that runs on the Word-Perfect word processor for IBM compatible personal computers. It can sort entries in the Tibetan alphabetic order and convert the Wylie transliteration into Tibetan characters, and subsequently print them out on an HP-Laserjet Series II compatible printer. But, of course, at this stage the question of hard- and software environment is secondary. Using a standard transliteration system for Tibetan and Sanskrit makes conversion from one system to another possible.
2. The Sanskrit original, if available, follows in the standard transliteration form. If the Sanskrit original has not clearly been retraced to an Indian source in this context, it should be left out or marked with an asterisk for further verification.
3. The German translation follows.
4. The English translation. In fact the German or English equivalents may be of secondary importance. Reasons for the choice of a particular equivalent can be given in one of the commentary fields below. More importat than the mere translation of a term will be the background information that allows translators to choose their own equivalents. Of course the equivalents should be standardized in this dictionary.

5. Other languages like Pāli or French can be cited.
6. Synonyms should be listed, at least in Tibetan, with cross-references to their explanations. It should be clear for which school of Buddhist thought such synonyms are relevant. This is one reason for making a number of smaller glossaries limited to certain sources or systems.
7. The source of a scriptural commentary should be given. The sources should occur in abbreviated form. There is no need to give the author's name because this can be traced from the Text and Author Indexes, already established. The scripture, page or folio and line have to be given. An example would be RLCHu, f7b.4 meaning *bsdus grwa Rigs Lam Chung ngu folio 7b,* Line 4. If a source is written in verses, the verse numbers should be given instead of page numbers. This is helpful for coordination between different editions. In general a standard edition is to be used for each text. Mainly the *lha sa bka' 'gyur* and *sde dge bstan 'gyur* will be used together with the monastery textbooks (*yig cha*). We will use those of Sera Jeh, as we study them ourselves.
8. The commentary is cited. This commentary should include definitions, divisions, etymology and further explanations of a term. It should be entered in Tibetan and, if possible, in German or English translation.
9. The source of an oral commentary is given, preferably with the details of where the passage is to be found on a tape, in a transcript or in a book. We have not yet worked out a clear system for collecting oral sources. Nevertheless, we think they are helpful and important. At the moment, our main source is Geshe Thubten Ngawang's teaching in the seven-year study programme.
10. The oral commentary is given in English or German.
11. The name of the researcher who made the entry.
12. The name of the one who checked the entry.

Entries can be made by hand or by computer. Methods have been developed so that one can copy passages of already existing files on computer into the entry form easily, for example, from the texts that have been translated for the seven-year study programme. In fact, while working on translations in a particular field, one can easily make entries from the same material without much extra effort. But I cannot go into the details of computing here. One version of an entry in its finished form, printed out from the laser printer, could probably look like the one in figure 2 below.

Entries with many citations may of course cover whole pages. To start with, it is planned that different persons fill in texts from the above-listed traditional sources they are most familiar with. Restriction to these limited number of sources all derived from only one tradition of Tibetan Buddhism is more systematic and will lead to more clarity. This is a more practical approach. It also makes it easier to trace a term back to its source and makes the meaning clear in its given context. Sources may be expanded later. It is not planned to cover the whole spectrum of Buddhism and we do not consider it to be realistic with our limited resources. Also a sort of new Mahāvyutpatti may not be realistic in the present situation. It may be rather the duty of all of us to save each tradition as a whole on its own ground.

(*bhāva**) - effective phenomenon, thing.
Definition: That which is able to perform a function
Effective phenomena are divided into three types: matter (æ), consciousness (æ) and non-associated compositional factors (æ). (Scriptural Source: RLChu, 7b. 4)
The function and effective phenomenon is able to perform is that of creatig an effect. According to this system of Sautrāntika, which asserts a truly existent object condition (æ) prior to perception, a main function of an effective phenomenon is to act as a cause for the direct perception of itself. (Oral Source: GTN, SYSP III).
Synonyms:æ

Fig. 2. An example of how the entry could look when printed.

Students of Geshe Thubten have already accepted to make entries for certain fields of studies from a limited range of sources alongside their studies. Many people working on the entries can make quick progress possible, but may also create coordination problems. It will be an important and difficult task to collect the different information and arrange it in a consistent final form.

When a certain text has been entered, it is possible to print out different versions of parts of the dictionary that deal with a certain field of study and that build a unit. Or one could even publish entries from only one text. This avoids having to wait many years for results as in the case of other extensive dictionary projects. Also summaries of explanations put into an easily readable style can be extracted for people not interested in the difficult philosophical language and too many citations, etc.

Working with an electronic database is not only helpful for printing out different versions, but also for continually extending and improving the entries and putting them into a layout for printing. Copies could be made and exchanged in disk form among scholars, if desired.

Another plan is to enter complete series of texts. In this way, indexes can be easily made. Terms would be simple to find and relevant passages could be copied into the dictionary file. In this connection we are considering installing a computer in Sera Monastery and training monks to insert texts.

3 *Request for contribution*

We think that we have gathered the necessary conditions to start the project by relying on the advice of Geshe Thubten and the scholars mentioned. People from the Tibetan Centre responsible for making entries have been found. But still we are looking for help among the scholars and institutions around the world, and this is one purpose of my being here. Please let me know or write to us if you are working in the same field or have already gathered material and experience so that efforts can be united. We are prepared to send you more detailed information. Scientific methods are indispensable in the project. By the way, I think the Tibetan tradition would benefit by adopting scientific methods that have proved to be very effective, for example in the field of library science.

We hope that we will be able to produce a dictionary that will be a sound basis for the translation and practice of Buddhism as it appears in one of the important traditions of Tibet.

A third long-term project, in which mainly the female practitioners of our centre are involved, is the revival, i.e. the establishment, of the Bhikṣuṇī Saṃgha in the Theravāda and Tibetan traditions. Two nuns have already taken the precepts from the Chinese tradition. They study the role of women and nuns in Buddhism and are doing a comparative study of the Vinaya, mainly between the Tibetan Mūlasarvāstivāda, the Chinese Dharmagupta and the Theravāda traditions. They have taken part in a conference and seminars in India, the United States and Germany and are translating parts of the Tibetan Vinaya under the guidance of Geshe Thubten Ngawang. They are publishing the results of these comparative studies and translations for fully-ordained nuns and people who are involved in the research. If you are interested or working in this field yourself, please contact them at the Tibetan Centre. They would be especially interested to have contact with people working on the Tibetan Vinaya.

For further informmation on the different projects, you can contact us:

1. Study programme : Bhikṣu Jampa Tenzin
2. Dictionary project: Bhikṣu Jampa Gyatso
3. Vinaya: Bhikṣuṇī Jampa Tsedroen

at:

Tibetisches Zentrum e.V.
Hermann-Balk-Str. 106
D-2000 Hamburg 73
West Germany
Tel. 040-6443585

or:

Foundation for Tibetan Buddhist Studies
Tesdorpfstr. 13
D-2000 Hamburg 13
West Germany

Appendix

"Examples of a dharma centre's contribution in the field of translation" (Dictionary project)

Source Texts for Difinitions for the brda dkrol bstan pa'i snang gsal Dictionary

These are the texts actually directly and intensively studied in the Geshe studies programme at Sera. They are the source materials from which the entries to the Dictionary upon each subject should be directly compiled. Full details including the Edition to be used are specified for each text. The distinctive abbreviation to be used in referring to each text is also given after it. When no further details are given, the text is part of the by (ChGy). If you wish to refer to the as such, you can either refer to it as (ChGYSB) or simply (Y) for. However, the abbreviations given after each distinctive section of the texts are quite sufficient in themselves as a reference, as their references are quite distinct within the entire scheme for the references for all texts. All the texts mentioned are available in the Library of the Zentrum. Appendix A gives the location of the texts in the Library. Appendix B gives the list of abbreviations used in just this document.

A: Preliminary Studies

(1) (DR) by (PC)
(Mysore edition:M) (RLChu)
(M) (RLB)
fol. (folios) 1-44 (M) (RlChe)
fol. 1-25 (M) (lR)
fol. 1-28 (M) (LR)
(2) fol. 1-17 (M) (DDC)
(3) fol. 1-17 (M) DDC
(4) fol, 1-20 (M) (SL)

B. (Pramāṇavārttika)

(1) (root text) by (Dharmakīrti) (Dh), Toh 4210 Ce (3) fol. 94b-151a), Verses to be numbered according to the vulgate edition of Miyasaki, 1977.
(2) fil. 1-122 (M) (LD).
(3) by (GTsh) Toh. No. 5442, YSSB fol. 1-93 (ፕKSGTsh)
(4) by (KHGr) Toh. No. 5501, YSSR () fol, 1-244 (DMS)
(5) by (Ts) Toh. No 5416 YSSB () fol. 1-23 (DJG).
(6) by (GGr) Toh. No. 5528 SB, Gangtok, 1981, fol. 1-212 (TshR).

C. (Prajñpāramitā)

(1) (Perfection of Wisdom Sūtra in 25,00 lines) Lh10, (Toh 9), Vols 26-28, fols () 1-558, 1-548, 1-537 (PVPS).
(2) (Abhisamayālaṁkāra) by (Maitreya) (M) fol. 1-18 (M), also Toh No 3786 Kas 2 fol. 1b-13a (A). But please quote verses and follow their numbering according to the critical edition of Stcherbatsky and Obermiller, Leningrad, 1929.
(3) (Sphutārtha) by (Haribhadra) (H) fol. 1-68 (M), also Toh No 3793 Ja 2 fol. 78b-140a (SA).
(4) by (Ts) Toh. No 5412 YSSB fol. 1-405 and 1-267 (LS).
(5) by (GyTsh) Toh. No. 5433 YSSB fol. 1-346 (NyGy).
(6) The divides in the following way according to the eight Chapters of the Abhisamayālaṁkāra:-

Chapter 1:-

(a) fol. 1-135 (M) (KD).
(b) (also known as fol. 1-46 (M) (GHNySh).
(c) fol. 46-73 (M) (ByL).
(d) fol. 74-105 (M) (R).
(e) (explains fol. 106-185 (M) (GGr).
(f) fol. 1-54 (M) DrNg)

Chapter 2:-

fol. 1-85 (M) PyD?)

Chapter 3:-

fol. 1-35 (M) (PyD3)

Chapter 4:-

fol. 1-47 (M) (PyD4)

Chapter 5:-

(a) fol. 1-37 (M) (PyD5)
(b) fol. 1-27 (M) (GL)

(c) fol. 1-37 (M) TBr)

Chapter 6:-

fol. 1-5 (M) (PyD6)

Chapter 7:-

fol. 1-7 (M) (PyD7)

Chapter 8:-

fol. 1-67 (M) (PyD8)
fol. 1-77 (M) (M) (ChK)

D. (Madhyamaka)

(1) by (Candrakīrti) (C) fol. 1-27 (M) (MM), also Toh No 3861 Ha fol. 201b-219a. But please quote verses and verse numbers from the critical edition of De la Vallée Poussin, St Petersbourg, 1907-12 Reprinted Osnabruck, 1967.
(2) by (Ts) Toh. No 5411 YSSB fol. 1-267 (GRS).
(3) by (Ggr) Toh. No 5526 SB Gangtok, 1971, fol. 1-53 (SM)
(4) fol. 1-162 (M) (BMPyD)

E. (Vinaya)

(1) by (Guṇaprabha) (GP), Toh No 4117 Wu fol. 1b-100a (VS).
(2) by (TshZ) (M) DTsh).
(3) by (GOR) Toh. No 5523 SB Gangtok, 1971, fol. 1-476 (RPr).

F. (Abhidharmakośa)

(1) by (Vasubandhu) (V) fol. 1-41 (M), also Toh No 4089 Ku fol. 1b-25a (AK). But Please use the verse numbers from the critical edition by Pradhan, (Sanskrit), Patna, 1967.
(2) (NG) by (a Sakya author) (CP).

(3) by (GGR) Toh. No. 5525 SB Gangtok 1971 1-227 (TLSGGr).

Appendix A: Location of Above Texts in Library

Lhasa Edition. *Life Wall of Shrine room.*
Derge Edition. Life Wall of Shrine room.
Alter wall of Shrine room.
Altar wall of Shrine room.

Mysore, Sera rJe Editions and other Tibetan editions of root texts and commentaries -Left side of Altar wall of Shrine room, bottom right corner. The texts are all marked.

Critical editions of root texts, together with various indexes, studies and translations into European languages of these texts, shelf on left *side of Library room.*

Appendix B: Abbreviations Used Just In The Above Text

For other Abbreviations see Texts and Authors lists.
M Mysore, Sera rJe Edition
SB
YSSB
Source: Geshe Thubten Ngawang
Research: Jampa Gyatso and Dr Peter Ebbatson
Written: Dr Peter Ebbatson.